PATRIOTIC MURDER

PATRIOTIC MURDER

A World War I Hate Crime for Uncle Sam

PETER STEHMAN

Potomac Books | An imprint of the University of Nebraska Press

Library of Congress Cataloging-in-Publication Data
Names: Stehman, Peter, author.
Title: Patriotic murder: a World War I hate crime for
Uncle Sam / Peter Stehman.
Description: [Lincoln, Neb.]: Potomac Books, An imprint
of the University of Nebraska Press, [2018] | Includes
bibliographical references and index.
Identifiers: LCCN 2017053879
ISBN 9781612349848 (cloth: alk. paper)
ISBN 9781640120983 (epub)
ISBN 9781640120990 (mobi)
ISBN 9781640121003 (pdf)
Subjects: LCSH: Prager, Robert, 1888–1918. | Germans—
Illinois—Collinsville. | Lynching—Illinois—Collinsville.
| Collinsville (Ill.)—History. | Coal mines and mining—
Illinois—Collinsville. | World War, 1914–1918—Social
aspects—United States.
Classification: LCC F549.C725 S74 2018 | DDC 977.3/86—dc23
LC record available at https://lccn.loc.gov/2017053879

Set in Janson Text LT Pro by Mikala R. Kolander.

This work is dedicated to my parents, Lucille and Milton Stehman, who taught their children to learn and respect local and U.S. history, to stay well-informed about public affairs, and to serve the community and nation in which they live. Never have those attributes been more necessary than today.

Contents

Illustrations

Acknowledgments

Since I was first told of the incident as child, I have always held a certain fascination for the story of the lynching of Robert Prager. I was probably drawn by the macabre sense that something that wicked, that sensational, had actually occurred in my hometown, where *nothing* ever really seemed to happen. To make it all the more mysterious, there seemed little to document the event—no memorials or books, just the story as related by my parents. They were too young to have witnessed the lynching, but they dutifully passed on what they had been told by my grandparents and others. But why was Collinsville the only place where a German immigrant was lynched during World War I? What were the ingredients that had cooked up so much trouble here?

For generations the lynching wasn't openly discussed in Collinsville, initially because those most deeply involved probably didn't want it brought up. It was kept tucked away by later generations, who felt no need to discuss something that may have shamed their families and certainly shamed the community. That the whole affair seemed Collinsville's open secret only increased my intrigue.

It was never a question of if I would write on the Prager lynching but simply a matter of when. I had two primary goals for the project. The first was to tell the complete story, including a description of the turbulent environment that allowed it to happen in Collinsville. The second was to provide the most accurate account of what actually occurred, an effort that would also require extensive research.

There are many people I wish to thank for their assistance,

whether it was a tip on a possible resource, answering some obscure question, providing technical advice, reading portions of the manuscript, or just providing overall support. My thanks to all of you for helping me tell this important story: Harper Barnes, Mike Bartsch, Charles Bosworth, Delores Cox, Francis Jo (Bruno) Elkins, translator Carmen Freeman, Patrick Gauen, Loretta Giacoletto, Steve Giacoletto, Annette Graebe, Paul Guse, Philip Herr, Robert Herr, Wayne Hinton, David and Marian Hoskin, Louis Jackstadt (rest in peace, Lou), Robert Johann, William Jokerst, Phyllis (Riegel) Kesler, Judy (Mueller) Kramer, Rev. Dr. Martin Lohrmann, Jeffrey Manuel of Southern Illinois University–Edwardsville Historical Studies, Randy Mitchell, Kay Monroe, Madison County coroner Steve Nonn, Madison County Trial Court administrator Teri Picchioldi, Hon. Philip Rarick, Mary Sue Schusky, Paige St. John, and Hon. Don Weber. If there are others whom I have neglected to individually mention, please accept my apology and also my gratitude.

In order to best reconstruct what happened in 1917 and 1918 Collinsville, I extensively relied on local and St. Louis–area newspapers. Most of these were found in St. Louis–area libraries on microfilm. Likewise regional and state archives broadened my knowledge of the regional wartime environment and provided further details from the Prager case. I was fortunate to have excellent library and archive facilities for my research. I naturally spent a significant amount of time at the Collinsville Memorial Library Center, and I appreciate the assistance from Leslee Hamilton and other staff members there. The Collinsville Historical Museum was an important resource, and I am grateful to Charlotte Knapp and the museum's other volunteers. I also appreciate the efforts of Mary Westerhold and others at the Madison County Historical Museum and Archival Library in Edwardsville. The St. Louis Central Public Library is truly a gem of the Gateway City, and I would like to thank staff members there too for their invaluable assistance. I extend that same thanks to the staffs of the public libraries in Belleville and Edwardsville.

Both the Illinois State Library and the Illinois State Archives in Springfield were more than helpful, as was the staff of the Abraham Lincoln Presidential Library in the same city. I gained valuable information at the Thomas Jefferson Library at the University of Missouri–St. Louis, as I did at the (Elijah) Lovejoy Library on the campus of Southern Illinois University–Edwardsville. Stephen Kerber was most helpful at SIUE's Louisa H. Bowen University Archives and Special Collections. I appreciate the individual efforts of Lesley Martin at the Chicago History Museum, Shawn Barnett at Concordia Historical Institute in St. Louis, and Tilo Bönicke of the State Archives in Dresden. I was also assisted in my research with information provided by the Missouri History Museum Library and Research Center in St. Louis and the Indiana State Archives in Indianapolis.

Words cannot express my thanks for my friend Brad Bugger and my brother, Jim Stehman, for their review of and commentary on the complete manuscript. Their critical insights and overall observations helped me to tell the story better, in a manner that allows readers to find their way more easily through all the permutations.

Like so much forgotten history, the story of Robert Prager's demise merits telling for the lessons it offers to today's world. Patriotism is a wonderful thing, but propaganda, nationalism, and xenophobia have no place in great societies. Sadly, a reminder of that message is as relevant today as it was in 1918. I thank my agent, Steven Harris of CSG Literary Partners, and acquiring editor Tom Swanson of Potomac Books at the University of Nebraska Press for sharing my belief that this story needed to be told.

Finally, like anyone who has engaged in a project of this scope, I appreciate the kind support of my family and their tolerance of my mind being focused for so many months on an event and characters from one hundred years ago. Thank you Barb, Courtney, Christopher, and Nathan for listening.

PATRIOTIC MURDER

1

It's Plain Murder, but What Can You Do?

One thing was conspicuous as usual, and that was the loudest talking agitators wanted somebody else to do the fighting. They were willing to hold the coats but their precious heads were not put in jeopardy.

—Editorial, *Collinsville Advertiser*, April 13, 1918

It was past 11:30 p.m. as motorman James Moore and conductor J. P. Harrison brought their East St. Louis and Suburban streetcar up and out of the Mississippi River Valley on the Caseyville Road, taking the long, steady incline into Collinsville, Illinois. Theirs was one of the last cars of the day headed out of the Edgemont Station, near East St. Louis.[1]

Given the time of day, passengers were few on the brisk Thursday evening of April 4, 1918. They included the young Reverend P. G. Spangler and his wife, Ruby. The day before had been their six-month wedding anniversary, and they had enjoyed the evening in St. Louis, a respite from the demands of being the wartime pastor of the First Baptist Church in Collinsville.[2] Patriotism ran high in the city, as did tension. Increasingly, Spangler was conflicted by his congregation's desire to support the war effort and his given call to spread the word of God.[3] Quite often the two did not align, at least in his opinion.

A few rows away, Maida Gilmore, eighteen and attractive, rested as she rode the interurban line to her parents' home. It had been a long day, first with her shift at American Carbon and Battery Company.[4] The plant was so busy with orders for the War Department it could scarcely find enough girls to hire. After work she and some of her coworkers visited a sick friend before seeing a moving-picture show in Belleville.[5]

The streetcar climbed the grade up into Collinsville, then turned onto the St. Louis Road east, headed toward Collinsville's Main Street. The car seemed to slow early for the next stop, at the West End Saloon and the Hardscrabble Mine of the Abbey Coal Company. It was unusual for this time of night. And the noise of a loud and boisterous crowd soon told the passengers why.

At the Hardscrabble stop, more than two hundred men and boys were cheering and shouting.[6] Two men carried the American flag in front of the disorderly procession, but the main attraction was held by two others in the mob. They brought a small man with thick brown hair and a moustache to the center of the streetcar tracks, allowing its bright white light to illuminate him for the passengers to see.[7] He was a prize worth showing off, the men said, because he was a German spy. A pro-German, the kaiser's man, the crowd said. But tonight he would share in their drink of patriotism.

His gaze was uneven, his face drawn with fear. Those on the streetcar didn't know quite what a German spy should look like, but it didn't seem it would be the slight and hobbled figure held before them tonight. As the mob paraded him down the side of the interurban, some of its members said he would meet with tar and feathers. Others said they would kill the spy. Whatever would happen, this mob would have its way.

The mob told the man to sing "The Star Spangled Banner" and shout patriotic expressions for the benefit of those on the streetcar.[8] Earlier there had been talk of placing the pro-German over the tracks and having the motorman run over him, but nothing came of it.[9] Unlike the man they held captive, the faces in the mob were familiar to the riders from Collinsville. Mostly they were coal miners. And mostly they were drunk. Many were but half-grown boys who whooped and hollered just for the fun of it all.[10]

One face in the mob was very familiar to Maida Gilmore. She moved to the window as she spotted her red-haired father amid the unruly troupe.[11] She didn't know what they were up to, but she knew it would not be good. "Papa, come on home now," she cried out to Calvin Gilmore in a trembling voice.[12] His response was to continue west with the mob. Maida went east on the street-car toward home.

So did Reverend Spangler and his wife. He didn't feel the pro-German was in great danger, or he would have made an effort to dissuade the mob.[13] Quite a few men like that captive had been paraded up and down the small-town streets of southern Illinois in recent weeks. A few had been tarred and feathered, but mostly they had just been made to display their patriotism to Uncle Sam. There was a war on, after all.

Robert Paul Prager, thirty, continued west with the mob too, but he had no choice in the matter. In his broken English, the German immigrant continued his feeble efforts to sing patriotic songs.[14] Tears welled up in his brown eyes whenever he kissed the flag for the men. He occasionally would shout out a patriotic phrase for the benefit of his captors. *"Three cheers for the red, white, and blue."*[15]

With a man on each arm, Prager was alternately pushed and dragged westward on the St. Louis Road, part of what was also known as the National Road. The two men holding him made it easier for the others to repeatedly hit Prager with their fists, sometimes hard enough to knock him down.[16] It had been this way since he was abducted from City Hall nearly an hour earlier.[17] And it would continue for nearly another mile, until the mob had him outside the city limits. *Until the boys had their fill of him.*

Whether he was truly a spy or merely pro-German, everyone wanted to teach him a lesson. Earlier some of the men had said that he planned to blow up the Maryville mine. But no one seemed to actually know him; it was just what they had been told. At this point it really didn't seem to matter. The mob was much too riled up to care.

The leaders at the forefront were holding their prey, beating him, pushing the meandering effort to create the night Collinsville would just as soon forget. They were spurred on by the cheers and jeers of the younger boys and the older men who challenged them to give no quarter.[18] Show the pro-German just how tough

Americans are. The agitators stayed behind the mob, never steering the wheel but surely supplying the fuel. Those crying loudest for action would not soil their hands by touching Robert Prager.

Most people in the mob were actually little more than bystanders. They may have shouted at the pro-German occasionally, but they were primarily just curious about what would become of him. Several cars followed, most containing young men with no intention of missing one of the most exciting things to happen in Collinsville for years.[19]

There seemed no particular plan of what to do except torment the man and get him out of Collinsville.[20] One of the cars following the mob contained four city police officers. Their goal was to see that nothing too wretched happened to the pro-German, inside Collinsville anyway, less the mob tarnish the city's fair name.[21] The police planned, one officer said later, to dash up and take Prager from the mob if it attempted to lynch him. All four were armed with revolvers, and no one in the mob was believed to have any type of weapon. Yet by the time they reached the western city limits, the officers had made no attempt to rescue Prager, and they simply returned to their station.

The motley entourage continued out the St. Louis Road and stopped about one quarter mile past the city boundaries, atop Bluff Hill. Where the pavement ended by the streetcar tracks, Prager was ordered to remove his socks and shoes so he would have to walk on the rough surface with bare feet.[22] Someone asked if there was any need to continue down the hill, but no one could offer a reason. By this time the crowd had thinned to about one hundred people, a few actively involved in tormenting the hapless prisoner but most passively watching.[23]

At first the leaders were uncertain of what to do with Prager.[24] Eventually, their inebriated kangaroo court decided a coat of tar and feathers would well suit the pro-German.[25] They believed tar could be found at Schmidt's Mound Park, a tavern and resort four miles west, between Collinsville and East St. Louis.[26] Never mind that the mob had walked within a stone's throw of a barrel of tar at the Hardscrabble Mine, less than a mile back.

One of the mob leaders approached an automobile driven by eighteen-year-old Harry Linneman. He was driving the service car for Bitzer Garage that night, but curiosity had gotten the better of him. He and some friends decided they would follow the midnight parade. Three or four members of the mob stepped onto the running boards and ordered Linneman to drive to Schmidt's Mound Park. He already had eight passengers and protested to no avail that the car would be overloaded, that he didn't want to go. Drive, Linneman was told, and he did.[27]

Schmidt's Mound Park was so named because it sat next to an ancient Indian burial mound. Its proprietor, John Schmidt, offered a tavern and beer garden, with fried chicken dinners also served. The interurban line stored tar at Schmidt's to maintain the roads and its rail beds.

When the overloaded car arrived from Collinsville, the men on the running boards jumped off and beat on the door of Schmidt's home. It was about midnight. Impatient—and on a mission—they began their search before Schmidt could come to the door. They found baled packages of asphalt, which they didn't take, but somehow overlooked fifteen casks of tar. We'll get it back in town, they told Linneman, and ordered him back to Collinsville.[28]

Atop Bluff Hill the mob leaders used the interlude to harass and interrogate Prager. Was he a German spy? Had he planned to blow up the Maryville mine? Why didn't he keep his date to meet with a miners' union official in Edwardsville yesterday? Prager denied their accusations. Some questions he did not answer.[29]

Returning from their fruitless journey, Linneman drove up the steep incline of Bluff Hill to the north side of the blocked roadway. The men jumped off, and the leaders once again discussed their options. One man went to the service car driven by Linneman. In the tonneau compartment, he found a length of half-inch manila rope, used for towing disabled cars.[30] At this early morning hour, it would serve a different purpose.

Mobs hold great power, not great wisdom. They have the ability to bring out the worst in all who partake. They pander to the loudest voices, the lowest thoughts, and the most abhorrent behavior. People of otherwise little account become leaders, become empowered. It was Joe Riegel, a drunk, impulsive troublemaker, who became a leader this evening. A twenty-eight-year-old army veteran, he was earlier at the front of the charge to take Prager from police custody. Since then Prager had scarcely left his grasp.[31]

"The mob," Diogenes said, "is the mother of tyrants." And so it was that the drunken Riegel was given unto the City of Collinsville that night. When he found the rope in the car, Riegel knew just what to do with it.[32] The German spy, Riegel said, would hang.

Rope in hand, Riegel walked over to a sprawling hackberry tree, barren of leaves, on the south side of the roadway. "This will do," he said.[33] He then scrambled up the tree like a squirrel, placed the rope over a limb about twenty feet in the air, and slid back down.[34]

These sobering preparations had the effect of stilling what had been a boisterous and rowdy crowd.[35] Many backed away, wanting no part of what they thought could occur next. Conspicuous now in their silence were those who had earlier called loudest for Prager to die, those who had been most vocal in demanding violence.

Also silent were a number of businessmen and community leaders, men whose curiosity had earlier gotten the better of them when they decided to follow the mob. Now in the instant when it seemed the affair would turn deadly, none stepped forward, individually or as a group, to lodge any protest. They included store proprietors, a city alderman, a barber, and both Collinsville newspaper publishers, who may have followed just to get the story. They were men of standing in the community, men whose word would be respected. Yet they would say nothing to the mostly younger, drunken men and boys leading the action. Driven by fear of the mob or perhaps disdain for the German alien, their quiet complicity would help leave a stain on Collinsville for generations to come. They, like the men who had been so vocal earlier, slipped back into the shadows cast by the newly risen half-moon.[36]

Harry Linneman felt increasingly uneasy too and started to drive back into Collinsville. But he was stopped and told to point the car toward the tree, so the headlights could be used for illumination. Some of the other drivers were directed to do the same.[37]

When Prager was finally led to the tree, he seemed resigned to his fate. Cecil Larremore, seventeen years old, searched Prager's pockets and looked for anything incriminating.[38] Asked if he had anything to say, Prager was stoic, "Yes, I would like to pray." He knelt on the ground, clasped his hands in front of him, and prayed fervently in German.[39] Those who understood said he called on God to witness that he was innocent and being made a scapegoat of unreasonable hate. Yet he also called on God to forgive those who persecuted him. Prager asked for remission of his sins, confessing that he had many faults, but said he was loyal to the United States. Hearing enough after about three minutes, someone pulled Prager to his feet.[40]

Unwilling to intercede yet knowing the hanging would be a travesty of justice, some onlookers still could not tear themselves away. One man said to another: "They ought not to do that." The other man agreed, saying: "It's plain murder, but what can you do?"[41]

Just before he was strung up, Prager asked that the Stars and Stripes be brought to him one more time. When his captors complied, he kissed the flag, tears again welling up in eyes. Prager lifted his head up and said: "All right, boys, go ahead and kill me," in his halting English. "But wrap me up in the flag when you bury me."[42]

With the noose secure on Prager's neck, Riegel called for people to help with the rope. In response most of the crowd stepped farther back. Riegel pulled up on the rope by himself three or four times, but he was unable to lift Prager. He called out to the crowd, "We've gone this far, boys. Don't let there be any slackers here."[43] Another appeal was made for people to at least touch the rope, to show they were all involved. Again many took a step backward.[44] But fifteen or twenty men did step toward the rope, and together they lifted Prager off the ground.[45]

But no one had bothered to tie his hands behind his back. As Prager was raised into the air and started to choke, he instinctively grabbed for the rope above his head to relieve the pressure on his neck. Riegel called out for him to let go of the rope, but Prager did not and continued to struggle. Another man in the crowd yelled, "Let him down. Let him say something if he wants."[46]

Once again on the ground, Prager was asked if he was going to tell who he was "mixed up with." Perhaps not understanding the question, Prager said he had three partners but refused to divulge any names. He also said his parents were living, and he wanted them to be contacted. "Brothers, I would write a letter," he said.[47]

It is uncertain whether Prager was trying to buy time or if he truly wanted to reach out to the family in Germany he probably hadn't seen in thirteen years, but the mob allowed him to write. Riegel and twenty-year-old Charles Cranmer led Prager over to the three surrounding automobiles. They moved to the front fender of Louis Gerding's machine, the only one with a spotlight.[48] Cranmer, who earlier had gotten off work at National Stockyards in East St. Louis, still had a pad of waybill sheets in his pocket. He gave Prager one of the sheets and a pencil.[49]

As Prager started to write the note in German, some protested at not knowing what he was writing. "All right," Riegel said, "let him go ahead."[50] Prager simply wrote that he was going to die and made a final request of his family: "Please pray for us, my dear parents." He said it was his last letter and "sign of life."[51]

After completing the note, Prager handed it to Riegel and gave the pencil back to Cranmer. Riegel scanned the note and asked Prager what it said, to see if the German was "putting anything over on him." Prager then asked Cranmer to write his father's name and address on the note.[52] Someone asked how they might get a letter to Germany during wartime. "Through Washington," Prager said.[53] With that Prager was escorted back to the tree.

Again he was asked if he had any local family members or partners in his alleged crimes. Prager shook his head no this time. He didn't seem to want to talk anymore. "Well if he won't come in with anything, string him up," someone said.[54]

This time Prager's hands were tied behind his back with a handkerchief. More men moved to the rope as he was lifted ten feet into the air. Five or six men then tied the working end of the rope to a roadside telephone pole.[55]

Hanging, done correctly, provides a means to quickly break a man's neck. The shock of the body weight against the rope will typically break one or more cervical vertebrae or perhaps stop all blood flow to the head. Breathing ceases, and the heart peacefully stops within a few minutes.

But the hanging of Robert Prager, like most lynchings, was not done in the most humane fashion. With no sudden drop to break his neck, he was left to suffocate on the rope, first struggling for air, then convulsively jerking due to lack of oxygen. The last desperate struggles of Prager served to drive most of the dwindling crowd even farther away from the tree or to leave. One man nonetheless walked up and pulled on the German's bare toes.[56]

For more than fifteen anxious minutes, his body grotesquely twitched and convulsed at the end of the rope.[57] Finally some of the men decided they would finish the matter. They untied the line and let the body fall three times before jerking the rope to try to break his neck. "One for the red, one for the white, and one for the blue," someone said, proclaiming their patriotic work done for now.[58]

Only a few men were left to watch Prager's final earthly moments. A handful quietly celebrated, but most broke off in twos and threes to silently make their way home.[59] The top of Bluff Hill was quiet once again, almost tranquil. In early April with the trees not yet full, those atop the bluff could see the lights from St. Louis, only ten miles west.

Just across the St. Louis Road from the hanging tree lay Hillside Park, where five days earlier Collinsville had celebrated Christ's resurrection with an Easter egg hunt. More than two thousand residents turned out for the event, called "one of the great successes of the kind ever given in this City."[60]

One of the highlights Sunday had been the performance by the Collinsville Concert Band. When it played "My Country 'tis of Thee," the whole crowd joined in singing.[61] Standing by the hilltop tree where Robert Prager's lifeless body now hung, one would have heard the lyrics:

My country, 'tis of thee,
Sweet land of liberty
Of thee I sing;
Land where my fathers died,
Land of the pilgrim's pride,
From every mountain side
Let freedom ring.

2

A Small Town, a Great War

My Tuesdays are meatless;
My Wednesdays are wheatless;
I'm getting more eatless each day.
My home, it is heatless;
My bed, it is sheetless,
They're all sent to the YMCA.
The barrooms are treatless;
My coffee is sweetless;
Each day I get poorer and wiser.
My stockings are feetless;
My trousers are seatless;
My God, how I do hate the Kaiser!

—The Poet's Corner, *United Mine Workers Journal*, January 24, 1918

From atop Collinsville's western bluffs, the growing St. Louis skyline could be seen in the distance. If St. Louis, a bustling city of over 750,000, was the Gateway to the West, Collinsville, looking down along the National Road, was perhaps the scenic Gateway to St. Louis. Three industrial river towns collared St. Louis on the Illinois side of the Mississippi River. With the river and excellent rail access, East St. Louis, Granite City, and Alton provided much of the heavy industrial muscle for the St. Louis region. There were mills for steel and other metals, chemical plants, packinghouses and the whole lot of industries that everyone needs but no one wants as a neighbor.

Collinsville was above those towns and St. Louis, but it was connected to them as conveniently as possible in 1918 by street-car lines and roads. Between Collinsville and the industrial towns west lie the American Bottoms, a floodplain with rich soil, ideal for farming corn, wheat, and beans. But the city was comfortably perched more than one hundred feet above the industrial fray and pollution that lie in the river valley. From the top of the bluffs, one could see to the east the great plain that comprises the lion's share of Illinois's topography. Just outside of Collinsville's limits, farmers plied their trade on fields where flooding was not a concern.

But it was an unseen geological feature that dominated Collinsville in 1918, a seam of bituminous coal about two hundred feet below ground. The first coal mine in Collinsville had been sunk in 1862, but the venture did not pay big rewards until the Vandalia Railroad ran tracks south and east of town.[1] The tracks were literally a stone's throw from the Cantine Creek area, which had a rich seven-foot-long vein of coal.[2] The chief entrepreneur of Collinsville's coal industry was initially Dr. Octavius Lumaghi, a convivial Italian physician. Smelting of metals generally required about two tons of coal for every one ton of ore, making it most feasible to have smelting works near coal mines. Lumaghi built a zinc smelter next to the railroad and adjacent to his first mine. His company would end up sinking four mines in Collinsville.[3]

The industrial demands of World War I provided the high water mark for Collinsville's coal industry.[4] Nine mines were located in or adjacent to the city. More than half of Collinsville's workingmen were employed at mines, and mining-related occupations accounted for many more jobs. Demand was high for experienced miners and laborers, which brought a flood of workers to the town, many of them immigrants.

Collinsville's population hovered near ten thousand, but immigrant whites or those with at least one immigrant parent made up more than half the residents—a far higher percentage than any other nearby Illinois city.[5] Likewise, Collinsville had a higher percentage of foreign-born whites (18 percent) than any of its neighbors, even the industrial towns to the west. Some employers had urged their alien workers to become U.S. citizens, and more than 130 began seeking naturalization in early 1917.[6] But the immigrant-heavy demographics provided for instability in the town on the bluffs. In 1918 they would arguably make Collinsville the most volatile town in the area after race riots had already boiled over in East St. Louis in 1917.

Collinsville was primarily developed around four streets, the St. Louis Road from the west, Main and Clay Streets uptown, and Vandalia Avenue headed northeast out of town. Most homes and businesses were built close to those streets as they were served by the East St. Louis and Suburban streetcar system. In 1917 and 1918, the system was the prime means of transportation and connected with most of the surrounding cities and St. Louis. Everyone used mass transit. Homes for sale were advertised with their distance from the rumbling streetcar line.

All roads fed onto the paralleled Main and Clay Streets, where stores and businesses of every sort were located in a six-block stretch. Streetcars ran on both streets, with Clay Street eastbound and Main Street headed west. The Orpheum Opera House on Main Street was the most imposing building in town, although the miner's labor temple, which was under construction, promised to rival that.[7]

The social scene was strictly small town. There were church and club affairs. Collinsville Community Band concerts cost ten cents. It was the same price for a balcony seat at the Orpheum, but a main-floor ticket cost twenty cents. When it was too hot for shows indoors, the operation moved to the Airdome across the street. Both hosted moving picture shows and vaudeville acts. Dances were held at Reese Hall, Collinsville Park, and other venues, but were illegal on Sundays. The town had dozens of saloons. Some bars had offered wine rooms in the back where ladies were welcome, but they had been ordered closed by the mayor, lest an unsavory situation develop. Collinsville also had pool halls and at least six restaurants and lunchrooms.

The city was cleaner and less dusty now that most of the outlying streets had been oiled.[8] Uptown streets and sidewalks were mostly brick or concrete, but most sidewalks outside that area were still dirt and cinders. Many fancier homes lined Clay, Vandalia, Morrison, and Church Streets, some with fenced yards. Most homes had outbuildings, perhaps a barn or shed. Older places had privies.[9]

But Collinsville was booming; there was little doubt about that. Collinsville Township included the city, the rural area around it, and the village of Maryville out on Vandalia Street, just north of Collinsville. In 1917 the township had seen seventy new homes built, mostly in the city.[10] But the most dramatic increase was in ownership of automobiles. In 1916 there were just 86 "gas wagons" in the township. That number increased to 186 in 1917. Still, less than 2 percent of people owned cars. As one businessman said, few people had them, but everybody wanted one.[11]

World War I had begun following the June 1914 assassination of Austria-Hungary's Archduke Franz Ferdinand and his wife in Sarajevo, but it seemed a remote issue to most Americans. The affair got more complicated following the May 1915 sinking of the *Lusitania* by German Unterseeboot 20, which killed nearly 1,200 people, including 128 of the 197 Americans on board. While the United States was officially a neutral country, a war in someone else's backyard proved a good thing for U.S. industrial and banking interests. By late 1916 American firms had done $2 billion in war-related business with the Entente nations of France and Great Britain, and American banks had loaned them $2.5 billion. By contrast just $45 million had been loaned to the Central Powers of Germany, Austria-Hungary, the Ottoman Empire, and Bulgaria.[12] Neutral indeed.

The *Lusitania* was indeed a passenger ship, but it was also a Royal Navy Auxiliary Cruiser carrying sixty tons of war màtèriel and sixty-seven Canadian soldiers.[13] Before it set sail, the German Embassy had published warnings that the ship was subject to submarine attack. After the sinking U.S. president Woodrow Wilson issued a stern protest. He told an audience three days later, "There is such a thing as a man being too proud to fight; there is such a thing as a nation being so right that it does not need to convince others by force that it is right."[14] Many, including former president Theodore Roosevelt, considered Wilson's response cowardly.

But Wilson's 1916 presidential campaign continued along those lines. It seemed the right message to a country that had seen the arrival of twelve million immigrants, mostly European, since the turn of the century and was not in the mood for war.[15] The U.S. economy was humming, and with the war some three thousand miles away, there seemed no need to get involved. Wilson's 1916 campaign slogan was "He kept us out of war."

Both political parties realized the folly of running a pro-war campaign. Republican nominee Charles Hughes and vice presidential candidate Charles Fairbanks advocated a higher level of preparedness for war. The Democratic position was left of that, with Wilson and running mate Thomas Marshall advocating continued neutrality. Marshall was perhaps as humorous as Wilson was, at least publicly, dour. After one U.S. senator had prattled on about what the country needed, the vice president could stand no more. "What this country needs," Marshall said, "is a really good five-cent cigar."

After a bitter campaign the Wilson-Marshall ticket won 49 percent of the vote compared to Hughes-Fairbanks's 46 percent. The 1916 presidential election was a close affair in Collinsville too. Women had won the right to vote on most elected positions in Illinois in 1913, and in 1916 in Collinsville they went for Wilson for president, 1,053 to 935.[16] Collinsville men voted in favor of Hughes, 626 to 480. Whether it was the novelty of the new vote or that they took their civic responsibility more seriously, almost twice as many women as men had turned out to cast their ballots in Collinsville on that election day.

Just as the Collinsville men had voted, Madison County and Illinois also went for the Hughes-Fairbanks ticket. Despite the party's loss in the presidential race, Republican officeholders were swept in at both the county and the state levels.[17]

Before President Wilson could even be sworn in for his second term, relations deteriorated rapidly with Germany, which had resumed unrestricted submarine warfare on January 31, 1917. The United States severed formal relations February 3.[18] In March three American cargo ships were sunk in a twenty-four-hour period. A telegram from the German foreign secretary was intercepted that encouraged Mexico to join Germany in war against the United States and offered military assistance. The release of the telegram and the revived U-boat attacks on American shipping were enough to finally force the administration to act. Fewer than five months after being elected with a campaign slogan of "He kept us out of war," Wilson planned to declare just that on Germany.

Wilson called the new Sixty-Fifth Congress into a joint session April 2, 1917, and spoke on the need to join the fray with the British, the French, and others, as "the world must be made safe for democracy." To not intervene would allow autocracy to spread, war proponents claimed.[19]

In the spring of 1917, the concept of entering a world war on foreign soil was hard to grasp for many U.S. citizens, as well as for a number of elected officials who would be asked to approve the operation. It was an era long before America saw itself as the world's protector and policeman and some thirty years before the Truman Doctrine.

The House first approved the president's declaration of war, followed by the Senate. On April 6, 1917, Good Friday, the United States was officially at war. There had been some debate from people like the Socialist senator Robert La Follette and others, but the Senate and the House voted overwhelmingly for approval. Tax funding for the war, a compulsory draft, and even prohibitions on free speech would be approved thereafter.[20] The limited debate that did occur in Washington reiterated many of the assertions of the common people, including that it was a rich man's war.[21] The belief was that industry and banks would reap huge profits from a conflict that would cost the lives of thousands of working-class men, and it was continuously cited by Socialists and other critics.

The implications of declaring war were unclear to many. Told of the cost and needed manpower projections, one senator at a committee hearing asked: "Good Lord, you aren't going to send troops over there are you?"[22] Many thought American involvement would be limited to patrol of the Atlantic Ocean or assumed military service would be voluntary. In the last great U.S. military affair, the Civil War, less than 6 percent of the troops had been drafted.[23] Yet those drafts had resulted in riots and other public unrest. But Wilson and military leaders realized how voluntary service had carved up a whole generation of young leaders in Great Britain who had rushed out early to serve in the war. Volunteering had also taken away men who were experienced in providing war-industry needs on the home front. And few army officials believed there would actually be enough volunteers to meet military needs.

After Congress approved war legislation, the task remained of how to convince a splintered nation that entering the conflict was necessary. More than a third of the population was either immigrant or had at least one parent who was.[24] Germans had been the predominant immigrant group for decades, and they had mixed feelings at best about waging war against the Fatherland. America had the second highest German population in the world.[25] The Irish tended to oppose anything that might benefit Great Britain. Nativists generally felt Great Britain should be supported, as did most Anglo immigrants. The lower classes tended to think the war would benefit only the wealthy. And all that any American had heard from Wilson's administration for the last two and a half years was that the United States should remain neutral. Wilson now not only wanted Americans' full support for the war effort; he also sought to establish war controls through voluntary means, not by executive orders. He wanted food and fuel prices set by agreement with the affected industries, not governmental authority. And the only way that level of pervasive patriotic thinking could be cultivated, Wilson believed, was by a wide-reaching public relations bureau. Others would call it simply a government propaganda agency.[26]

Woodrow Wilson's name for this agency was the Committee on Public Information. It was created April 14 and chaired by longtime Wilson supporter, muckraker, and public relations man George Creel. The CPI was composed of Secretary of State Robert Lansing, Secretary of War Newton Baker, and Secretary of the Navy Josephus Daniels. Given the other members' wartime responsibilities and Creel's autocratic ways, it was essentially a one-man committee. In fact, it had just one meeting.[27] It was often appropriately referred to as the Creel Committee and would help create a wartime nation teeming with paranoid, hysterical patriots.

Creel built an organization intended to galvanize American support for the war, and he did so by controlling nearly every form of communication to U.S. citizens. He wanted to increase the American war will and get everyone involved in the effort.[28] There had to be shared sacrifice for everyone to buy in, he believed. Just one week after the CPI was created, ten-by-twelve-inch "information" cards titled "What the Government Asks of the Press," were distributed to newspaper and magazine editors nationwide. Concurrent with Wilson's thinking, requests such as these would be considered not government censorship but *guidelines*.[29] Any form of press restriction would be self-imposed. The only judge, Wilson and Creel said, should be in the court of public opinion.

News announcements on war efforts were most always positive and came in the form of some six thousand major news releases. More than twelve thousand smaller papers, such as the *Advertiser* and the *Herald* in Collinsville, got a weekly digest in galley form, ready to be used in print.[30] But it would be only months before many U.S. editors adopted the term *Creeling* to describe CPI reports that were based more on wishful thinking than on fact.[31]

CPI bureaus were created to produce everything from Liberty Bond posters to flyers alerting people to beware of German spies in their midst. One enduring creation of the era was the image of Uncle Sam saying, "I want you for the U.S. Army." All told, 122 illustrations were created for streetcars and windows, 310 more for newspaper and magazine use, and 1,438 graphics were designed for buttons, seals, and the like.[32] Patriotic ads, often promoting the purchase of Liberty Bonds, were developed for newspapers—with local patriotic companies paying for the advertising space.

All public information related to the war effort went through Creel's office. Photographs were distributed at the rate of seven hundred per day. Over two hundred thousand slide images were created.[33] War expos—described by Creel as having "all the attraction of a circus and all the seriousness of a sermon"—were held in major cities and drew a total of ten million people.[34] Adults paid twenty-five cents for admission, and the expos helped improve Liberty Bond sales.

A plethora of printed materials were made, ranging from thirty-page booklets designed to steer the beliefs of the educated businessman to heavily illustrated Loyalty Leaflets for distribution to the working class with their weekly paychecks. An estimated seventy-five million specialized booklets were printed in eighteen months.[35] Propaganda materials were literally tailored to each type and class of worker. Traveling salesmen, for example, were given *The Kaiserite: 101 German Lies*. It told of 101 rumors about the war and described how they were untrue. The salesmen were asked to challenge these rumors if they were to hear them told on their route. If they found the original source of the rumor, they were asked to report it to the CPI office in Washington. "Swat the lie," they were told. "Don't be satisfied with hearsay or rumor. You are summoned as specifically as if you were enlisted in the Army or Navy to aid the national cause. Our troops will meet the enemy abroad. You can meet him at home."

By the fall of 1918, a sixteen-page newspaper had been created for America's schoolchildren; it reached an estimated twenty million homes.[36] A suggested elementary school teaching plan included themes of patriotism, heroism, and sacrifice. Students were also shown how the horrors of war had hurt France and Belgium and were told the same thing would happen here if Germany attacked the United States.[37]

Magazines and newspapers were the prime purveyors of mass communication in 1917 and 1918, and the federal government controlled nearly all of what was seen by the naive eyes of Americans. The government could not necessarily stop the printing of publications by war opponents, such as the Socialists. But it did stop their national distribution through the U.S. Post Office. Postmaster General Albert Burleson was empowered by the Espionage Act to halt delivery of any publications that he believed could damage government efforts to prosecute the war.[38] Burleson, a heavy-handed Texan, took it a step further by not allowing distribution of any publication that even embarrassed the government.

Organizations that relied on national mail communication were stymied in their efforts to share their antiwar beliefs, even though they did not directly impede government efforts. Burleson was greatly criticized by socialists, including novelist Upton Sinclair. In a letter to Wilson, Sinclair said: "Your Postmaster-General reveals himself a person of such pitiful and childish ignorance . . . it is simply calamity that in this crisis he should be the person to decide what may or may not be uttered by our radical press. . . . It is hard to draw the line, Mr. President, as to the amount of ignorance permitted to a government official; but Mr. Burleson is assuredly on the wrong side of any line that could be drawn by anyone."[39]

And the censorship of mail was not just an issue on the national level. Some local postmasters took it upon themselves to view, censor, delay, or destroy inbound or outbound mail from people or organizations they deemed suspicious.[40]

War Secretary Newton Baker set a nationwide draft registration day, and it was a big affair in Collinsville. The Commercial Club and the City Council would lead the effort for men to "answer the call of Uncle Sam, when that call comes." On Tuesday, June 5, registrations started at 7:00 a.m., and a 10:30 a.m. parade brought two thousand people down Main Street, while thousands more looked on. From there the draft-aged men moved on to registration stations, based on their precinct. The crush of men was so great that one of the stations ran out of registration cards.[41]

The excited young men, ages twenty-one to thirty, filled out registration cards with their name and address, physical characteristics, and date of birth. They were also required to list their occupation and employer, as those in war-critical positions might be eligible for exemption. They were asked for their marital status and whether they had parents, a wife, or children under twelve who were solely dependent on them for support. The registrants were also asked if they were natural-born or a naturalized citizen of the United States. The form was to be marked "Declarant" if they had taken out their first immigration papers and pledged to become a U.S. citizen. Those who had not taken out any immigration papers were marked as "Alien."[42]

One reporter focused on two of the registrants in Collinsville: "One blond-haired German miner, who had taken his first papers and who said he was the sole support of his mother, father and sister, said nothing in answer to the questions, but a steely glint in his eye showed that he was made of the heroic stuff that puts country above all other considerations." Another was a Lithuanian miner who had a wife and three children and also his brother's three orphaned children in his household. When asked if he had any exemptions, he said: "Only my family. If somebody care for them, I go."[43]

Another newspaper reported on a Russian alien who had lived in the United States for nineteen years but still "indicated his lack of affection for the land."[44] The man gave numerous excuses for why he could not serve, not least among them that he was supporting a wife, three children, two parents, and six siblings back in Russia.

Copies of President Wilson's war declaration speech were distributed to the men. The city council had provided flags and pins stating, "I am Registered, are you?" which young women from the retail clerks' union or the hosiery workers' union gave to each of the registrants. The registrants also received green cards as proof that they had fulfilled their patriotic duty.[45]

"Throughout the day the City wore a holiday aspect," a newspaper reported. Most businesses and industry closed, but confectionaries and saloons remained open. "While there was no jollification, there was little air of depression among either the men registering or among the citizenry at large."[46]

In all 1,079 men from Collinsville would register that day, nearly half of whom declined to list any exemption that might preclude their having to go to war. Nearly 400 indicated that they had dependent family members. Among the registrants were 176 aliens, only two of whom were from Germany.[47] Altogether 9,660,000 men across the United States registered on that day; of those, 800,000 would get occupational deferments.[48] And to the surprise of some, there was no large-scale draft resistance nationwide. That is not to say everyone agreed, however; the Illinois National Guard was dispatched to Rockford for three days due to antidraft demonstrations in that city.[49]

Another registration day was held one year later, followed by two more in August and September 1918, bringing a total of more than 24 million registered men; 2,810,296 would later be inducted by 4,650 local draft boards nationwide.[50] The total male population of the United States in April 1917 was some 54 million.

A Collinsville newspaper noted that on Monday, June 4, the day before registration, there had been an uptick in the number of marriage licenses issued to draft-eligible men. But no aspersions were cast on these men: "While many of the men seeking matrimony were of conscription age, they are not to be regarded as slackers."[51]

The list of eligible Collinsville men was created in the following weeks, but some men would not wait for the exemption and draft process. Probably the first to enlist was Lester Dorris, a tall, red-haired twenty-year-old student at the University of Missouri School of Mines and Metallurgy in Rolla, who reported for the army on May 4.[52] By August Dorris would be promoted to second lieutenant. Forty Collinsville men enlisted together in early July to serve in the Third Illinois Artillery and reported to camp in early August. One of them, Jules Field, had served as secretary of the Collinsville Commercial Club and would later be appointed lieutenant in the Headquarters Company.[53]

The patriotic call to serve seemed contagious on all social levels in the community. Six Collinsville physicians, including Mayor John Siegel, had signed up and been declared eligible for the Medical Officers Reserve Corp.[54] If all had been chosen to go, only two physicians would have been left to serve the town of about ten thousand.

On Friday, July 20, a blindfolded War Secretary Newton Baker, at the Senate Office Building in Washington DC, drew a black capsule from a glass bowl. It contained the first draft number, 258.[55] The Collinsville man with that number was Emil Gerken.[56] An anxious community was informed of the drawn numbers by the *Collinsville Herald*, which published two extra editions that evening listing the numbers for all the local registered men. All five hundred copies of the first extra were sold as soon as they came off the press.[57]

The *Collinsville Herald* tried to find Gerken for comment and learned he had left his laborer position at St. Louis Smelting and Refining. It speculated that "Gerken had a hunch" his number would be called and implied he had left the area to avoid duty. The newspaper noted that his name was probably Austrian or German.[58] Learning what had been printed about him, Gerken sought out the publisher and told him that he had taken a job for a gas company and resented the suggestion that "he might sympathize with the Teutonic Allies," despite his name. The *Herald* reported, "He insists he is an American through and through and is ready to fight any time. He is a big, well-built man of 23, and looks every inch a fighter. He has no dependents and waits the pleasure of Uncle Sam."[59]

Gerken and some 229 other registered men from Collinsville and the surrounding township would be examined for their fitness to serve in the National Army beginning August 11.[60] Shortly thereafter 600 others on the list would receive their notices.[61] Charles Maurer had the unique perspective of serving on the local Draft Exemption Board and saw the transition of public opinion from mostly opposed to the war and the draft to supporting the war effort later in 1918. "A lot of people thought it was a moneyed-man's war, which made it a lot harder on the men that were to go and harder on the people who were doing their duty." Once the United States declared war, however, the attitude changed to "we had gotten into the war and the only way out was to fight, and to fight hard." As the war progressed, Maurer said, more-reluctant soldiers came in line as they did not want to be labeled as slackers by townspeople and those already serving.[62]

On August 17 the *Herald* published a list of all those who had claimed family support exemptions from serving, mostly due to a dependent wife or children. By the end of the month, it was announced that Collinsville's district, Madison County Draft Division 3, had surpassed its draft quota.[63]

Most of Collinsville's clergy openly supported the war effort, essentially considering it God's work. Rev. Willis Cleaveland of the Christ Episcopal Church said that the United States faced despotism and the loss of democracy if the war was not won by the Allies, that the soul of America was the hope for the world. Rev. Theodore Cates of the First Methodist Church said it was the "will of God" for the United States to take up arms.[64] Some churches had more to prove than others, namely, their patriotism. Membership in the Holy Cross Lutheran and Jerusalem Lutheran Churches and St. John Evangelical Church was predominantly German, and those churches offered German-language services in addition to English. Times being what they were, there were suspicions. Holy Cross hosted a Lutheran regional celebration of the four hundredth anniversary of the Reformation on September 2, 1917. The 1,500 people in attendance heard church leaders proclaim that Lutherans were loyal to Uncle Sam, not the kaiser.[65] Still, Holy Cross thought it best to cover its stained glass, which had German printing.[66]

The local papers were filled with patriotic stories, letters, and artwork, much of it supplied by the CPI. The "Star-Spangled Banner" made one edition, while Edward Everett Hale's "A Man without a Country" ran as a regular column.[67] One edition printed James Whitcomb Riley's poem "The Name of Old Glory."[68] Another column reported on the busy day on a battleship, while the Liberty Loan Committee provided a letter from a Canadian soldier under the title "A Glorious Feeling to Die for Democracy."[69]

The first eleven of Collinsville's drafted men reported for induction on September 5. Before leaving town they were given an informal reception at the Masonic Temple in the Red Cross rooms.[70] Each of the men received a comfort bag from the Red

Cross before Rev. W. D. Vater of the First Presbyterian Church and Rev. M. F. Bierbaum of St. John Evangelical spoke to them. Mayor Siegel, wearing the uniform of captain in the Medical Reserve Corp, asked the men to uphold the honor of Collinsville while in military service. Then Siegel and two members of the draft board used their automobiles to transport the men thirteen miles west to Madison, Illinois, where they would board a train bound for Camp Zachary Taylor in Louisville, Kentucky.

Yet for all the public display of patriotism on registration day and hullabaloo over the release of draft numbers in July, the first eleven men who reported on September 5 bore little resemblance to the first eleven local men whose names were drawn in the July draft. First pick Emil Gerken, draft number 258, was on that train. But whether the cause was deferment, family support exemption, war work exemption, or another reason, the next lowest numbered man, Earnest Adams, was 30th on the local list.[71] The next lowest man had the 103rd local number drawn. The 11th and final man in the initial contingent had his number drawn as the 265th local pick in July. For all the over-the-top public enthusiasm shown since the war had started, Collinsville's drafted men were in no hurry to be on that first troop train out of town.

When five times as many of Collinsville's young men reported to join the others at Camp Taylor two weeks later, the departure became much more emotional. Perhaps it was the large number of draftees or the fact that many of the families went to East St. Louis and watched them board the train, maybe seeing them for the last time. But the impact of the young men leaving September 19 was much more unsettling to the community. The Tuesday evening before their day to report, a farewell meeting planned for city hall had to be moved to the outdoor Airdome on Main Street to accommodate the huge crowd. The following morning seemingly the whole town turned out to see them off outside city hall.

"Mothers, sweethearts, wives and male relatives surged about the place seeking to say a few words to their dear ones," a reporter noted. One draftee's elderly mother "clung to his neck with convulsive sobs shaking her frame." The mood was somber and serious. "There was no braggadocio in evidence. The scene was too solemn for that."[72] At 9:30 a.m. the recruits marched to a line of motorcars for the ride to East St. Louis, and many family members and friends followed.

"They've gone," another newspaper reported. "Bathed in the tears of relatives, their ears ringing from the shouts of goodbyes from the whole city, and followed by hundreds of prayers and good wishes from hungry, vacant hearts, 55 men, the first main contingent of Collinsville's selected men for the National Army, left Wednesday morning and rolled out of East St. Louis for Camp Taylor." As a band at the train station played the "Star-Spangled Banner," the men struggled to pull away from their families and friends. "One pathetic scene after another was enacted throughout the crowd. Few men there were dry at the parting."[73] An awkward half-hour delay of the loaded train at the platform only seemed to make matters worse.

On the heels of the emotional departure of so many of its young men, Collinsville became less tolerant of remarks favoring the Central Powers. "All unexpectedly there has broken out in a few quarters of Collinsville, pro-German utterances which are generally regarded as unpatriotic." J. O. Monroe, the eccentric new publisher of the *Collinsville Herald*, noted that at least two different people in the city had made offensive remarks in public. "The mass of public sentiment in Collinsville at present is in no humor to listen calmly to light remarks about the soldiery or insinuations regarding the unjustness of the war we are waging."[74]

Two weeks after the contingent of fifty-five men left, twenty-nine more would depart on October 3.[75] Another Tuesday evening send-off was well attended, but this time the crowd was much less emotional. The men were taken to their train again by Mayor Siegel and other leading citizens in their machines. Fewer families went to the train station.

Thirty men had been scheduled to report that Wednesday morning, but Joseph Stapen, a twenty-four-year-old Lithuanian miner, was not among them as expected.[76] After the drafted men were sent off that morning, Police Chief Tony Staten went in search of Stapen. He found him asleep in bed. Acquaintances said he had not worked in three months, depressed because of the pending draft. He had told them he would not be drafted. Chief Staten told Stapen he would personally take him to the draft induction center the next morning and to be prepared. Before Staten would return, however, the miner put a gun to his head and ended his own life.

There had been twenty-two other recent draft no-shows in the district, two of them from Collinsville.[77] Officials listed their names and offered $50 for each deserter turned in to authorities. When the slackers were arrested, they too were sent off to fulfill their obligation starting at Camp Taylor.

Immigrants seemed the most opposed to the draft and the idea of fighting in the European war, Draft Exemption Board member Charles Maurer said. No matter where the immigrant had been born, Maurer generally saw little difference in attitude: "The Italian was hard to handle and also the Poles and Russians were nearly all slackers. If they had no children they would borrow someone else's to get exemptions."[78] Children who could not be verified were also reported.

Language barriers also may have made it difficult to fully understand the draft requirements and exemption process. In some cases the immigrants had left their native countries just to avoid such military service. Two months after Stapen killed himself, an Italian immigrant who worked at one coal mine was told he would soon get a draft questionnaire. Witnesses said he "went crazy" and spread out his clothes after undressing outdoors on a cold December day. He then proceeded to swim and bathe in the mine's pond. "How he failed to freeze to death is not known." An ambulance was summoned, which transported the man to a hospital.[79]

Others who were escaping any service requirement were aliens who had not filed their first U.S. naturalization papers. These men were effectively in citizenship limbo and by law could not be required to fight for a nation that they were essentially just visiting.[80] "This situation has made the draft harder to bear for boys who have been called to go," a local publisher said.[81]

As a draft board member, Maurer noted a different perspective on patriotism as it related to inductees: "There was always plenty of patriotism from the fellow that did not have to go. He was continually out to show his patriotism. But the fellow that had to go to camp was always a little, more or less, the other way."[82] The same applied for the draftees' families. And when a young man was drafted, his family often immediately questioned why a neighbor's son had not also been sent.

As training camps swelled with the initial call of draftees, the next batch of Collinsville men would not report until February 25, 1918. Those twenty-six men would also be driven to the train station in Madison by civic leaders after a community send-off.[83] The army rushed to set up thirty-two new cantonments to handle the influx for training, and that process had just begun to gain momentum in the fall of 1917.[84]

Draft classifications, those delinquent from registering, those sent to camp, and those who had gotten the various types of exemption continued to be big news in the Collinsville newspapers, which continued to publish long lists of the names of those affected. Madison County would easily meet its quota of 1,284 men for the first call of the Federal Conscription Act of 1917, which was for 687,000 men nationwide.[85]

Most draftees would get perhaps six months of training stateside before being sent out on a miserably overcrowded troop ship. Another two months of training would be attempted in France, where the English and the French would teach the doughboys about trench warfare. Each new soldier earned $25 a month as a second-class private. Parents were promised that two "safeguards [were] thrown around the Army: Prohibition (and) suppression of social evil."[86] The quintessential doughboy of World War I was a white male in his early twenties, with little education and no prior military experience.[87] Yet as the war progressed and manpower needs increased dramatically, training would be significantly reduced. In the second half of 1918, some of the new troops would be sent to France never having fired a rifle.

The war effort entailed other costs besides flesh and blood. On

October 3, 1917, Congress passed the War Revenue Act, which imposed federal taxation on single persons with net earnings over $1,000 per year and married couples netting more than $2,000. Even at those limits, only 5 percent of the population would be required to pay income taxes.[88] At the minimum, the tax rate was 2 percent. It increased to 5 percent for net incomes between $5,000 and $7,500. The new graduated schedule provided for continued increased taxes as earnings rose. The tax rate for the top bracket rose from 15 to 67 percent.

But an immediate influx of funds would come from four Liberty Loan bond sale drives conducted after U.S. entry into the war. Bond interest ranged from 3 to 4.5 percent, always below what banks were paying, but interest earnings were tax free. The Liberty Bond sales were tremendously successful nationwide, over-selling the intended goal of $17 billion. And the bonds provided an outlet for everyone to show his or her patriotism, whether they served in the military or not. Newspapers, clubs, unions, and employers implored people to buy bonds. Moving-picture star Douglas Fairbanks, most recently appearing in *A Modern Musketeer*, used a cross-country train trip to raise more than $1 million. Theda Barr, star of *Cleopatra*, helped sell $300,000 worth in one day in New York City.[89] The first Liberty Loan drive began May 14, 1917. The St. Louis Smelting and Refining plant in Collinsville reported nearly half of its employees had purchased Liberty Bonds and that at $23,500 the facility had sold more than any other National Lead plant. But the response in the rest of the Collinsville was not so good, with banks reporting only a limited number of buyers except for the Lead Works employees.[90] A newspaper publisher took local residents to task: "Many people who would not hesitate to invest money in a new automobile stock or a wildcat mining venture appear to be afraid to trust Uncle Sam with their money. This is all wrong. It is neither good business nor good patriotism."[91]

The second Liberty Loan drive, which started October 1, followed the same trend in Collinsville. A local newspaper promoted the campaign to buy bonds "until it hurts" and included a proclamation about the drive from President Wilson. Madison County had been targeted to raise $2,780,000 but had total sales of $3,731,250 from 9,508 different subscribers.[92] Collinsville had been targeted to raise $250,000. Madison County did its part and then some; Collinsville did not.[93]

The two banks in Collinsville sold $201,950 in bonds to 503 subscribers, nearly 25 percent less than its goal. But the much smaller, perhaps more affluent communities of Highland and Edwardsville had bought some $345,000 and $528,000 in bonds, respectively.[94] Reasons for the poor bond sales in Collinsville could have ranged from poor local organization and promotion to silent opposition to U.S. involvement in the war. But in 1917 no community wanted to be pegged as not fully supporting the war effort. U.S. Treasury secretary William McAdoo, speaking to a crowd in California during the second bond drive, said: "Every person who refuses to subscribe or takes the attitude of let the other fellow do it, is a friend of Germany and I would like nothing better than to tell him to his face."[95]

As the Collinsville economy thrived, the war impact was similarly felt throughout the nation. Coal was in demand, which meant the mines were in full operation, when labor matters did not interfere. The first industry to settle in Collinsville to be near the coal supply, the Collinsville Zinc Smelter, then of the Picher Lead Company, abruptly stopped operation on April 23, 1917.[96] The closure was blamed on the more than thirty nearby property owners who had filed suit against the smelter for damages. Heavy pollution caused by the plant just east of town had given many people health problems and killed crops in the area, it was said. In a nearby Italian neighborhood, grapevines would no longer produce fruit for making wine. But with the economy booming, the loss of the three hundred jobs and a $40,000 monthly payroll hardly impacted the city.[97]

The Lead Works of St. Louis Smelting and Refining had taken steps to avoid similar lawsuits in 1917 by building a 386-foot smokestack, at a cost of $75,000, to discharge its pollutants higher in the air, so the locals would be less affected.[98]

Just two months after the closure of the Zinc Smelter, it was announced that coal was drawing another industry to the city. Alunite Company of America, headquartered in Kansas City, had acquired forty acres below the bluffs just southwest of Collinsville for construction of a potash plant that would employ 1,500 people.[99] Potash, a munitions component needed for the war effort, was made from firing wood ashes and the burned refuse of sugar beets. Raw materials would be shipped in from Colorado, but coal would be provided by local mines.[100]

The war effort hadn't affected just mining and heavy industry. Brooks Tomato Products had been asked to reserve 18 percent of its tomatoes for government use in 1917.[101] Tiedemann Milling Company was grinding soft wheat flour for government use; about 2,500 barrels had been produced by the close of 1917.[102] Few local industries saw a negative impact from the war. Blum Manufacturing, which produced livestock bells, had some shutdowns due to metal shortages, however.[103] But jobs were not in short supply. The draft had taken some of the workforce, but the active coal mines and high demand elsewhere meant no slacker could complain of being unable to find work.

Illinois in 1918 was the top food producing state in the nation. But in the spring of that year, farm labor shortages were severe enough to prompt the Illinois High School Association to cancel sports so that all the boys could work on farms.[104] Farmers got top dollar for their wheat in 1917, $2.25 a bushel. It was said that some got greater profit per acre than what they had paid for their farmland.[105] Female workers also enjoyed high employment rates. Chester Knitting Mills on Main Street used a primarily female workforce and constantly sought new employees. On May 29, 1917, it had set a production record by knitting 1,053 pairs of hosiery.[106]

Baseball fans enjoyed watching their local teams, the Maroons and the Candy Kids, but they also got some distraction by reading about the World Series, then in its fifteenth year, in the St. Louis daily papers. Collinsville's Art Fletcher played shortstop for the New York Giants, but they had dropped the first two games at Chicago's Comiskey Park to the White Sox October 6 and 7 and would go onto to lose both the game and the series, 4–2, at the Polo Grounds in New York on October 15.[107] Fletcher played in all six games and had twenty-five at bats, but hit just .200 in the series.

• • •

The American Expeditionary Forces (AEF) in France were under the command of General John "Black Jack" Pershing. He sailed for Europe on May 26, 1917, with an explicit order that he maintain a separate, unique, and distinct American army.[108] Wilson, Pershing, and other U.S. military officials wanted no part of the trench warfare stalemate that the Great War had become. Artillery and machine guns gave great advantage to defensive positions, and Pershing wanted to drive the Germans into the open and engage them. But with the draft just having started, some months would pass before America would be able to ship significant numbers of trained troops abroad.[109]

The British and the French governments lobbied hard to have the American troops simply amalgamated into their armies, a bone of contention that would last nearly the whole war.[110] But Pershing would have none of it. Aside from having an insufficient number of trained troops ready for combat, a major obstacle became how they would be shipped across the Atlantic. Britain, which dominated world shipping at that time, had the capability to move the troops but not the inclination, since the men would not be amalgamated with other Entente troops.[111] Pershing finally allowed some of the meager flow of the first arriving U.S. troops to help reinforce British and French soldiers before a separate American army could be assembled in France.

Between getting American troops processed and trained stateside and getting them shipped, the flow of doughboys into France was much more a trickle than a flood in late 1917 and early 1918. Four U.S. divisions were either in France or on the way in January. Nine months after Wilson's declaration of war, this amounted to 183,896 troops, including many noncombat soldiers.[112] Pershing's initial goal of one million doughboys in France by early summer 1918 was not to be.[113]

Among those to be amalgamated and see the earliest American combat action was the army's First Infantry Division, the Big Red One. At the start of the war, it was a mix of "veterans" and those who had volunteered after war was declared—those who wouldn't wait for the draft. Among them was Charles Massa, son of Anna Rossman of Collinsville. The First Division was one of a very limited number of U.S. troops considered ready to go. Massa was nineteen years old when he enlisted on May 9. An adventurer and daredevil at heart, he would later become an airplane wing-walker and make over one hundred parachute jumps. His adventure in 1917 would begin with being sworn in May 12 at Jefferson Barracks in St. Louis and then shipped to Fort Bliss, Texas, for less than two weeks of stateside training. By June 1 he was on a train bound for Hoboken, New Jersey, and subsequent shipment to France.

Perhaps the greatest asset this first batch of doughboys brought to France was goodwill and hope, badly needed commodities in a country that had been ripped apart by three years of war.[114] With at least some of its soldiers badly undertrained, the First Division would spend part of the next four months learning from the French Alpine Chasseurs, the famed Blue Devils, at Gondrecourt. Assigned to Company F, Second Battalion, Sixteenth Infantry, Massa had been among those to arrive with much fanfare, parading through Paris on July 4, the toast of the town. But on the cold, rainy, miserable night of November 2, he and his comrades had been slipped under cover of darkness into the trenches in the Sommerville sector near Barthelemont. There were no cheering crowds.

Company F, then consisting of forty-six men, was placed that evening along one hundred yards of the forward-most line to relieve French troops.[115] Carrying one hundred pounds of gear, they slogged into trenches half-filled with cold water. The area was considered a quiet sector with no serious fighting in over two years. But the opposing German troops knew that the untested

Americans were moving in and had their own reception waiting. The Germans were from the Seventh Bavarian Landwehr Regiment, which had acquired a reputation as some of the kaiser's most brutal troops. At about 3:30 a.m., sixteen German batteries used ninety-six guns to unleash a forty-five-minute box barrage that effectively isolated Company F. This gave way to a half-circle barrage at the rear of the trench to prevent it from being reinforced. By then some 242 Bavarians where right on top of Company F.

At least two of the Germans were reportedly dressed as American soldiers. In the fifteen-minute raid, three Americans were killed, one with his throat slashed, and seven were badly wounded. The main goal had been prisoners, perhaps for intelligence, and eleven doughboys were captured. The Germans also took all the American equipment and removed all their own killed and wounded before retreating. Down to twenty-five men, Company F would not be relieved for another nine days. Charles Massa and fourteen of his compatriots were cited for offering the most stubborn resistance and given the Croix de Guerre, the highest military honor France awards to foreign soldiers.[116] Despite their efforts Company F yielded the first three American battlefield deaths of the Great War: Corporal James Gresham, Private Merle Hay, and Private Thomas Enright.

The American deaths made big headlines in the Allied nations. The *Chicago Herald* banner announced, "Huns Kill 3 Pershing Men." The *London Daily Mail* said in an editorial, "Never again will it be possible for Americans to think they have one set of interests and Europe another."[117] *Life* magazine published a poem by Christopher Morley:

> Gresham and Enright and Hay!
> There are no words to say
> Our love, our noble pride
> For these, our first who died.[118]

Massa's battle engagement would make Collinsville headlines in late November, as would the pneumonia death of another enlisted man, Sergeant Humphrey Leighton Evatt. He would become the first Collinsville man to die in the war effort on November 20 in Rouen, France. Evatt worked with Base Hospital 21, which was organized at Washington University School of Medicine in St. Louis and had shipped out just six weeks after the United States entered the war. A Collinsville Township High School graduate of 1912, at the time of his enlistment Evatt was in dental school in St. Louis. He had previously worked in the office at St. Louis Smelting and Refining but felt destined to do greater things.[119]

Evatt was remembered at the Township High School homecoming held in December, just before the Christmas break. It was normally an occasion of much celebration with graduates home from college or work and preparing for the holiday. But homecoming festivities were tempered this year by the absence of forty-nine young men who were serving their nation, at least one of whom would never return. "A solemnity never felt before pervaded our halls and classrooms that day," said School Superintendent Charles Dorris.[120] The school created a roll of honor of those serving in the military. Alongside Evatt's name was a star with the footnote, "Died in France for His Country."

Collinsville stores, primarily centered around Main and Clay Streets uptown, reported strong business during the holidays, with many having record years. Many shoppers sought to buy items they could send to the soldiers in camp.[121]

The New Year brought new regulations from the federal government that required registration of German aliens, often referred to as enemy aliens. These immigrants had not made application for citizenship. Mayor Siegel had the police department handle the matter. The immigrants would be photographed, fingerprinted, and a physical description noted, with one copy kept locally and another sent to federal marshals. The alien would in turn be issued an identification card, which he was required to carry at all times.[122] A U.S. marshal's notice published about the program said, "Persons required to register should understand that in so doing they are giving proof of their peaceful dispositions and of their intentions to conform to the laws of the United

States."[123] The regulation applied only to males fourteen years and older. By mid-February twenty-six Germans had registered with the Collinsville Police Department.[124] German women and Austrian men and women would later be required to go through the same process.[125]

Illness would claim two other local soldiers in early 1918. Private Eugene Kohler, twenty-three, died New Years Day 1918 at Camp Taylor of pneumonia, which was rampant in military camps. His remains were brought back to his hometown for burial January 5.[126] Pneumonia also claimed Private James Dukes on February 22 in France. He had enlisted in May. The twenty-four-year-old Dukes was survived by his parents, four sisters, and one younger brother. They were grief-stricken, his mother inconsolable. "He was a big strong fellow," said a press report, "much admired by his friends both for his fine physique and his manly ways."[127]

Disease would be the big killer early for the AEF as its troops were trained and slowly amalgamated into Allied fighting forces. By March 15, 1918, nearly one year after the United States entered the fray, just 136 Americans had been killed in action while 641 had died of disease.[128] Yet many young men nationwide, and in the Collinsville area, yearned only to serve. St. Louis papers told of a boy, fifteen years old, who came 150 miles from the hamlet of Kansas, Illinois, to enlist at St. Louis. Told he was too young, he stripped and walked in to the Mississippi River and drowned himself, leaving his clothes neatly bundled with an address on the riverbank so that they might be sent to his parents.[129] Back in Madison County, Dorris, the Collinsville school superintendent, told of speaking with a man from the same graduating class as Evatt in early 1918. The man had just registered for the draft. He essentially managed the family farm for his elderly father. Knowing this Dorris stated he should have no difficulty getting an exemption. The man looked at Dorris with resentment and responded, "Do you know I can't look a soldier in the face when I meet him on the street? Why I would be in the service now, had it not been that the folks at home persuaded me to stay and take care of the farm a little longer."[130]

All but three of the young man's 1912 classmates were now in the military. He told Dorris he had read the popular war books *Over the Top* and *Private Peat* and registered without exemption. "I think it will be glorious to fight in this war, and I want to have a part in it," he declared. Dorris thought perhaps he had underestimated the patriotism of many young men who were not yet in uniform.[131]

At least one of the local papers pledged to send free newspapers to the hometown soldiers. Both papers occasionally published letters home sent by Collinsville soldiers. Leonard Ritter wrote November 4 of the damage he had seen in France, including graves that German soldiers had dug up to get metal from the coffins. "I am glad the war is not in America for I would not like to see America blown up like this place," Ritter commented. "When Fritz leaves town they take all the young girls and young men with them, then they blow up the place."[132]

Sergeant Claude Kitson wrote from Fort McPherson, Georgia, that he had bought a $100 Liberty Bond, as had most of his comrades.[133] "When will we go to France?" was a common question for those troops. Kitson described himself as a Sammie, a nickname based on Uncle Sam but later dropped for the term *doughboy*.

William Selkirk was a sergeant in officer's training at Fort Bliss, Texas. His account of a raid on a U.S. border town by men suspected to be connected with Pancho Villa was reported in a Collinsville newspaper. Soldiers jumped at the chance to be able to go after the raiders. Selkirk remarked, "You can plainly see the boys in khaki are anxious to have a little mix up."[134]

The Collinsville draftees ended up at Camp Taylor in Kentucky, as did all the early conscripted troops from southern Illinois. This prompted a visit from August Schimpff, the editor and publisher of the *Collinsville Advertiser*. He was struck by the size of the camp, thirty-five square miles, just south of Louisville. The camp was clean, he reported, and the boys were well fed and played baseball and basketball during free time. Home to forty-thousand troops, it had ten YMCA buildings and five Knights of Columbus buildings that provided homelike settings with pianos, record players, comfortable furniture, and the like. The men could go into Louisville but were not allowed to drink. Schimpff wrote, "The demeanor of the boys in training camp is that of a young colt, full of playfulness, and such training as they have had, has made all the boys vastly changed in appearance. No protruding stomachs are to be seen, but the men look like conditioned athletes."[135] The most requested thing by the Collinsville troops: letters from home.

In the early part of the twentieth century, clubs, lodges, and societies provided some disability and death benefits and played a major part in the social life of any town, and Collinsville was no exception. It was home to about forty such organizations in this period, ranging from the Order of Owls, Collinsville Nest 1247, to the Daughters of Pocahontas, Leota Council 18, to the Woodmen of America, Camp 373.[136] The group meetings, usually two evenings per month, provided much of the out-of-family social contact. Meetings were usually hosted at halls above local businesses, often saloons that could provide refreshments or meals. Many of the groups seemingly competed to do as much as they could to help the war effort, primarily by contributing to the Red Cross, the Salvation Army, or the YMCA. The Improved Order of Redmen, Tallapoosa Tribe 101, voted to contribute $100 to help the state association of Redmen provide a Red Cross ambulance for military use.[137]

A new Red Cross chapter was formed in Collinsville in June, and it provided the outlet for many women, including those who had sons in the military, to do their part. R. Guy Kneedler, city attorney and former mayor, was elected chairman, although most of the active members were female. The group provided comfort bags to soldiers upon induction, and at Christmas time it again sent comfort kits to the local boys. Listings of those who had joined or donated as little as twenty-five cents to the Red Cross filled the columns of the *Collinsville Herald*.[138]

The Red Cross used rooms at the Masonic Temple to collect and prepare donated sheets and linen for bandages and to knit sweaters, socks, mufflers, and the like. The work was considered important enough that women who had previously refrained, for religious reasons, from doing any "fancy work" on the Sunday Sabbath regularly made an exception for their own war effort.[139] While some questioned the legitimate value of all the women knitting across the nation, others saw it as critically important to the military. When a prominent evangelist suggested that a German spy had entered the Atlanta Red Cross headquarters and damaged nineteen sweaters, local leaders allayed his overwrought fears: "Germans had nothing to do with it. Mice did it."[140]

Red Cross membership in Collinsville was 197 in June, helped when more than 50 employees of the Chester Knitting Mills joined en masse.[141] In December 1917 the local chapter boasted of 1,810 members. By the end of World War I, the American Red Cross nationwide would have nearly four thousand chapters and over thirty million members. The Commercial Club decided to cancel its annual fall festival and instead give the money to the Red Cross. A charity baseball game was held in July between the Moose Lodge and the Eagles Lodge, and nearly two thousand people attended, raising $1,400 for the local chapter. The navy sent several sailors and its St. Louis Fife and Drum Corps to the event and left with the names of fourteen potential recruits from Collinsville. With nearly four thousand members by war's end, the Red Cross would be Collinsville's largest support organization, giving residents a public opportunity to show their patriotism, although the chapter's War Fund collections would pale in comparison to many Illinois communities.[142]

Community expectations of patriotism only increased in 1918, when more and more American troops reached foreign soil. Collinsville's teachers were required not only to sign a pledge of their loyalty to Uncle Sam but also to participate in groups such as the Red Cross and the State Council of Defense and to purchase Liberty Bonds.[143]

One of the biggest controversies for the Wilson administration during the war was prompted in part by the brutally cold winter of 1917–18, when high industrial and foreign demand and rail distribution problems left many unable to buy coal.[144] Local officials elsewhere commandeered coal trains moving through their areas while ships blocked East Coast harbors, unable to be loaded with coal. The situation was not a problem in Collinsville, where local mines supplied all the coal that was needed.

But the crisis out east would force a January 17 mandate from Wilson's fuel administrator, Harry Garfield, who ordered all factories east of the Mississippi shut down for four days to allow bottlenecked coal supplies to reach eastern ports.[145] That measure may not have been enforced in southwestern Illinois, but officials did restrict use of coal for most businesses on Mondays, starting January 21 and continuing for the next ten weeks. This meant most businesses would close both Sunday and Monday.

There were a few exemptions for industries that ran seven days per week, but in Collinsville it appeared the regulation would most significantly affect the lead smelter and the Chester Knitting Mills. The only businesses that would be exempt were those heated by natural gas, which was uncommon in 1918.[146] Local businessmen bristled at the new regulation, which they felt should not apply to communities that had local mines selling coal for regional use. "The only thing to do," a local newspaper opined, "is to make the best of the situation."[147]

There was also much complaint about the industrial shutdowns on the national level, not just from Republicans but also from Wilson's own Democrats. Opponents attacked the Wilson administration's organizational abilities. Whether because of political pressure or logistical brilliance, the coal supply bottleneck was quickly broken and the industrial shutdowns were discontinued.[148] But the Heatless Monday program continued. Most Collinsville businesses, even saloons, did close for four Mondays beginning January 21, as the grumbling continued. "The fellow with the burning thirst was also disconsolate at finding all the thirst parlors closed," a Collinsville newspaper reported.[149]

There was less outcry when the government enacted the Standard Time Act, a 1918 version of Daylight Savings Time, as an energy-saving measure beginning March 31. Most Collinsville stores and businesses complied, although the law was unpopular nationally, and the nation reverted to traditional standard time at the end of the war. Earlier restrictions barring the use of electric sign advertising two nights a week drew little complaint. With few automobile drivers, gasless Sundays later in the war would likewise ruffle only a few feathers.

The fuel crisis was just another example, critics said, of the Wilson administration's inability to efficiently prosecute the war. Troops shivered in U.S. camps and abroad while stocks of winter clothing went undelivered. Hundreds of millions spent to design and build military ships and planes by early 1918 had not resulted in any delivery of either.[150] It didn't help matters when Quentin Roosevelt, the son of Wilson critic and former president Teddy Roosevelt, was shot down and killed flying a second-rate French Nieuport 28.[151] One U.S. Army general compared the nation's war effort to a new driver learning to operate a stick shift, with both the clutch and the accelerator simultaneously engaged: "The engine is whirling around and a tremendous noise is being made, but there is no application of power."[152]

One of the first home-front agencies created by the federal government after the declaration of war was the Food Administration. Wilson appointed future president Herbert Hoover food administrator. Food demand had increased as the United States helped supply Allied nations, while some poor crop yields in 1916 and 1917 reduced available foodstuffs.[153] Building the new U.S. Armed Forces would further strain the food-supply system. Grumbling also resulted when Hoover ordered a 30 percent reduction in grain used by breweries, reducing the alcohol content of beer to no more 2.75 percent.[154] But like Wilson, Hoover did not want rationing; instead he relied on promoting meatless, sweetless, and wheatless days and hoped patriotic enthusiasm would get the job done.[155] In a letter to food retailers, Hoover asked for "cooperation rather than coercion." Press releases appeared in local papers, calling for women to conserve food. One story denied the report that the government could seize the food stocks of housewives: "These rumors were originated partly by pro-German propagandists and partly by conscious-less grafters."[156]

Lumber company owner A. C. Gauen was appointed Collinsville food administrator. He worked with a committee of grocers, bakers, butchers, and others beginning in January 1918 to set a range of prices that buyers might see for foodstuffs and list prices that the retailer had paid buying in bulk.[157] The list was regularly printed in the local papers in the hope that prices would not range too far above state averages.

Sugar sales were limited to fewer than five pounds per week. By February the committee had worked with local grocers to incorporate a program in which shoppers would be asked to buy one pound of cornmeal or other substitute for every pound of flour purchased. A Collinsville newspaper columnist took to task a buyer who complained of having to purchase the same quantity of substitute meal. The man had told the grocer he would have laid in several hundred pounds of flour had he known the restrictions were coming. The columnist remarked, "How patriotic some people are with their eating habits was shown in a striking and unconscious way Friday morning by one of the indirect friends of the Kaiser."[158]

Lunch counters and restaurants were reminded that the new "regulations" applied to them too. Collinsville grocer Sam Galinat fell under scrutiny when it was learned he had sold three hundred pounds of flour to one person. Galinat was forced to reclaim the flour from the buyer and refund his money.[159] The flour was then confiscated by the food administrator. The irony of the enforcement effort in Collinsville was that the dealers, restaurateurs, and public were apparently deluded into thinking that they could be charged with violation of federal law if they disregarded the restrictions. In actuality the heaviest sentence a scofflaw could have gotten would have been a rebuke in the court of patriotic public opinion. Still the local newspaper columnists continued their rants: "The time has come to enforce the rulings with a strict hand, and those who imagine that they can pull the wool over the eyes of the government will find that heavy punishment is in store for them."[160] People were urged to report violators to the local food administrator.

Inflation drove up most prices after the war began, but wages had increased too. Just as the farmers had benefited from the agreed-on price for wheat, coal miners benefited from the higher price that had been accepted for coal. The local economy flourished. In the winter of 1918 in Collinsville, Isenberg's store sold men's pants for $2.98 and women's silk skirts for $5.98. Ford dealer J. C. McLanahan sold touring cars for $360, sedans for $695. A haircut would cost a man 35 cents weekdays, 50 cents on Saturdays.

One of the most successful Committee on Public Information programs was the Four Minute Men, so named because the participating men were allotted four minutes to speak in the time it took to change reels at a moving-picture show, in what was a live patriotic commercial at the theater. The unpaid speakers were community leaders, nominated by local officials and approved at the state level. They were given topics and guidelines for their speeches but were largely unscripted. Their patriotic themes promoted such things as buying war bonds, conserving food, or fuel or vilified Germany's leaders or its army.[161]

Collinsville did not come on board with the Four Minute Men program until February 1918. Its speaker's list was a who's who of influential men from the city, headed up by A. C. Gauen. The Collinsville Four Minute Men included former Mayor Kneedler, School Superintendent Dorris, two pastors from prominent churches, both newspaper publishers, and four others.[162] One man would speak each night of the week, except Sunday, when there were movies or other productions at the Opera House or the Airdome.

By the Armistice there would be seventy-five thousand Four Minute Men nationwide who gave more than 7.5 million speeches.[163] The young film industry also helped bolster domestic support of the war, ferreting out any theme that might be deemed unpatriotic. It helped build the growing anti-German frenzy with films such as *Draft 258*, *The Beast of Berlin*, *Face to Face with Kaiserism*, and *The Slacker*.[164] With the nearly subservient movie industry and the Four Minute Men, the CPI took advantage of the one last form of mass communication that was not already under tight government control. There seemed no escaping the CPI's patriotic messages, which were bludgeoned into the minds of every American in 1917 and 1918.

Superintendent Dorris's involvement in the Four Minute Men was most appropriate, as his was probably the "first family" of the war effort in Collinsville. Like many in the community, he was not initially in favor of U.S. involvement but jumped in with both feet when war was declared. Aside from his school duties, he was an accomplished speaker and community leader, active in the State Council of Defense, the Red Cross, and the Salvation Army, and he served as a registrar on the draft board. He was also an "operative" of the American Protective League.[165] Dorris's wife, Susan, was active in the Red Cross and chaired the local Women's Committee of the National Council of Defense, which concerned itself primarily with food conservation issues. Both of their sons had enlisted; Lester Dorris was the first local man to enter the service, and Milburn Dorris joined the navy later in 1917. When the Armistice was signed November 11, 1918, word would not reach Collinsville until after 3:00 a.m. But when it did, Dorris would awaken and walk seven blocks to ring the bell at Webster School to let the city know.[166]

In early 1918 Dorris strongly believed that many in Collinsville did not do enough to support the war effort. In a speech given February 2, he described a common local affliction:

> We are patriots so long as we can capitalize our patriotism. We join the Red Cross and hang 100 percent signs in our windows. We subscribe to the YMCA and get our names published in the newspaper, and charge it up to advertising. We wear Liberty Bond buttons and hang our service flags when our clerk goes to war. We swear at the German people generally and the Kaiser in particular and think we are patriotic. But we raise a terrible fuss when Mr. Hoover places a limit on the profit on the food we sell, or when he asks us to eat corn bread once a week, in order that our soldiers may not suffer. Our patriotic ardor cools considerably when

the government reduces the amount of alcohol in our beer and when it asks us to promise to eat less meat and more potatoes.

The hostile reception which was accorded the fuel conservation order of Dr. Garfield a few days ago was a disgrace to the citizenship of this country. . . . Our people are for the war, but so far have not shown a willingness to pay the price necessary for its prosecution.[167]

Disease was a prevalent killer of people of all ages in 1917 and 1918. Young men living in close quarters for the first time in military camps and society's increased mobility can be blamed to some degree. Pneumonia and typhoid were common. By mid-1917 over 1,300 cases of tuberculosis had been reported in Madison County.[168] The Spanish influenza would not become pandemic until later in 1918, but Collinsville would suffer through a smallpox epidemic starting in December 1917.[169] The city physician, Dr. M. W. Harrison, ordered those who had a skin eruption that might be a smallpox lesion to notify a doctor. Although smallpox had been considered under control since the turn of the century in the United States, the epidemic continued in Collinsville through March 1918 because a handful of residents refused to be treated or remain under quarantine. Some doctors had also failed to report cases to Harrison or state health officials.

By February the state was assisting with a vaccination program, which was mandatory for school children and strongly recommended for adults. Approximately 2,500 residents, 90 percent of them children, had been immunized by late February, when there were still twenty-four known cases in Collinsville and eleven more in nearby Maryville.[170] A nine-year-old boy from the city died in April due to the aftereffects of smallpox, but by early March the disease was largely under control.[171] Five people were charged with not complying with quarantine or reporting requirements.[172]

It was all typical 1918 wartime life in Collinsville, with problems not unlike those found in small towns across the nation. What escalated tensions locally was the firm grip coal mining and the coal miners maintained over the Collinsville community.

3

United We Stand

Every ton of coal that can be produced is sorely needed. Coal is food; coal is clothes; coal is steel; coal is guns; coal is transportation. . . . No miner able to work has the right to lie idle when the success of our country's cause depends so largely upon the production of coal.

—Editorial, *United Mine Workers Journal*, December 13, 1917

Coal mines fairly well surrounded Collinsville in 1918. It was said a man could walk from one end of the city to the other, underground, if he took the proper connecting mine tunnels. But the older mines under the city center had been largely exhausted by this time, and the lion's share of mining was done on the periphery of town.[1] Mines were in two categories, local mines that supplied coal for area residents and businesses, and the larger shipping or distributing mines whose output was primarily transported on railcars for distant industrial or heating use.

The most visible symbol of a mine above ground was its tipple, a superstructure for the hoist, towering perhaps fifty feet over a main shaft opening of about twenty feet by ten feet.[2] The hoist raised and lowered two cages simultaneously in the shaft to take men and equipment into and out of the mine and to bring mined coal to the surface.[3] Adjacent conveyor belts then moved the off-loaded coal for sorting and distribution to railcars and trucks. The whole arrangement was usually enclosed with roofs and siding for protection from the weather. Other buildings powered the mines, burning their own coal to generate electricity and steam to operate the hoist. Railroad tracks and roads for trucks wound their way around the coal-covered complex. A slightly smaller ventilation and escape shaft was nearby, and a large fan provided for a regular exchange of air in the mine. Though the mines' topside footprints were relatively small, underground maps show that they were vast entities sprawling for miles, right up to the mineral rights of competing coal companies.[4]

The five big shipping mines locally ranged from Consolidated Mine No. 17 on the south end to the Donk Brothers Coal and Coke Mine No. 2, just north of Collinsville in Maryville. In between were the Lumaghi Coal Mine No. 2, Lumaghi Mine No. 3, and Donk Mine No. 1.[5] All were outside the city limits, so for all the jobs they provided, they directly produced not one cent of revenue for the city of Collinsville.

The only mines actually in the city were two smaller operations, the Abbey Coal Mine, located on the St. Louis Road, and the Bunker Hill Mine. Previously both had been local mines, but with the price coal was bringing in wartime, Abbey became a distributing mine. Locals often referred to Abbey as the Hardscrabble Mine, so named, the story goes, after a late nineteenth-century conversation between two miners in what was then a small, struggling mine. "Do you think this mine will make it?" one miner asked his partner. "I don't know," said his friend. "But it will be a hard scrabble."[6]

In the short winter days of 1917 and 1918, a vivid parade of bobbing orange lights could be seen along the brick sidewalks on the east end of the city heading toward the Lebanon Road, as miner's made their way to the big Lumaghi mines in the early morning darkness or back home in the early evening. Most of them used the carbide lamps on their hats to light the way.[7] As they trudged along in their heavy boots, they carried metal lunch pails with water in the bottom and food on top. In addition to drinking, the water was used to feed the miner's carbide lamp.

Once at the mine, men changed into their work clothes if their mine had a shower house. Then they waited to be lowered in a cage about two hundred feet in the mine shaft by the coal hoist. There were two cages; one landed on the mine bottom when the other arrived at the surface.[8] Those who operated the hoist were notified when there was human cargo, so that more caution might be exercised. The bottom of the shaft served as the mine's underground operations center, and supplies and a repair shop were located there. From the shaft bottom, the miners were taken out to the room where they would work for the day, usually in a pit car powered by an electric motor. That trip could take a while, since some of the mines would eventually cover more than 1,500 acres underground as the rooms and corridors were mined outward from the bottom of the shaft.[9]

The miners typically worked in pairs. When they arrived at their assigned room, an experienced miner knew to take his pick and tap the roof. He could tell by the sound if rock or coal was loose and therefore dangerous to work under. Mines in the Collinsville region had a seam of bituminous coal measuring six and a half to eight feet.[10] From this seam rooms were cut, approximately twenty feet wide, in the coal vein. In a vocation filled with hazards, perhaps the most dangerous was making the undercut, when one of the two miners would lie on his side and use his short-handled pick to cut out a step of coal about twenty inches high and six to eight feet deep, extending across the room.[11] As the miner worked his way in, his entire body would eventually be under a bank of coal weighing several tons. A few small struts were placed underneath, but the process was still perilous because soft spots or other faults could cause the bank to fall. For the miners keen eyesight and hearing were critical to detect the telltale sights and sounds of eminent collapse.

While the miner was making the undercut, his partner would prepare to drill into the top of the vein, over the undermined area.[12] The drill was anchored before six or more 1 1/4-inch holes were drilled along the top. The top holes were angled so they would end in the center of the undercut in an effort to throw the coal outward. The remaining holes and those along the side edges, called rib shots, were drilled straight in. A charge was made by pouring black powder into paper to make a cartridge; a fuse was added, and the charge was tamped using a special rod. Each hole was then backfilled with dirt to concentrate the blast. Fuses were lit at different lengths both to push the coal outward and to alert the miners if one of the charges did not fire. If one charge did not sound, the room would not be worked for a period of time.

After the coal was loosened, their pitch-black bounty was loaded into the pit cars, which carried about two tons of coal. Since the miners were paid by weight of the coal, a pit tag was placed on each car to indicate who got credit for the load when it was weighed. The two-person teams alternated in placing their tags on each loaded car. Mules moved the cars back to the hoist, and they were taken topside to be emptied. Working together two men could fill seven or eight cars on a good day.[13] The men had to work in a crouched position, and the job was damp and dirty, true, but the pair of miners could usually work most of the day on their own in a sixty-degree temperature. They could think and act independently, with no bosses breathing down their necks.[14]

A blast on the steam whistle signaled the end of shift. If the miners heard three blasts, it was good news; it meant the mine would be working the next day too. Before going up miners would first collect the pit tags they had left at the bottom of the shaft, so the bosses would know they were out of the mine. In this manner everyone in the mines' far-reaching rooms was accounted for at the end of shift. After the cage trip back to the top, the shower house allowed the miner to remove the black coal grime that covered him before returning to town. Men whose mines did not have a shower house would return home nearly as black as the coal they had wrestled all day.[15]

About 90 percent of the men employed by a coal mining company worked underground.[16] Most were miners, who were paid by the ton. But there were also laborers and drivers for the motors and mules that hauled out the coal. Other employees included men who operated the hoist, the cages, and special machinery; timbermen; and track men. Some mines also had dedicated shot firers. Boys of sixteen or seventeen were employed as trappers, the requisite name for those operating the mine's trapdoors. All the positions except the miners' were paid daily rates.

Wartime demand meant record production for Illinois coal mines, whose output nationally was exceeded only by Pennsylvania and West Virginia.[17] In 1915 Illinois produced 58 million tons of coal, but by mid-1918 production was up to 90 million tons.[18] The number of mines had grown from 779 to 967, and number of miners from 76,000 to 91,000, with everyone wanting a piece of the action. There had been a 14 percent increase in production in Illinois mines in just the last year.

The biggest Collinsville-area coal producer in the 1918 reporting year was Donk Mine No. 2, in Maryville, at some 731,000 tons. It also produced jobs, 605 of them in 1918. The Donk Mine No. 1, also called Cuba Mine for its proximity to Cuba Lane, produced 500,000 tons with 369 men.[19] The other three shipping mines produced from 191,000 to 494,000 tons and a total of 1,022 jobs. The upstart Abbey Mine produced 65,000 tons using 56 men. The three oldest mines, Donk No. 1, Lumaghi No. 3, and Abbey, were considered hand mines and had less modern machinery.[20] All the Collinsville-area mines were at least partially reliant on mules to move coal underground in 1918, the largest of them using forty animals.

Railcar shortages nationwide bedeviled the coal mining industry more than any other single issue in 1917 and 1918, and they played a big part in the coal supply fiasco in early 1918.[21] To ease the supply crush, local homeowners and businesses had been encouraged as early as the spring of 1917 to fill their coal bins for the coming winter. Few did. Some of the national press and mine operators elsewhere blamed "slacker" miners for the shortage, but they usually were not the guilty parties. Some rail workers blamed rail company logistics, as empty coal cars also congested many rail yards.[22] Whatever the cause railcar shortages meant that production often had to be cut at all the Collinsville-area shipping mines except for the two Donk's mines, since the company had its own rolling stock.[23] Some days the mines did not work at all; other days they were forced to half-time operation.[24]

Illinois coal mining thrived after the turn of the century, but some of that growth came at expense of safety. The 1909 Cherry

Mine disaster, which claimed the lives of 259 men and boys in northern Illinois, prompted state lawmakers to require firefighting and rescue stations in mining areas and later pass occupational disease protections and the first version of the state's Workmen's Compensation Act.[25]

Mining jobs remained dangerous, nonetheless. Nine Collinsville-area men lost their lives in the mines in 1917 and early 1918.[26] William Hedger, Jonah Mayer, Samuel Alex, and William Ward were killed by falling coal or slate. Alex had just finished his last undercut of the day when the room fell in on him.[27] Louis Wille, George Tumat, and Charles Dolzadelli died after being run over by either pit cars or a motor. John Larremore was electrocuted. Another Collinsville man, Marshall Sangrelet, had been a manager at Donk Mine No. 1. He had recently taken the same position at a Fairview mine when he was killed in a motor accident. All told, they left eight widows and three children. State law provided for a one-time payment to the widow and children of double the miner's annual salary, up to $4,000.[28] A $100 death benefit was also paid by the miner's union, and sometimes fellow miners would take up a collection for the survivors.

When production went up, so did miner fatalities and injuries in Illinois. In the year ending June 30, 1918, 259 deaths were reported, up 25 percent from the prior year.[29] It was the deadliest year on record, excluding the 1909 disaster at Cherry Mine. Yet the tonnage produced and the number of employees in 1918 had only increased about 14 percent. Statewide, pit car accidents and falling coal were the leading causes of death, and inspectors said the miners' carelessness was largely to blame.[30] The men working in the mines, however, seemed to accept the large number of deaths and injuries as just part of the job.

In addition to the nine local men killed, at least 144 Collinsville and Maryville miners sustained serious injuries in 1917 and early 1918.[31] The number of men injured in Illinois rose to 2,161, an increase of 32 percent in 1918. And the state only tracked serious injuries, those that caused a man to lose thirty days or more of work. The average time off work was nearly two months. The

Illinois Coal Report said that adequate safety laws were in place: "It seems the only recourse now left is to educate the miner and impress upon him the necessity of taking every precaution for his safety, and to compel the operator to rigidly enforce the provisions of the law in regard to the operation of his mine."[32]

The comprehensive list of injuries for Illinois coal miners in the prior year was both gruesome and alarming, with 546 broken bones, 49 amputations, 25 burns, 5 eyes "destroyed," and hundreds of other traumatic injuries. It did not include 234 cases reported as "Body Injured," which could have included any combination of those afflictions.[33]

Coal mining work had always been inherently erratic, and the employment irregularity was certainly a drawback. But the money was good. The miners could thank the war and the United Mine Workers unions for that. They had to provide their own tools, lamp carbide, and blasting powder, but take home pay for miners was never higher than in the spring of 1918.[34]

Even if a war had not been raging, few men planned on going to college in 1918, when just finishing high school was somewhat a feat. When boys were strong and big enough to be called men, most went to work. The minimum age of employment in the mines was just sixteen.[35] In Madison County just 37 percent of sixteen- and seventeen-year-old boys were in school, less than half the number attending at ages fourteen and fifteen.[36] Children had a greater chance of attending school longer if both of their parents were native born, a lesser chance if one or both of their parents were foreign born, and the least chance of attending longer if they themselves were foreign born. For immigrants America was indeed the land of opportunity but not necessarily of higher education. In 1916 forty-eight boys and forty-one girls made up the Collinsville Township High School freshman class. Four years later just fifteen boys and twenty-eight girls would graduate.[37] Even black males, segregated and clearly relegated to second-class status, received more schooling than white males at ages sixteen and seventeen in Illinois.[38] But only 3 percent of Illinoisans were considered illiterate; however, a person stood a nearly four times greater chance of being illiterate if he or she was foreign born.

Most young men and women of the era lived with their families after they began working, contributing toward household expenses. Not until marriage, and sometimes not even then, did most young people leave home. Likewise, older family members typically joined the households of their children in later life. It was not uncommon to have three generations living in the same home, with two generations, in Collinsville, working in the mines. It was possible to have three or four miners living under one roof.

A number of miners, however, tended to be more transient, foreign born or native, frequently on the move for better paying or steadier work. They ended up in hotel or boardinghouse rooms or sometimes rented homes. Staying anywhere to put a roof over their heads, they weren't particularly discerning. Perhaps they sent some of their earnings to support family in the old country, perhaps not. But without the anchors of local family or close friends, they contributed to the instability that existed in Collinsville in 1917 and 1918.

• • •

When physician Dr. James L. R. Wadsworth became mayor of Collinsville in 1907, he tried to enlist support for sanitary sewers and paved streets uptown, but the city's residents would have none of it. They did not want to pay the cost. He told his son-in-law of the quandary. "Why you've got Collinsville in the hollow of your hand," the young man reportedly said. "All you have to do is tell them you'll close the saloons and they'll do whatever you want."[39] It is unknown exactly what persuasive techniques Wadsworth used, but by 1909 the uptown area had its sewers and paved streets.

As in most cities, drinking was a significant part of the workingman's life in Collinsville in early 1918. It was the saloon era, a time frame that inspired Jack London's alcohol-fueled autobiography, *John Barleycorn*, in 1913. London wrote: "In the saloons, life was different. Men talked with great voices, laughed with great laughs, and there was an atmosphere of greatness. And there was something more than the common every day, where nothing happened. Here life was always very live, and sometimes even lurid. . . . Terrible saloons might be, but then that only meant they were terribly wonderful."[40]

The city had at least nineteen saloons in the uptown area alone, many located near the *Y* intersection of Clay and Vandalia Streets. The place was so named because the streetcar tracks coming from the north on Vandalia at this point intersected the tracks that looped around Clay and Main Streets uptown. And most men returning from work at the Lumaghi mines came this way on foot. Those working at the Donk's mines or the Lead Works likewise could jump off a streetcar here.

For the men returning from a hard day's labor, it was town center—not quite at the center of uptown but the place to be. Martin Fulton's Y Saloon was there on Clay Street, as was Adam Boneski's and John Baltrasat's Bar. Just a block over on Main Street were saloons operated by Charles Salel, Sam Pelepot, Dom Bertino, August Balsat, Jules Schiller, and John Szillat. The Commercial Hotel and the St. Nicholas Hotel were also there, both with bars. The rest of the uptown saloons were sprinkled west down the next three blocks of Main Street.

Farther north on Vandalia Street, there were another five saloons. Eight more were in Maryville. Another six were in the area of Cuba Lane and the lead smelter. These bars had the first shot at working men coming from the Donk's mines or the Lead Works. Toss in another nine saloons in various other neighborhoods, and the total comes to at least forty-five saloons serving the Collinsville area.[41]

The twenty-nine bars inside the city limits alone provided about one saloon per one hundred men above the age of twenty-one. Most all workingmen of the town considered one or more of the saloons their favorite haunts.

For Collinsville the saloons were more than just meeting places for the local men. The tavern dramshop license fees provided the city with its largest single source of revenue. In 1918 the fees accounted for 23 percent of the city's revenue, almost $23,000 of the nearly $97,000 received.[42] For as much as the coal mines and smelter works influenced the community, most were outside the city limits and not subject to taxes or fees. And the city could have used the money; in 1918 it spent nearly $111,000, or 13 percent more than it had brought in. An increase in electric rates and the loss of the dramshop fees during Prohibition would nearly bankrupt the city several years later.

How much did the Collinsville men drink in 1918? There are no exact figures, but one businessman posed the question of the miners' discretionary spending to another longtime Collinsville business leader who well knew local habits. He ventured that one-third of the income went to St. Louis merchants and mail-order houses, one-third went to Collinsville merchants, and one-third went to local saloons—not necessarily in that order.[43]

A saloon in 1918 was much more than just a place to get a drink. There one could learn the news, whether by reading a newspaper or by word of mouth. It served as the mailing address for many. It was a place to find out when a mine or business might be hiring. It was the gathering place before a lodge, club, or union meeting—and the place to go afterward. In an era when some working-class men did not trust banks, saloons served as a place where paychecks could be cashed. One manufacturer in Joliet, Illinois, reported that 3,599 of the 3,600 paychecks issued one payday had been endorsed at local bars.[44] With the First National Bank and State Bank nearby, it is doubtful that many in Collinsville used the bars to cash checks. But the bars seemed to always be open, something the banks could not match.

Above all, saloons provided an atmosphere of sociability, commonality, and conviviality. Perhaps it was just the gossip and song, but in an era of traditional marriages, the only way a man could talk with those he considered his equal was to seek out other men.[45] Working-class men did not attend dinner parties or private clubs, but they did have the saloon—the Poor Man's Club.[46] It was not uncommon for married men to return home after working all day, eat with their families, and then go to meetings and/ or the saloon for the evening.

At midday the saloon's served free lunches, often provided by the brewery whose beer was on tap. Offerings might include sausage or lunch meats, cheese, or soup and bread—not a large meal, but enough to hold a man over until dinner. And it really wasn't free; there was an expectation that the customer would buy at least one beer. At five cents for a ten- or twelve-ounce glass, it was not a bad deal overall.[47] The lunch offerings tended to be salty, encouraging the men to have a second glass or more. Working two hundred feet below ground, Collinsville's coal miners were not able to enjoy the free lunches on workdays, but many men did.

As varied as communities were in the United States, bars were strikingly similar. In urban areas many had been constructed by breweries, but the same general model was often followed from coast to coast. And it included many comforts a man could not have at home.[48] The bar itself, generally of oak or mahogany, ran nearly the length of the building and sometimes had an intricately carved front. Men stood at the bar resting one foot on a brass or wooden rail, making it comfortable to stand for a longer period of time. In 1918 there were usually no stools. The back bar too could be intricately carved, with shelves and cabinets often surrounding a large mirror. Spittoons were placed throughout, with sawdust covering the nearby misses and spilled drinks on the wooden floor. Tables and chairs were placed in the other half of the room, for those wishing a seat or to play cards.

If the bar did not have a second floor, there was often a small meeting room in back, sometimes called a wine room. Lodges and clubs were free to use the rooms, a practice that gave the saloon owner a captive audience before or after the meetings. Most saloons usually had a side or rear door too, often called the ladies entrance, where women might arrive for a meeting without the stigma of being seen entering a bar. Lights and fans hung from embossed tin ceilings. Often the saloon had a pool table and always wall décor provided by the breweries. The beer and alcohol smell and lingering cigar smoke only added to the ambiance.[49]

Side entrance notwithstanding, women weren't welcome, for their presence was a violation of social code that would not be broken until Prohibition. It also happened to violate a Collinsville ordinance, enacted in 1917 no doubt after some women made themselves too welcome in the wine rooms. Fifteen years old was generally recognized as the drinking age, about the time most boys had given up their schoolwork and gotten jobs.[50] It was an affirmation of manhood to be able to amble up to the bar and buy a round of drinks for one's friends. Continuing bar tradition dictates that once a man had bought someone a drink, that person was bound to stay at least until it was his time to buy a round. And a man was expected to keep the drinking pace of his compatriots; to not do so said something about his manhood or lack thereof.

With no private clubs for the wealthy in Collinsville, the saloons also served as a place where the working class could mingle with the business owners and the upper crust. No doubt workingmen predominated, but the saloons at least afforded men of different social strata an opportunity to meet in a social setting. After all drinking habits were similar for most men. Despite the elaborate back bars and numerous liquors they held, beer and whisky were the predominate choices. Italians, of which Collinsville had its share, were also known to favor red wines, perhaps something that passed as a Chianti.[51]

The saloon provided men with entertainment and escape from responsibility, along with laughter and fun, as reward for their six days of hard work each week. Drunkenness wasn't the norm, but there were certainly those who had more than their share. And saloons were not the place for timid drinkers; annual beer consumption for those fifteen and older in the United States averaged an estimated three gallons per capita in 1915.[52] While drinking was steady at saloons throughout the week, Saturday nights, with no work the next day, brought the biggest bash of the week. One writer has referred to Saturday-night drinking in saloons in the early twentieth century as "a riotous communal binge."[53]

Ultimately, the time and money spent by working-class men

in saloons were the impetus for many women—wives, daughters, and mothers—to fight for Prohibition. The battle to make alcohol illegal had been going on for years, but it picked up steam after passage of the Revenue Act of 1913. This law provided for a federal income tax, making the government no longer dependent on liquor excise taxes. When Illinois women got the vote in 1913, it was the start of significant effort throughout the state to control alcohol use. Thereafter, local option votes prohibiting drinking alcohol were approved in certain cities and townships.

Local option election battles on the dry or wet issue remained contentious in Illinois. In Lebanon, about fourteen miles east of Collinsville and home of Methodist-affiliated McKendree College, "wets" won a 478–407 victory in April 1917.[54] A celebration parade turned into a near riot when it went to the home of a professor who was a particularly vocal dry supporter. Rocks were thrown and several pistols flourished, but no shots were fired. About twenty people were injured, including the professor when he tried to placate the crowd. By late 1917 twenty-three states had voted to go dry.[55]

State and local efforts mattered less, however, after the December 18, 1917, passage of the national Prohibition amendment by the U.S. Congress. Just twenty days later, Mississippi would become the first state to ratify the Eighteenth Amendment.[56] Notably, the same state would not officially ratify the Thirteenth Amendment, which abolished slavery, until March 1995—some 130 years after it become law.

Only the most optimistic "drys" would have predicted the rapid success in winning Prohibition ratification by the states. It was helped by the growing disapproval of all things German, and the beer-brewing industry fell under intense criticism. Fifteen of the requisite thirty-six states would be on board by the end of 1918. When Nebraska approved the Eighteenth Amendment in January 1919, it became law.[57] The ratification had taken just 394 days, half as long as it took eleven states to approve the Bill of Rights.

It would end the saloon era, which had so wickedly influenced Collinsville's workingmen in early 1918. But perhaps Prohibition was to be expected. "The non-drinkers have been organizing for 50 years and the drinkers had no organization whatever," one writer declared later. "They had been too busy drinking."[58]

• • •

In 1917 and 1918 no group dominated the Collinsville area as much as the five locals of the United Mine Workers of America. The 605 men from Donk Mine No. 2 (Maryville) made up Local 1802, while the 460 men at the Lumaghi Mine No. 2 made up Local 685. The 369 men of Donk Mine No. 1, the Cuba mine, composed Local 848. Consolidated Mine No. 17 had 367 men in Local 264. Lumaghi Mine No. 3 men, 195 of them, made up Local 826.[59]

The pendulum that brought organized labor was initially pulled by low wages, long hours, and poor and unsafe working conditions. No doubt it had swung too far in favor of greedy business interests and industrialists. The downswing would seem equally extreme in the coal miner's favor, pummeling Collinsville—like all industrial communities—as it tried to find some sense of balance. Together the miners in the Collinsville area were some two thousand strong, and when organized they wielded their power like a bludgeon. They were an embodiment of the UMW slogan, "United We Stand, Divided We Fall." There were few things the miners' unions in wartime Collinsville could not control, but one of those was their own members.

The miner's locals, which had all grown with war production, had no meeting places to call their own in Collinsville. Four of the locals instead used city hall, usually twice a month in the evenings. Three locals decided in 1917 to build their own labor temple at the corner of Main and Clinton Streets uptown; the fourth would join the project later.[60] Funding would come from the state UMW and would be repaid by a 1 percent assessment from each miner's wages. The Miners Institute, as it would be called, would be much more than just a meeting place. It would be a measure of the miners' presence, an edifice to their power in Collinsville. An imposing three stories, with two large meeting rooms, business offices, retail space, and a 1,500-seat theater, its construction cost nearly $100,000. Its front on Main Street was built in Renaissance Revival style with brick and terra-cotta panels and pilaster corners and surrounds.[61] Above the meeting hall entrance were embedded statues of two seated miners holding a United Mine Workers emblem atop the curved canopy. The elegance continued inside the theater, with ornate plasterwork and marble walls. The new building opened in late 1918 and hosted vaudeville shows and silent movies, complete with five-piece orchestra.

Even before the United States joined the fray in Europe, America's economy was booming. Industrial production was up just supplying the domestic market and the Entente powers with the tools of war. U.S. entry into the war made demand all the greater; it meant coal production had to significantly increase. Inflation was an issue, as prices rose for most common goods. Coal mine operators in April 1917 announced that they would pass along a ten-cent-per-ton pay increase to miners and sixty cents per day for other laborers.[62]

Concern about keeping a reliable, continuous coal supply prompted the Illinois State Council of Defense to begin discussion with coal mine operators in June and July. The coal operators questioned the involvement of the State Council and appealed to the federal government for assistance.[63] Another meeting in Chicago in August between Governor Frank Lowden, coal operators, and miners led to a State Council of Defense recommendation of federal and state control of coal production, pricing, and distribution.

The concerns of the State Council of Defense were not unwarranted. Standing on mines of black riches while the nation went to war, Collinsville-area miners went instead on a series of wildcat strikes in the summer and early fall of 1917. The strikes were not endorsed and hardly understood by the UMW local leadership. Sometimes impacting one mine, sometimes all mines, and led by just a handful of radicals, the impetuous actions would continue for nearly three months.

The first was on July 26 at Lumaghi Mine No. 2, where miners questioned the accuracy of the scales on which their coal was weighed, claiming that the scales favored the company, perhaps to the tune of 25 percent.[64] The scales were checked by both city officials and UMW officers and found to slightly favor the miners. The malcontents, said to be mostly Austrian and Italian immigrants, didn't believe them. The county mine inspector, UMW district board member Mose Johnson, and even state UMW president Frank Farrington could not persuade the men to return to work. Johnson said the strike was unsanctioned and without merit and ordered the men back to work on July 28. The result was a near riot at the mine on Lebanon Road that Saturday morning, with the majority of the 460 men wanting to return to work and a few radicals threatening them if they did. A newspaper headline said the radicals "are in small minority, but have other miners frightened."[65] Several strike-related fights were reported.

A Local 685 meeting was called for the night of July 30 at city hall to try to resolve the dispute. The meeting was described as "one of the stormiest ever known" there.[66] Older, reputable members of the local were hissed down when they tried to reason with the younger men behind the strike. A continuation of the meeting the following night had the same result.

Lingering hostility from the Tuesday-night meeting carried over to Main Street as the men went to the saloons afterward. Mose Johnson, the UMW district board member, had worked hardest to try to resolve the dispute. He also caught the brunt of the anger from the union radicals. Two of them tried to rough up the fifty-one-year-old Johnson, who was a longtime miner and union official.[67] A newspaper said Johnson "used force" on the men, who were half his age. One of them, Joe Riegel, twenty-seven, had his right forearm broken or dislocated. The other was Henry Shereikis, a twenty-five-year-old Russian miner from Consolidated No. 17. City police charged both Johnson and Shereikis with assault and battery.

The fight reinforced the notion that those responsible for the strike didn't want any settlement and were egged on by outsiders who seemingly had no stake in the matter.[68] Johnson had earlier told a newspaper the malcontents were paid agents of the German government, deliberately seeking to obstruct operation of the mine. One local newspaper account of the strike was placed adjacent to a national news story stating that German money was funding the efforts of the Industrial Workers of the World (IWW), a socialist union that had no apparent connection or relevance to the Collinsville area. Company management of Lumaghi Mine No. 2 thought it best to let union officials resolve the matter internally. And they tried, even under the threat of having their UMW charter revoked as the mine remained closed into a second stormy week.

The strike was finally settled August 9 when another UMW district board member, Leo Franke, met with the men of Local 685.[69] Perhaps it was because Franke could communicate better with the Italian miners.[70] Perhaps it was just because Franke was not Mose Johnson. Whatever the reason this time the miners approved the same settlement that Johnson had proposed earlier.

Almost as if a footnote, it was reported that Johnson could not attend the meeting because he had been stabbed in the abdomen three days earlier by someone in a group of five or six men who argued with him on Main Street.[71] Johnson recovered from the five-inch knife wound, and no public mention was again made of the attack. In the future Johnson was known to carry a pistol when dealing with wildcat strikers.[72] The men returned to work on August 10.

"The news that the mine is to work will be welcomed by the entire city, inasmuch as the strike has had an unsettling effect on business and industrial conditions during the past two weeks," one newspaper reported.[73] Another editor lamented the misrepresentations of the wildcats who had caused the walkout: "The men have lost thousands of dollars in wages and for no apparent reason that could not have been adjusted in a half day, if hotheads had not been in the middle."[74]

Normalcy would be brief. The same day that Lumaghi No. 2 resumed operation, drivers at Donk Mine No. 2 started an unauthorized strike for higher wages. By Monday it had spread to all

Collinsville-area mines and, in fact, to thirty-two of forty down-state mines.[75] Drivers made $3.60 a day and motormen and laborers made $3.88 per day. The drivers reportedly sought $1 more per day, a 28 percent pay increase, even though the contract was not open for negotiation. By August 17, after union officials struggled to get the men back to work, most Collinsville mines resumed operation. Donk Mine No. 1 was still closed, but according to one report the drivers there had "quietly" agreed to return.[76]

As with the first wildcat strike, union and company officials had trouble determining the specific complaints at Donk No. 1, the Cuba mine. Grievances ranged from not liking the mine manager to driver wages to wanting the company to build a washhouse. The newspaper report said, "German agents were stirring up the faction and allowing them to use any pretext that was available." A union official gave credence to that theory and said he felt the same thing was happening all over southern Illinois.[77]

Illinois UMW president Farrington had seen enough of the wildcat actions and sent telegrams to fifty-eight local presidents after being given an ultimatum by mine operators. Farrington said that anyone refusing to resume work should be expelled from the union. He added that workers who refuse to replace miners who have not reported to work should also be expelled from the union. "Whether he is successful will depend on what is done by Socialist leaders in the organization," a newspaper reported. "These leaders are bitterly opposed to Farrington and they may seize the present opportunity to bring about his undoing."[78]

By August 21 even the miners at Donk Mine No. 1 had returned to work. A state mine inspector had posted a notice requiring a shower house at the Cuba mine, perhaps placating the men. Miners throughout the region agreed to press their concerns through formal negotiations, but there was general, continuing resentment that mine operators were profiting too much from the increased coal demand, and not enough of those profits were being shared with miners and other union members.[79] Some felt mine operators themselves had a hand in the recent unrest by paying extra money to miners to increase production. The operators' intent was to lure miners from competing mines to theirs. The bonus payments had many miners on the move in southern Illinois and signaled others that their work was undervalued.

Many miners felt that a special state convention of the UMW should be called to consider new pay scales. The local from the Black Eagle Mine in nearby Fairview had passed a resolution to that effect, and it was followed by a similar resolution from Local 848 of Donk Mine No. 1.[80]

Peace and calm at the local mines lasted just twelve workdays before the men at Lumaghi No. 3 decided they too would strike for a washhouse.[81] Never mind that the Lumaghi company, noting the trouble at Donk Mine No. 1, awarded a contract for the construction of the building and that the contractor had as yet been unable to begin the job. Again the strike was not sanctioned by the union, which threatened to fine its members who did not return to work.

Having seen enough of the wildcat actions, the Lumaghi Coal Company decided it was the opportune time to close Mine No. 3 for needed repairs, despite heavy demand and the rapidly approaching heating season.[82] The day after the wildcat strike began, September 4, the company announced it would install new cages in the shafts and make other repairs. Some of the miners realized they had overplayed their hand and contacted Mose Johnson for assistance in getting the mine operating again. "Can't you get things started?" they asked. "I didn't stop 'em," was Johnson's laconic response. "The company didn't stop and it will be up to you to do the starting." A newspaper noted, "By the time the repairs are finished the men will be more than glad to go back to work." The wildcat strike and subsequent shutdown for repairs would cost the miners at least another ten days of work.[83]

UMW officials and coal mine operators alike were hopeful that federal fuel administrator Harry Garfield would lead the government effort to set coal pricing and wages for the duration of the war, as opposed to any federal takeover of the mines. Optimistic union officials promised quick action after meetings began in late September. But a decision would not come soon enough for the miners. The officials agreed in Washington on October 6, 1917, that the mining prices for coal should be increased 10 percent and that most day laborers would be paid $1.40 more per day and other workers would get increases of 15 percent.[84] It would take time, however, to calculate the exact coal prices for the different types of coal and the wages per ton that would be allowed by the federal government. Expediency was not served when Garfield's mother became seriously ill in Cleveland, requiring him to recess the hearings for several days.[85] Miners had earlier been told they could expect pay increases by mid-October.

Many words could be used to describe southern Illinois coal miners in 1917, but *patient* would not be among them. Realizing they would not be paid at the new wage scale, on October 16 miners in Collinsville and elsewhere in Illinois again walked off the job. Statewide forty mines were shut down and fifteen thousand miners went on strike. Nationwide the great majority of miners stayed on the job. In Washington Garfield was irked. The whole agreement had been predicated on a policy of no tolerance of strikes. He immediately stopped the hearings on coal pricing and said he would resume only after all miners had returned to work.[86]

Local industries began to shut down due to lack of fuel.[87] Miners' locals were again threatened with UMW expulsion if their men did not return to their jobs.[88] The Collinsville miners would miss at least five workdays before they could be corralled back following a Sunday, October 21, regional meeting. There was great dissension within their ranks, but the miners voted to allow Garfield time to set the higher coal prices that would fund their raises. They also passed a quixotic resolution demanding federal takeover of the mines, getting in one more dig at the abhorred mine owners.[89] All the miners were back at work October 22, but two of the smaller Collinsville operations, with more reasonable miners, restarted sooner.

For all the erratic job actions in 1917, the October strike may have been the easiest to justify for the Collinsville miners, yet it attracted the most national criticism. The strike met with at least the tacit approval of local UMW officials. The miners had been told pay hikes would be coming October 1, then October 16—but both estimates were overly optimistic. "They've been promising us a raise for weeks," said an exasperated Robert Bertolero, president of the Local 685 miners of Lumaghi No. 2.[90] Even Mose Johnson could sympathize with the miners this time. He doubted the strike was legal but would not order the men back to work.

Ironically, the Collinsville miners would strike just four days after state UMW president Frank Farrington came to town to participate in laying the cornerstone for the new Miners Institute on October 12. The event was preceded by a grand parade, with two bands, it was noted. It was a holiday for the miners, but not all showed up for the ceremony in the piercing cold that day.[91]

Farrington denounced the recent wildcat strikes in the area and again blamed pro-German influences for the "misdirected agitation." He acknowledged the dissension among the members: "There are some in the ranks who are not satisfied and think the United Mine Workers of America ought to be abandoned for a more militant organization. I don't agree with them."[92] He continued:

> Men who start illegal strikes, bodies that adopt immature and unwarranted resolutions, agitators who go about seeking to call special conventions, stirring up the men and creating a distrust of their officials, are the miners' worst enemies. And I call on the conservative and thinking men of Collinsville to come to the front and put down any such agitations when they arise here. Things have been done in the miner's ranks during the past few months which would not have been tolerated by any other labor or fraternal organization in the country. The guilty men would have been cast out of any other organization. The greatest outrage of unionism is independent action. It is not unionism at all. It is disorganization of the worst sort.[93]

Garfield finally announced the new coal pricing structure on October 27, 1917. The prices would go into effect November 1, but miners would not see the raise reflected in pay checks until November 30.[94] The miners would get an increase of thirty-five cents per ton over their current wages and coal prices would increase by the same amount.[95] The agreed on pricing would remain in effect until the end of the war.

Collinsville Herald publisher J. O. Monroe welcomed the agreement for the calm it would bring to the city:

> Conditions are again normal in the Collinsville industrial field. With the granting of increased wages for miners for the period of the war and the fixing of new prices for coal by the government, it is believed there will not be a recurrence of the strikes and uneasiness which have marked the past few months.
>
> With industry humming and the bounteous crops around us, there is no reason for Collinsville people to worry about the economic situation for the winter. . . . While prices will be higher, wages are much higher—in some cases double what they were two years ago—and with the demand for every ton of coal that can be produced, everyone ought to have the wherewith to buy. Collinsville can count itself fortunately situated.[96]

The rebellious nature of the Collinsville-area miners, however, had impacted local coal production. During the period in 1917 and 1918 when Illinois produced 14 percent more coal than the prior year, three of the five big Collinsville-area shipping mines, Donk No. 1 and No. 2 and Consolidated No. 17, actually had lower production. Lumaghi No. 2 and No. 3 both increased output.[97] The number of workdays, whether reduced by wildcat strike, railcar shortage, or maintenance, were likewise down in three of the five big Collinsville-area mines, while statewide workdays were up 7 percent.

With the local dissension in the Illinois UMW ranks, it perhaps should have been no surprise that a Collinsville man would challenge Farrington for the state UMW president position in December. Frank Hefferly had been state vice president previously and fell four thousand votes shy of knocking off Farrington when the approximately fifty-two thousand votes were tabulated.[98] Men at Consolidated No. 17 alleged that the results had been doctored, but nothing came of it.[99] Also surviving the election was district board member Mose Johnson, who withstood a spirited challenge from Dan Slinger.

In January 1918 the price for coal had been set at $2.75 per loaded ton and the mines were operating regularly.[100] The miners were well paid, and everyone knew it. Many of the workingmen in Collinsville who were not currently miners had worked the mines previously, giving credence to the phrase, "once a miner, always a miner."[101] So it was when Officer Mike Dooner resigned from the Collinsville police force to take a job at Consolidated No. 17. He was replaced by Harry Stephens. At this point miners were making about twice what policemen earned. "It is understood that others are considering exchanging the billy for the pick," a newspaper reported.[102]

The demand for coal and the related prosperity continued to the point that the February 15, 1918, payroll at the Collinsville mines was the largest ever, estimated at about $150,000, for coal mined from January 15 to January 30.[103] At the smaller Abbey mine, the pay for that period had been 30 percent higher than normal.[104]

As volatile as the United Mine Workers of America were in the Collinsville area and elsewhere, the miners were a critical part of the U.S. economy in 1918. And the UMW was a political force to be reckoned with as well, with more than 405,000 members nationwide. Collinsville would shine at the union's convention starting January 15 in Indianapolis, as a former local miner, Frank Hayes, would preside as national president. War and the federal price agreement had brought both wealth and rare stability for the UMW; for the first time in twenty years it would open a convention without a general strike in progress.[105]

A forty-eight-by-seventy-five-foot service flag hung over the convention hall in Indianapolis, adorned with 19,135 stars for miners presently serving in the military. Of those serving 3,269 had come from Illinois by way of volunteering or conscription.[106] Illinois UMW membership was more than 87,000, of whom some 14,000 were still subject to the draft. The wartime convention in Indy was reported to be the world's largest labor assembly to date. Among that number were ten delegates from Collinsville-area mines, making sure the local men's voices would be heard.[107]

4

You Are Either for Us or against Us

The scab is a traitor to his God, his mother, and his class.

—Labor union saying

The volatile labor environment of 1917 and 1918 was not just a hindrance in the coalfields of southern Illinois but a problem to be dealt with nationwide. The booming war economy created a tight job market for nearly every industry, just at the time when many young men were drafted or enlisted in the military.[1] Labor unions worked to solidify their gains from President Woodrow Wilson's Progressive Era and take advantage of a political landscape designed to maintain or increase industrial output for the duration of the war. Meanwhile, inflation continued to skyrocket, and quite often wages didn't keep up with the cost of living.

In the first six months of the war alone, more than 2,500 significant industrial strikes were reported nationwide.[2] While many of those disagreements were simply about higher wages, a greater number of job actions were called to win union recognition for employees or closed-shop agreements. One of those battles for unionization would be fought in Collinsville at the St. Louis Smelting and Refining (SLSR) plant. And for all the chaos wrought by a handful of miners for the UMW and local mine operators, it would pale in comparison to the citywide mayhem to win union recognition at the lead smelting works. That fight would rage almost concurrently with Collinsville's wildcat coal mine strikes in 1917 and make the city a steaming cauldron of labor militancy.

The Lead Works, as the plant was known to locals, located northeast of the city in 1904 to also be near the abundant coal supply.[3] Lead ore was shipped in for smelting into ingots, sheets, and powdered lead for further refinement and industrial use. There was naturally heavy wartime demand for the product. East of Vandalia Street on Cuba Lane, the Lead Works was a vast complex of homes, industrial furnaces, and related buildings. The entryway to the plant on Cuba Lane was lined with stately white post-and-rail fences before reaching the six manager's homes on either side of the road. The homes were large bungalows, most with wide dormers and hip roofs, befitting Superintendent William Newnam and the other plant managers who lived there. It was nearly a company town when one adds in some smaller homes built farther down the lane for employees and the Harry Schnick Grocery. The residential areas also included a large boardinghouse. Perhaps alluding to the wage levels of its residents, the boardinghouse was sometimes referred to as the Welfare Hotel. It compactly housed about 130 of the workers and their families.[4] In the area around the Lead Works, it wasn't difficult to discern the haves from the have-nots.

After smelter rates were increased, workers at the plant were given raises in April 1917 that paid them from $2.30 to $2.65 per day. Newnam explained, "It is our desire to retain our present efficient force and their contentment and well-being shall be our first consideration." But these rates were still well below what miners were earning.[5]

Some effort had been made to make the plant safer, as workers had complained of respiratory problems, and nearby farmers said the lead fumes hurt their crops. Three new smokestacks were constructed in 1917, the largest of which stood at 386 feet.[6] The *Collinsville Herald* proclaimed the improvements signified "the passing of the day when industries were slave drivers and man killers, who brushed aside the human wreckage of their enterprise and called for fresh forms to mangle."[7] It was hoped the stacks would be high enough to prevent more pollution lawsuits too. The plant was also expected to be 25 percent more efficient with the upgrades.

The Lead Works had upward of four hundred employees, but five of them in particular caught the ire of company officials in the summer of 1917. When management learned they were attempting to unionize their coworkers, they were promptly fired. But the efforts at organizing, and the underlying employee discontent, brought more voluntary concessions from SLSR on July 28, including a 10 percent wage hike and a reduction to eight-hour workdays.[8] It was said to be the third voluntary pay hike in a year's time.

On Sunday, July 29, two hundred of the smelter employees met with representatives of the International Mill and Smelter Workers Union at an organizational meeting at city hall.[9] A committee had asked Superintendent Newnam for reinstatement of the five organizers, but he refused, calling the men "undesirables." Meanwhile, more than 125 men had signed the petition seeking recognition of the union as the employees' bargaining agent.[10]

The union organizer said the men were not making within fifty cents per day of what they should be earning, even with the recent increases. He said the shortage of labor made it an "opportune moment" to press their concerns.[11] UMW state president Frank Farrington also spoke to the benefits of unionism and said the worker's efforts would be fully supported by the miners' unions. He too agreed it was the right time to unionize, as the government would not let the Lead Works shut down, even if it wanted to. Farrington denied reports that black workers would not be allowed to join the union and characterized the latest company wage hike as "inconsequential" and a "sop." Smelter workers conditions in 1917 mirrored those of miners twenty years prior, Farrington said.[12]

Locked in a stalemate, the employees made their move on August 4, when a large number quietly walked out of the plant at the sound of the noon lunch whistle.[13] Newnam and SLSR continued to say that they would not reinstate the five discharged men or recognize the union as bargaining agent. In fact, Newnam refused to meet with anyone who was not a Lead Works employee. The departing workers were paid their wages due when they left that day. But without enough men to operate the facility, Newnam elected to close. The company said working conditions, hours, and wages were appropriate and that it would remain closed until the labor matter had been resolved.

The Collinsville Trades Council, an organization of union groups, said, "The central body of the City and all its branches are backing the striking lead smelter workers." That backing would include financial support as the five Collinsville-area miners' locals began signing on to create a strike fund.[14] With a 1 percent deduction from each miner's paycheck, the fund could potentially yield $2,000 a month.

As the strike entered its third week, union organizers advertised the wages paid at St. Joseph Lead Company's smelting plant in Herculaneum, about fifty miles south in Missouri. The plant was unionized and much better paid. Farther from St. Louis and more rural, theoretically Herculaneum should have had a lower cost of living. But the wage comparisons were telling. Furnace tappers were paid $2.80 per day in Collinsville, $4.55 per day in Herculaneum; furnace helpers received $2.60 in Collinsville, $4.11 in Herculaneum; motormen earned $2.60 in Collinsville, $4.29 in Herculaneum. The wage disparity of about 60 percent made it easy to understand why SLSR had so quickly offered pay hikes in an attempt to avert the strike. "We as a body of men realize that we have been imposed on and have been suffering from the pressure of working under unbearable conditions," the union ad said.[15]

The Collinsville Trades Council assisted the strikers by helping pitch a tent city where unmarried strikers could camp outside the plant and be available to serve as pickets when needed.[16] The council had arranged credit at stores for the strikers to use for necessities. Mayor John Siegel had tried to get the two parties together again to negotiate but to no avail.

The city council would become further involved when it was asked at a special meeting August 21 to adopt a resolution by the trades council that criticized SLSR for threatening to move the operation to another town. "This company ought not deny to its employees the right to belong to the organization of their craft," the resolution said.[17] Mayor Siegel questioned whether council action was appropriate and suggested that the company be given an opportunity to present its side to the council. Alderman R. C. DeLaney, a weighman at the Donk's Mine No. 1, said he would rather see the company move than continue to pay low wages.[18] Siegel would later say the resolution was passed illegally and was null and void.[19]

Forty-five-year-old Dr. John Siegel had served as mayor since 1915, having won reelection in April 1917. His medical practice on Main Street was well established in the community, his home just six blocks away on Morrison Avenue. The mayor's wife, Stella, eleven years his junior, had borne him a son, Vivien, now fourteen.[20] As a businessman Siegel was less apt to adopt the union line. The workingman's favorite in the last mayoral election had been former mayor James Mathews, who had alleged that Siegel did not want the new labor temple built in Collinsville. Siegel denied the charge, adding, "Voters should remember that every man cannot get on the police force, even if they are promised before the election."[21]

Siegel would make another attempt to bring the parties together by taking a committee of three strikers to Newnam's office to negotiate.[22] They met for about an hour, and the company agreed it would allow an open shop, which would permit union membership. But it would not consent to dues checkoff or allow a union business agent to collect dues at the plant. Also the company would still not agree to reinstate the five organizers.

There were some last ditch efforts to break the stalemate. One included a September 5 meeting at the home of city physician M. W. Harrison.[23] It was announced that the union had requested a 30 percent wage hike, about half the difference between the Collinsville and the Herculaneum salaries. Newnam rejected that percentage but did agree to some increase. The smelter workers backed away from the demand for reinstatement of the five original leaders. The major sticking point was now union recognition, and the workers were not bending on that. Determined to keep a nonunion shop, neither was Newnam. After the meeting a large number of smelter workers convened in the meeting hall above Salel's Ye Olde Corner Bar on Main Street to discuss their next moves, but they were not holding the cards.

State mediators met with the parties on September 13, but as with the other sessions, to no avail.[24] By that time Superintendent Newnam's decision had been made. While the smelter workers, miners, and city officials fretted that St. Louis Smelting and Refining would move to another town, Newnam had another plan. He would stay and fight.

He would wage that battle in a town where more than half the workingmen were union miners, in a town where there were unions for barbers, bartenders, brewery workers, butchers, carpenters and joiners, cement workers, hod carriers and building laborers, hosiery workers, laborers, musicians, plasterers, railway carmen, retail clerks, sheet metal workers, teamsters, and wood, wire, and metal lathers.[25] And if Collinsville did not have a union for a given craft, it was a good bet that a nearby town did. Nearly every family had a union member in the household or at least a close friend who belonged to organized labor.

The Lead Works had peacefully existed in the community for thirteen years, but there had been no prior attempt to unionize— and that changed everything. With the talk about town since the start of the strike, Newnam and SLSR well knew what they were up against. But they would reopen the plant with no union labor. The company's first step on Monday, September 24, was to quietly seek a federal injunction in Springfield against anyone who would try to interfere with operation of the plant.[26] Specifically named in the injunction were national and local officials of the International Union of Mine, Mill and Smelter Workers. But the injunction also named state and local miners' union officials, labor council members, and even two Main Street saloon keepers.

Federal district judge J. Otis Humphrey's injunction prohibited any activity that might interfere with operation of the smelter, including intimidation or harassment of company employees, prospective employees, or those conducting business with SLSR.

The company announced its intentions on Tuesday and said the plant would restart the next day.[27] Federal deputy marshal John Murray arrived Tuesday to serve the injunctions. Because the Lead Works was outside the city limits, police protection should have been provided by Madison County sheriff Jenkin Jenkins. Instead, the sheriff informed Newnam that he would withdraw all his deputies from the area if the plant was restarted with non-union labor. Jenkins would allow Lee Thompson, the Lead Works security guard, to remain a special deputy and would also deputize Newnam and other executives to make arrests if they felt the need. With that the sheriff and his men left the plant area. Despite the strikers camped just outside SLSR's door, the message to the company from local law enforcement was effectively, you're on your own.

The U.S. deputy marshal said he expected to stay the week to see that order was preserved. Thompson, Newnam, and the U.S. marshal did arrest sixteen-year-old Alex Winters for throwing a rock at a car driven by company office employees.[28] He was arraigned Wednesday and taken to the county jail in Edwardsville for consideration of the grand jury.

The first day the plant was to restart, September 26, one hundred men applied and were put to work.[29] Another three hundred would be needed to fill all positions. But the newly hired men could start eight of the eighteen Scotch hearths, light the refinery, and begin cleaning the blast furnace. Some of the rehired men had originally signed to join the new union, but seven weeks without pay had taken the fight out of them just as surely as it had emptied their wallets.[30] Many other experienced smelter workers had left the area and would be difficult to replace, but most of the plant's positions could be handled by unskilled labor.

The men restarting the plant worked eight-hour shifts, and with a pay increase. But SLSR could not give any more, Newnam said, and he considered it pointless to continue negotiating with the strikers.[31] The president of the smelter workers' union that was not to be, Zenas Lockhart, said the plant would never get enough men to operate. Lockhart, thirty-one years old, had tried to support a wife and four children on the Lead Works wages.

77

The strategy of local union officials was to try to keep prospective employees away from the Lead Works. Those signing on the first day saw and heard from the pickets, but they weren't dissuaded. All the men hired on the first day returned for the next, Newnam said, when still more men signed on.[32]

The lead smelter strike in 1917 was not just a battle to create better-paying, union jobs in Collinsville. A principal concern was the fear of the plant using "imported" workers, which was largely a euphemism for blacks being brought in to take the jobs, as a strikebreaking move. That had been a primary cause of the East St. Louis riots three months earlier, which brought the deaths of at least forty-eight people and the burning of some three hundred homes and other buildings.[33] Other estimates claim fatalities were over one hundred, since the deaths of many blacks were not documented. Company agents sent thousands of unskilled blacks from southern states to that city by train, with the promise of good-paying jobs and better treatment. Neither ended up being necessarily true.

In East St. Louis a congressional committee investigating the riots said that the Aluminum Ore Company, the Armour Meat Packing Company, railroads, and other industrialists had "pitted white labor against black." Only making matters worse was the deep-seated public corruption and indifference in the town of sixty-five thousand residents. The final U.S. congressional report on the East St. Louis riots stated, "Sodom and Gomorrah were model Christian communities in comparison."[34] Collinsville did not have the extensive industry or the wide-open corruption of its neighbor to the west, but its residents still feared blacks being brought in to take jobs in the community.

A number of Collinsville blacks worked at the Lead Works prior to and after the strike. The positions did not pay well, but blacks had no access to the better jobs in the coal mines. If more black workers came in now, would it just be the first step to them getting the coveted coal miner's jobs? Many white men from Collinsville had also worked at the smelter. Prior to the strike the smelter workers were considered simply men who worked second-tier jobs. After the strike the smelter workers were considered scabs, an anathema to most union men. More repellent yet were the out-of-towners, mostly black, who would take the jobs that the miners and others wanted to see unionized. The men feared Collinsville would end up like East St. Louis.

From atop the bluffs in early July 1917, it was easy for Collinsville folks to look down their noses at the scandalous river town to the west. When the East St. Louis riots had just started, a mob stopped a streetcar operated by two Collinsville men. They could only watch as Albert James, a black employee of the Lead Works, was pulled off the car and nearly beaten to death. "A few dangerous demagogues have led half grown boys and denizens of the half-world in an orgy of blood," *Collinsville Advertiser* publisher Gus Schimpff said. "It was the act of a pack of hyenas traveling en masse. But East St. Louis must pay the price, and pay dearly."[35]

J. O. Monroe, the young publisher and editor of the *Collinsville Herald*, weighed in too: "There is scarcely a city in this section which might not have been the scene of similar disorders under similar circumstances. . . . Even Collinsville cannot claim that she might not resort to violence under certain provocation. Every city which shelters a mixed population is subject to the eruptions which develop from the irritations of different bloods." He went on to note that Collinsville had no "bad" district and that the mayor and police chief did fine work in keeping bad characters out of the city. At the Lead Works a similar service was performed by the special deputy there. "Thompson simply will not permit 'bad' negroes around the place," Monroe said. "Without turning the scornful lip at East St. Louis, Collinsville may be thankful that she has such a law-abiding class of citizens," the editor myopically wrote.[36]

The two newspapers in Collinsville, Schimpff's *Advertiser* and Monroe's *Collinsville Herald*, generally provided reliable information for readers during the era. But the turbulent events of the last months of 1917 and first half of 1918 in Collinsville would test the journalistic integrity of any small-town newspaperman. The story as told in the local newspapers from this point particularly lacks the perspective of s l s r Lead Works management and employees, no doubt owing to pressure from the unions and the community.

Tensions ran high in Collinsville after the Lead Works reopened on September 26. The union men of the city had a parade and rally Sunday morning, September 30, in support of the striking smelter workers. The parade formed after the arrival of two streetcars full of Maryville miners. Kreider's Military Band led the parade, and one thousand men marched through the downtown streets while thousands more watched. The men carried all variety of banners and flags, one calling for the overthrow of the "Czar of Labor in Collinsville," referring to the Lead Works' Newnam.[37] Another banner left no room for the indecisive: "You Are Either for Us or against Us."

The orderly parade concluded at the park behind city hall, where eleven days earlier the city had held an emotional send-off for fifty-five departing soldiers. The president of u m w Local 685 of Lumaghi Mine No. 2, Robert Bertolero, spoke first to the large crowd and told of the union's commitment to support the smelter workers, who had "quit the smelter to try to force enough in wages to buy bread." He urged nonviolence, lest the workers turn public opinion and law officials against them. One of the smelter workers' national union leaders said that in his thirty years of organizing, he had not seen anyone who "assumed as arrogant an attitude as that taken by Supt. Newnam" and likened him to a king or czar.[38] He said the right to organize was the biggest issue, but that wages should be about twice what they were at the Lead Works.

Monroe, the *Collinsville Herald* editor, praised the uptown saloon keepers for voluntarily staying closed during and after the parade and speechmaking, to avoid alcohol influencing the thinking of the frenzied crowd. "They probably forestalled trouble which might have resulted in violence or bloodshed or both. Many a good man loses his sense when inflamed with liquor and oftimes one or two irresponsible drunks can start more trouble than all the good citizens of the town can stop," Monroe said, quite prophetically this time.[39]

There had been trouble at the plant and in the surrounding area since the reopening. According to the local papers, nearly all of it was caused by the black employees brought in as strikebreakers. At Evanoff's Saloon there had been a report of black employees from the Lead Works creating a disturbance and displaying weapons. No one had been arrested, but six bars near the Lead Works were ordered closed indefinitely on Monday to avoid problems.[40] City police searched and harassed men going to or coming from the smelter using the interurban streetcar line. One black man, Collinsville resident Frank Thomas, was arrested on the streetcar and sentenced to twenty-one days in the county jail. W. C. Nessen was found with a blackjack and fined $25 and costs. After several days of the police harassment, the Lead Works sent cars to shuttle the strikebreakers from the streetcar stop just outside the western city limits. In this manner the strikebreakers avoided harassment by the Collinsville police and miners on the interurban cars traveling through town.

By the first week of October, the Lead Works had hired two hundred men, enough to fire up two more Scotch hearths.[41] Newnam denied that he was bringing in strikebreakers and claimed he was merely hiring former workers who had elected to return. SLSR was also literally gaining ground outside the plant, as a fire destroyed some of the striker's tents in their encampment at the gates, probably due to nearby burning cornstalks. Lead Works private security agents quickly moved in to occupy the land previously held by the strikers.

For all the interest local police had in the strikebreakers, the U.S. District Court was more concerned with the striking men and their attempts to interfere with plant operations. U.S. marshal John Murray summoned six of them to report to Judge Humphrey in Springfield for violating the injunction against harassment of SLSR.[42]

The following week the Lead Works had 250 employees, with more coming on board daily. Tension continued to rise between the union men and SLSR's employees, but the strikebreakers and Newnam appeared to be winning the battle. The area saloons had been allowed to reopen, leading to another fight at Schreiber's Barrelhouse on Vandalia Street. Sheriff Jenkins ordered saloons in the area closed once again.[43] The six men who had earlier been ordered to appear before Judge Humphries in Springfield demanded a jury trial. With a busy docket Humphries deferred hearing the case, reminding them that the injunction was still in effect and to keep their noses clean.

For what it was worth, the Collinsville Trades Council endorsed a resolution stating that SLSR was "harassing and intimidating strikers who have at all times conducted themselves in a most orderly and peaceful manner." It said the company had "hired gunmen and imported vicious and undesirable characters who go about the community armed, discharging firearms, and threatening the lives of peaceful citizens," no doubt referring to the private detectives and guards hired by SLSR to provide at least a modicum of protection.[44]

There were reports that a "riot" had erupted outside the plant when strikers chased some departing workmen, and a few rocks had purportedly been thrown. An out-of-town newspaper said that brickbats had been thrown, but the *Collinsville Herald* dismissed that report as "lurid." With the strikers apparently having the upper hand that day, police again were nowhere to be seen.[45]

Madison County sheriff Jenkin Jenkins had removed his deputies from the area around the plant on September 26, never mind his sworn duty to enforce the law in that part of the county too. Jenkins, age forty-six, was born in South Wales and had become a naturalized citizen.[46] He was a coal miner who had taken a "more or less lively interest in local political affairs"; he became a deputy in 1912 and was later elected sheriff. Jenkins and his wife, Edith, had two daughters and two sons, one of whom was a superb baseball player, enough so to draw interest from Branch Rickey of the St. Louis Cardinals. Roy Jenkins's parents had to decline a tryout offer, however, because the twenty-year-old was serving in the U.S. Army's new Aviation Corps.[47] The Jenkins family had previously lived in Collinsville, and within two years Jenkin Jenkins would be out as sheriff and working in a Collinsville mine once again. During the labor unrest of 1917, there was little doubt where his sympathies lay.

Jenkins's decision to withhold protection from the SLSR plant was not entirely unprecedented in the area. In nearby Granite City, the police chief and the mayor would find themselves indicted for omission of duty and malfeasance for failing to protect a nonunion sewer contractor and his workers from union activists who harassed and beat them also in the fall of 1917.[48] In that case a county grand jury ended up handing down thirty indictments. Granite City mayor Marshall Kirkpatrick, a Socialist, had similarly refused to protect company interests in that town during 1913 and 1914 labor strikes. And he was unapologetic for his actions, asserting that most residents approved.[49]

But the harassment of incoming workers by strikers, police, and other union men was not having the desired effect at the Lead Works, as production continued to ramp up closer to plant capacity. By mid-October the union men changed their strategy in fighting SLSR. Sheriff Jenkins decided he would once again *protect* the Lead Works. With the Collinsville police no longer able to search or harass incoming workers on the interurban rail lines, Jenkins planned to make sure that happened before they entered the plant. He sent deputies Vernon Coons and Hannah Jokerst to do the job and also swore in three special deputies, Steve Britton, Tom White, and Tom Wilson. Of course the special deputies were miners, except for Wilson, who sold coal mine supplies.

On Jenkins's order, the men searched everyone entering and leaving the Lead Works for weapons starting October 15.[50] Fourteen arrests were made the first day. One man was charged with driving a car carrying five workers around the deputies and into the plant. Coons jumped on the car and was reportedly injured before he could get the man to stop. The driver was charged with assault and fined $50 by a justice of the peace. A black detective from a St. Louis agency, which had been hired by SLSR, was charged with carrying a concealed weapon and also fined $100 by a justice of the peace. Twelve others were taken to the Madison County Jail, eight of them black, and most were checked to make sure they had registered for the draft.

The next day thirteen more men were taken to the county jail on trumped up charges, eleven blacks and two whites. Special deputy White even stopped J. A. Castleman, vice president and general manager of the plant, and searched him for weapons. Castleman submitted to the search under protest and was then allowed to enter the plant.[51] A local newspaper reporting on the arrests said, "As most of the names given by these men were probably fictitious, it is hardly necessary to publish them."[52] The SLSR attorney filed writs of habeas corpus for the twenty-five arrested employees still being held in the county jail. Jenkins, after conferring with the state's attorney, released the men with no charges filed.[53]

Sheriff Jenkins's newfound enthusiasm for law enforcement at the Lead Works didn't particularly please J. Otis Humphrey, the U.S. district judge in Springfield. He once again dispatched Federal Marshal Murray to Collinsville, this time to summon Sheriff Jenkins and his five deputies to court Thursday, October 18, for violating the restraining order.[54] Jenkins and three of the deputies boarded a train for Springfield while Special Deputies White and Britton were notified in Joliet, where they were attending a State Federation of Labor meeting.

Judge Humphrey sharply reprimanded Jenkins and his deputies in the Springfield courtroom, saying the plant's production was critical for the war effort. He told them to do their sworn duty as law enforcement officers and ordered their return to Springfield on October 29, when all the injunction cases would be heard.[55]

The union men of Collinsville were obsessed with the notion that workers, especially black men, were being brought in to take the Lead Works jobs. Jenkins said that the arrests had been made to protect the city and that the imported men "were of the vilest type, and many of them were criminals and of the lawless element."[56] The sheriff claimed that he was primarily after the agents responsible for bringing the workers in by automobile. "He had feared that the importation of strike breakers, particularly the negroes, would cause trouble."[57] Either from fear of violence and crime or fear of losing this labor battle, there was a sense of foreboding in Collinsville.

It was suggested that the city hire more policemen to prevent trouble. Mayor Siegel said he had tried recently to bring in more officers, but the low salary made it difficult to fill the positions. Miners' Local 685 president Bertolero, with a fox-guarding-the-henhouse solution, proposed that the striking smelter workers would perhaps be willing to do the job without pay. Siegel declined the suggestion.[58]

At age thirty-eight Robert Bertolero was a respected man in the community and at Lumaghi Mine No. 2. Born in Italy, he had become a naturalized citizen. In 1917 he and his wife, Minnie, and their eleven-year-old son, Robert Jr., lived on Burroughs Avenue near School Superintendent C. H. Dorris. Robert Jr. would follow his father's career in mining at Lumaghi Mine No. 2 six years later. Shortly after getting his first mining job, Robert Bertolero Jr. was crushed between two pit cars, and the seventeen-year-old reportedly died cradled in his father's arms.[59] (The year 1923 would be a particularly treacherous at Lumaghi Mine No. 2, as four miners in all would die there.)

By the week of October 22, less than a month after the reopening, Newnam announced that the Lead Works had 360 employees, all it could use at the moment, and that other men were available if needed. For all their efforts the strikers and their union brethren had been unable to stop the flow of workers needed to operate the smelter. Having been unable to stanch the tide of workers, at least one union man would try to cut off the flow of the commodity that first brought the smelter to Collinsville: coal.

UMW Local 826 president William Brockmeier of Lumaghi No. 3 notified the mine superintendent not to make any more coal deliveries to the Lead Works.[60] The superintendent passed the request up the line, as mine owner Joseph Lumaghi was away on a hunting trip. Newnam, of SLSR, learned of the request and said such action would also be in violation of the federal injunction. The contract between SLSR and Lumaghi stipulated that coal had to be delivered whenever the mine operated. It was thus implied that Lumaghi Mine No. 3 would not have to deliver coal if the mine was closed by strike. Despite Brockmeier's threat, the coal continued to flow to the Lead Works. Other miners' local officers let it be known that Brockmeier did not speak for their unions.[61]

Jenkins, his five deputies, and twelve other men who had been charged with contempt got their days in court from October 29 through November 1 in Springfield. And generally it did not go well for them. Judge Humphrey was unmoved by Jenkins's plea that he was just trying to keep the peace. The sheriff and his deputies all were found guilty of being in contempt of the federal court injunction. Jenkins was fined $1,000—no small sum in 1917—and court costs, while the deputies were each fined $100 and costs.[62] Humphrey ordered them held at the McLean County Jail until they could pay up. Their attorneys promised an appeal, and Humphrey allowed bond for the men, which was quickly paid by "prominent citizens of Edwardsville."[63]

The other defendants didn't fare much better; nine of the twelve men were found guilty that week.[64] Two men, including would-be lead workers' union president Zenas Lockhardt, were sentenced to ninety days in jail; another would get sixty days. Sentence was yet to be determined for six of the men. Three were found not guilty. Confident in their cases, all the men had requested jury trials. But early in the proceedings, they asked that the jury be dismissed, figuring they were better off taking their chances with Judge Humphrey. In eight of the nine guilty judgments, the bench or jury took the word of the black men who had been harassed over that of the white defendants, a newspaper noted.[65] Fifteen other cases were still to be tried by Judge Humphrey.

There was outrage at the convictions in Collinsville, where UMW State Board member Mose Johnson said the union had paid at least some of the defense costs. He forecast a "storm of protest among union men all over the state," but it never arrived.[66] Some people also called for the removal of Judge Humphrey and the U.S. attorney. J. O. Monroe, the *Collinsville Herald* editor, criticized the judgments too.[67] He drew an analogy to East St.

Louis's riots, saying that a congressional committee had faulted officials there for not searching men on the streets for weapons.

Jenkins's legal problems also spilled over into civil court, where the vice president of the Lead Works had filed suit against him for his false arrest and search without cause.[68] Up to fifteen others were expected to join in the lawsuit.

The union men lashed out at those they felt had a hand in their losses in court and at the Lead Works. *Herald* editor Monroe, thin of build but not lacking confidence, felt compelled to write a column defending his newspaper: "The *Herald* is a union shop, its editor and owner is a union printer, carrying a union card. He joined of his own volition when a mere youth while working in an unorganized town where there was no incentive except to show his regard for the principles of unionism." In fact Monroe owed no apology to the union men—far from it. The *Herald*, like the competing *Advertiser*, had failed to report on nearly all the harassment of St. Louis Smelting and Refining and its employees done by the union men and the Collinsville police and Madison County sheriff's deputies. Nevertheless, Monroe wrote, "Every man and every cause will have space for a fair hearing."[69]

The former Lead Works employees, now out of work for more than two months, weren't giving up the fight, however. They passed out various circulars letting the public know the strike was still on and identifying "scabs" in Collinsville.[70] There were reports that a committee of miners was calling on the Lead Works employees at their homes, *asking* them to quit.[71] Local stores were asked not to extend any extra service to Lead Works employees or their families. Under pressure most Collinsville stores agreed to stop offering credit and making home deliveries to Lead Works employees.[72] The nonunion workers could make only in-store purchases and only with cash. A local insurance man who moved into a home owned by a Lead Works employee was asked by union men to move out, and he did so two days later.[73] One of the UMW locals ordered one of its members who rented to a Lead Works employee to have "the boarding scab sent away."[74]

Highland Brewing agreed with the Strike Committee's request

to stop selling beer to the saloon of Mrs. John Berta, which was frequented by Lead Works employees.[75] She had gotten a temporary supply of Hyde Park beer and was now seeking beer from the Heim Brewery in East St. Louis. The company had agreed to supply her, but its union drivers would not deliver to the establishment.[76]

At the Lead Works Newnam denied that these actions in the community were having any great effect on morale and said his workforce was full, with four hundred men on board.[77] The smelter also reopened its white lead plant, which had been closed since March.[78] And, adding insult to injury, the plant announced that all employees would be getting Christmas bonuses and that eighty Christmas baskets had been given to employees' children.[79]

Not everything had been going in St. Louis Smelting and Refining's favor. Lawsuits had been filed by twenty-one nearby farmers, alleging that their crops had been damaged by pollutants from the plant, despite the new, higher smokestacks. SLSR asked for a change of venue, citing the unionism of the area and the harassment it had suffered.[80] SLSR also cited a statement by Sheriff Jenkins, who opined that the pollution had destroyed enough crops to have fed the U.S. Army for six months. But the request for a different venue was denied.[81]

Smelter workers continued to cause disturbances in Collinsville, at least according to city police and local newspapers. A drunken Lead Works guard, discharged from his position, reportedly came to the uptown saloons and boasted of being a scab herder. After getting into an argument with two union men, he flourished a knife and was severely beaten by a number of union men. He was charged with assault and weapons charges.[82] Another smelter employee, a Spaniard, was charged with carrying a knife while drunk.[83] A black Lead Works employee was charged after a confrontation in which he reportedly cut a miner with a knife on an interurban car.[84] Another black smelter employee was charged with using "obscene and profane language" with one of the strikers and also for obstructing an officer. Four other Lead Works employees, one black and three Mexican, were arrested on a stalled interurban for being intoxicated, becoming "familiar" with a female rider, and threatening other passengers.[85] The local newspapers also diligently reported that six former Lead Works employees, all black and from Collinsville, had been charged with robbing forty employees of Federal Lead in Alton.[86]

All those incidents got prominent play in local newspapers. In none of the cases was a striker or other union member arrested or found at fault; all the trouble continued to be blamed on the smelter workers. In fact there is no indication that any strikers, miners, or other union men were ever arrested by local authorities for the duration of the labor disturbance at the Lead Works.

Federal authorities were still paying attention on November 24, however, when a large group of union men intimidated and forced smelter workers off a streetcar. The workers, mostly black and at least one Mexican, were followed off the car by some of the union supporters. A Lead Works employee was beaten, and another cut one of his attackers.[87] No arrests were made by local authorities, but union men Tom Smith, Robert Smith, and William Barton were later charged by U.S. marshals with violating the federal injunction. Tom Smith was sentenced to four months in jail, his brother Robert to one month. Barton got off with a warning from Judge Humphrey.[88]

The latest attack on the interurban line was perhaps the last straw before St. Louis Smelting and Refining finally appealed to the Illinois State Utilities Commission on December 14, charging the East St. Louis and Suburban Railway with not protecting its passengers.[89] The commission had the power to force the company to increase security. At least two hearings were held in January 1918 on the complaint, and slsr was prepared to have more than one hundred witnesses testify to the ongoing harassment and intimidation of smelter employees on the streetcars.

Collinsville's coal miners had largely given up on the battle to unionize the Lead Works by January 1918, when the umw locals discontinued their 1 percent wage deduction to support the slsr strike.[90] Their moral support for the union cause would continue, but no longer their financial assistance.

Just as interest in the lead smelter strike was waning, Collinsville's union men became involved in another labor dustup, this one involving five female operators at the Central Union Bell Telephone Company. After one woman felt that she was treated unkindly at work November 13, she and four others walked off the job.[91] When cooler heads prevailed the next day and the women wanted to return to work, they were told they would have to reapply for their positions.[92] What had started as a minor squabble turned into another three-month fight for union recognition and better wages. Two phone companies served Collinsville in 1917, Bell and Kinloch. Phones on one system typically could not connect with phones on another. Not entirely unrelated was the fact that the Kinloch Company voluntarily hiked wages just after the Bell walkout.

By late December the Collinsville Trades Council and union electrical workers were distributing a circular calling the Bell Company unfair and asking people to remove their Bell phone service.[93] The flyer said the women were seeking a "living wage," better work conditions, and reinstatement of the operators.

By late January the unions in the city had bonded together to force the phone-company issue. They published a list of eight "unfair" businesses that had not removed their Bell telephones; fifty had agreed to do so.[94] Both newspapers agreed to remove the Bell phones, but that did not stop the *Herald*'s J. O. Monroe from writing a column on the difficulty of running a business with just one of the phone companies. He noted that even the UMW offices in Springfield only had Bell phones.

The pressure on local businesses was enough to force the Bell Company to settle, reinstating the women who had resigned and granting a pay hike.[95] Among those negotiating the settlement was the ubiquitous miners' union state board member Mose Johnson. It was not a big win for unionism in Collinsville but certainly better than the beating the union cause had taken in the Lead Works affair.

Perhaps buoyed by the success of the Bell operators but certainly feeling the effects of wartime inflation, teachers at the 230-student Collinsville Township High School threatened to strike in March

1918. Fearing that graduation could be interrupted, the cash-strapped school board agreed to pay an additional $11 per month to the cths teachers.[96] A $5-per-week increase had previously been given to grade school teachers, who taught 1,412 students at five other city schools.[97] A local columnist compared teachers' salaries with those of miners in the region and found that the miners, most often with little schooling, could earn up to four times as much as the college-educated teachers.[98]

The labor unrest of 1917 and 1918 beat down Missouri and Illinois just as it did the rest of the nation. The Illinois National Guard had to be deployed in 1917 to quell streetcar operator strikes in Bloomington and Springfield, in addition to the race/labor riots in East St. Louis.[99] Although union matters had reached a tenuous calm in Collinsville by early April 1918, a number of strikes were either in progress or pending in St. Louis. Labor officials from that city had gone to Washington to speak with Secretary of Labor William Wilson about strikes involving chemical and garment workers, cabinetmakers, and employees of two hardware companies, a biscuit company, and a large grocer.[100] Eight other strikes were pending, which could leave an additional 7,700 out of work. The union men hoped more could be done to end the wartime disputes.

Five strikes, which had kept some 13,500 people out of work, had recently been settled in St. Louis.[101] Among those were strikes held by streetcar men and department store clerks, who won union recognition. And employees at munitions maker Wagner Electric and tobacco company Liggett and Myers were now also allowed to unionize.

5

A Little Tar Might Help

I had always hoped that this land might become a safe and agreeable Asylum to the virtuous and persecuted part of mankind, to whatever nation they might belong.

—George Washington, letter to Rev. Francis Vanderkemp, 1788

It is difficult to overstate the impact of German immigration on the United States as it entered the twentieth century. Germans would end up constituting the largest part of the massive influx of new immigrants in the late nineteenth and early twentieth centuries. Between 1850 and 1909, nearly 5 million Germans became naturalized Americans, nearly 1.5 million more than the next largest European group.[1] With their strong ties to the old country, they raised their children in accordance with German culture, often with German being the primary language of the household.

The favorable descriptions of America that early German immigrants sent back to the old country also had an impact on future waves of immigrants; in both the 1910 and the 1920 censuses, the greatest number of foreign-born U.S. residents reported were Germans, despite heavy immigration by Russians, Italians, and Irish.[2] In 1910 foreign-born Germans made up a full 26 percent of the total white population in the United States.[3]

German cultural influence could be found everywhere in American society. One need only consider the cultural impact of composers such as Johann Sebastian Bach, Ludwig von Beethoven, and Richard Wagner or of philosophers such as Immanuel Kant, Max Weber, and Friedrich Nietzsche. The German influence in everyday life extended beyond sauerkraut and schnitzel to things as thoroughly American as hamburgers and frankfurters, reportedly developed in Hamburg and Frankfurt, Germany. Concepts ranging from kindergarten to Christmas trees were all introduced by the new immigrants. German culture was well received in the United States and before the onset of the Great War in 1914; indeed the Germans were probably the most esteemed immigrant group.[4] They were higher thinkers, clean, hard-working, and responsible—what was not to like?

Earlier German immigrants were well entrenched in the St. Louis region and included many business and factory owners. German Americans famously dominated the beer-brewing industry in cities like St. Louis. Many others settled to farm the more-rural areas of Illinois and Missouri.

But most of the new immigrants ended up in midwestern cities like Chicago, Cincinnati, Milwaukee, and St. Louis, which already had high concentrations of German residents. In St. Louis, the sixth-largest city in the nation, 24 percent of inhabitants were foreign born in 1910, but the number would decrease to 17 percent by 1920 as the immigrants moved out to suburban and rural areas.[5] Thanks largely to Chicago, Illinois would become home to more German- and Austrian-born residents than any other state.[6]

Gathered in urban neighborhoods of like nationality, immigrant groups could keep some connection to the old country. Germans formed hundreds of social and political organizations, ranging from the Liederkranz choral groups, to the Turnvereine, or Turner organizations, which were gymnastic and athletic clubs. In St. Louis alone there were six thousand Turner members; branches of the organization were also established in the nearby Illinois towns of Belleville and Columbia, both south of Collinsville.[7]

The clubs provided for a more cohesive German community, where members could maintain some cultural identity and tradition, but these benefits probably came at the expense of assimilation into American society. One newspaper described the conflicting allegiances of German immigrants in the phrase, "Germania Our Mother; Columbia Our Bride," seizing on the adage that a man did not have to forsake his mother to embrace his new wife. Perhaps so, another writer noted, so long as the mother and the bride weren't feuding.[8]

That wasn't the case after World War I started in July 1914, when the *neutral* United States gradually went all in for the Entente nations. The sinking of the *Lusitania* nearly one year later didn't help matters. The German societies that had formed to help maintain German culture provided a basis for other groups to become politically active in fighting Prohibition and later for American neutrality. In 1904 a branch of the Deutsch-Amerikanischer National Bund (DANB; National German-American Alliance) was formed in St. Louis and included Illinois residents from Alton in the north to Belleville in the south. With dues of $1 per year, it would boast twenty-two thousand members before the Great War.[9]

The Bund's first challenge was to fight local-option dry laws in Missouri, which made it illegal to drink on Sunday. Perhaps more than any other immigrant group, the Germans took the dry Sundays as a direct attack on a culture that vigorously embraced its *bier*.[10] As with other workers who put in six days a week, German immigrants chafed at the Sunday prohibition, which made it impossible to drink with family and friends at local clubs, saloons, or *Biergärten* on their one day off.

The other great cause of the Bund alliances was to advocate for continued neutrality in World War I. In May 1915, when 128 American passengers died on the *Lusitania*, along with them sank any real chance of America staying out of the European fray. The local DANB shutdown in 1917 essentially coincided with the end of free speech for Germans—and most other Americans—for the duration of the Great War.[11]

The response of most German immigrants or those with German sympathies, whether in St. Louis or Collinsville or nationwide, was to keep their opinions to themselves. If they had any feelings for the Fatherland, they were best expressed only at home. Public displays of any allegiance to the homeland, and sometimes German tradition and culture, fell away. In Glen Carbon, eight miles north of Collinsville, even the Liederkranz group disbanded, as one newspaper explained, "having decided last week there was not much to sing about in the German language nowadays."[12] The group gave the $10 in its treasury to the American Red Cross.

Churches that had predominantly German membership were targeted in many communities in southern Illinois; some were disbanded. A number of Lutheran parochial schools and churches were vandalized; some had "Kaiser School" or "Kaiser Church" painted on them.[13] Other Lutheran churches had men and boys listening outside, straining to overhear any phrase that might be twisted into something unpatriotic. Students from the schools were harassed and beaten by other children. Ministers and teachers were sometimes followed, and their every move was watched with suspicion. There was no documented violence against the Holy Cross Lutheran, Jerusalem Lutheran, or St. John Evangelical churches in Collinsville during this period. But like many public schools nationwide, those in Collinsville no longer offered German-language classes in the fall of 1918.[14] The twenty-five enrolled students would have to learn the language elsewhere. Holy Cross Lutheran would soon follow suit at its parochial school.[15]

When America began ramping up for war, the perpetual whipping boy of immigration was brought front and center by federal officials. Most of the fury was naturally directed at Germans and Austrians, but other immigrant groups who had found a home in America in recent years were also targeted. While the United States was still neutral, German agents had reportedly sabotaged some goods for shipment to the Allies and tried to stir labor troubles.[16] The plots were quickly discovered, and some German officials were deported. In 1915 President Woodrow Wilson spoke of those "born under other flags but welcomed under our generous naturalization laws to the full freedom and opportunity of America, who have poured the poison of disloyalty into the very arteries of our national life. . . . Such creatures of passion, disloyalty and anarchy must be crushed out."[17] World War I's iteration of xenophobia was just getting under way.

Increasingly it was argued that the country no longer had a place for hyphenated Americans—no Irish Americans, German

Americans, or Polish Americans. Only "true" Americans would do, and every immigrant needed to toe the American line. Former president Teddy Roosevelt would later say, "Every man ought to love his country . . . but he is only entitled to one country. If he claims loyalty to two countries, he is necessarily a traitor to at least one country. We can have no 50-50 allegiance in this country."[18] One conservative group, the National Security League, coined the phrase "100 percent Americanism" to promote the idea of immigrants wiping clear their old world identities.[19]

For their part the recent European immigrants were in a state of international limbo, neither necessarily wanting to fight America's war nor wishing to return to their homeland. "They were strangers in a strange land," historian David Kennedy observes, "awkwardly suspended between the world they had left behind and a world where they were not yet fully at home."[20]

Congress passed the 1917 Immigration Act in February, over-riding a veto by President Wilson, and imposed a literacy test on new immigrants and severely barred immigration from many Asian countries. An $8 tax was also required of each new immigrant.

In 1918 most of the immigrants working in Illinois coal mines were English, but the second-largest immigrant group was Italian.[21] Collinsville became home to many of them, with a number of Italians settling just east of the city, where rolling hills would bring proper sunlight to their grapevines for "dago red" wine making.

When the United States entered the Great War, Germans and anything Germanic became the primary targets of the hysteria. Hamburgers became liberty sandwiches; sauerkraut became liberty cabbage. St. Louis schools discontinued German classes. In St. Louis Berlin Avenue became Pershing Street (for General John Pershing). Kaiser Avenue and Von Versen became Gresham and Enright respectively, in honor of two of the first three Americans killed in France.[22] Classical German symphony and opera were looked on with disdain. Later in 1917 St. Louis police would bar an Austrian musician from performing. And in the hallmark move of all intolerance and xenophobia, German books were burned in many communities.[23] Many German-print newspapers closed. Given the lofty place that German culture held before the war, the fall was precipitous. One historian called it "the most spectacular reversal of judgement in the history of American nativism."[24]

There was widespread paranoia that German spies were harbored in the United States, seemingly lurking behind every bush, in places ranging from New York City to St. Louis to Collinsville. "The Hun within our gates masquerades in many disguises," Theodore Roosevelt said in 1917.[25] "He is our dangerous enemy; and he should be hunted down without mercy." In his declaration of war speech to the joint session of Congress, Wilson noted that millions of people born in Germany or with German sympathy lived in the United States. He said most were loyal to their new home, but that "if there should be disloyalty, it [would] be dealt with with a firm hand of repression."[26]

Ads were placed in local newspapers to warn of the threat. "Every German or Austrian in the United States, unless known by years of association to be absolutely loyal, should be treated as a potential spy," said an item in Collinsville's *Advertiser*. "Energy and alertness may save the life of your son, your husband or your brother." It cautioned that news was being sent to Berlin and lies were being spread about early peace or the morale of the U.S. military. Readers were told to contact the Collinsville police or the Department of Justice whenever "any suspicious act or disloyal word comes to [their] notice."[27]

It was the job of George Creel's Committee on Public Information (CPI) to foment the groundswell of public support that Wilson wanted behind the war effort. CPI publicity delivered an inescapable message from coast to coast: real Americans supported the war effort, and traitors did not. The CPI message no doubt helped sway many who were unsure about U.S. involvement in the European war. But it also helped develop an ironic patriotic hysteria that would set personal liberties on their ear in the United States, all while U.S. troops were being sent abroad to save democracy in Europe.[28] Thus in 1917 began an American dark age for democracy, a low point that would not be overcome for years after the war's end.

Just two months after the U.S. declaration of war, the Espionage Act gave the federal government the primary tool it would use to suppress those who opposed the war.[29] It provided for fines up to $10,000 and twenty years in prison for anything that obstructed military operations during wartime. It also provided for the postmaster general to deny mail services to those who might communicate an antiwar message. In an era of very limited mass communication, the mail restriction left little way for opposition groups to communicate with their members.

There were opponents to the Act in Congress, but they were few and far between. A New York Socialist was one of them. "There is nothing more oppressive in the world than a democracy gone mad, than a democracy which has surrendered rights to an individual," Representative Meyer London said. "Let men speak freely. Do not drive them into the cellar of conspiracy. Do not turn people into hypocrites and cowards. Let us not, while we talk of fighting for liberty abroad, sacrifice and crush our liberties here."[30]

The law was liberally interpreted by federal courts to mean that any statement or sign that might discourage a man from submitting to the draft or enlisting in the armed services effectively obstructed the military. That essentially meant that any person or group who opposed the war was fair game for arrest. It became open season on Socialists and others who opposed the war on philosophical, political, or religious grounds. Jehovah's Witnesses leaders were jailed. Teachers found themselves under fire if their lectures didn't sound patriotic enough. Another prime target was the Industrial Workers of the World (iww). The Wobblies, as the union was also called, held radical socialist views. Wobblies and Socialists were seemingly linked in headlines to any anonymous or unexplained threat or uprising during the war. Those two groups would suffer some of the greatest political oppression doled out in the history of the United States.

The federal government's effort to put everyone on the lookout for spies was primarily orchestrated through distributed Committee on Public Information materials. In addition to the State Councils of Defense and Neighborhood Councils of Defense, a myriad of other groups cropped up to defend the homeland from the perceived interloping spies and saboteurs. The largest of these was the American Protective League, which by June 1917 already had units operating in six hundred cities.[31] Membership was primarily made up of leading men of the community who paid seventy-five cents or $1 for the authority to say they were working with the U.S. Department of Justice on investigations, using the title of the Secret Service.[32] Some were originally issued "Secret Service Division" badges. Despite concerns by Wilson and others in the administration, they were allowed to continue their Patriotic Police efforts for the duration of the war, eventually growing to 250,000 members nationwide.

Other vigilance groups included the All-Allied Anti-German League, the American Anti-Anarchy Association, the Boy Spies of America, the Sedition Slammers, and the Terrible Threateners.[33] The Anti-Yellow Dog League, all one thousand units, was open to boys over ten years old, and members were encouraged to listen for unpatriotic talk wherever they went and report anything suspicious to authorities.[34]

President Wilson spoke of "vicious spies and conspirators" who "sought by violence to destroy our industries and arrest our commerce," and throughout the war he encouraged continued vigilance. Picking up on that theme, one newspaper editorialized: "You do not require any official authority to do this and the only badge needed is your patriotic fervor."[35]

Attorney General Thomas Gregory in the summer of 1917 already bragged of having "several hundred thousand" private citizens spying on neighbors and coworkers. At about the same time, he privately acknowledged at a cabinet meeting that talk of German spies was little more than hysteria.[36] Gregory said the programs generated about 1,500 complaints per day to the Department of Justice, but just 5 percent of those cases might justify prosecution for unpatriotic talk.[37]

Whipped into a paranoid, flag-waving frenzy, many claimed

that the Espionage Act was not strong enough. People could make an unpatriotic statement or say something negative about the president or the government and there remained no federal statute to use to arrest the miscreant. Increasingly acts of violence had been directed at those who disapproved of the war, and it was said that people felt they had to take the law into their own hands because the government would not act.

The Sedition Act debated in the spring of 1918 and enacted in May was an even more draconian set of laws. It was actually an amendment to the prior year's Espionage Act, and it doubled the fines of the prior statute and made it illegal to utter false statements about the military or bond sales or incite disloyalty or deter enlistments.[38] Also banned were "disloyal, profane, scurrilous, or abusive language about the form of government of the United States, the constitution of the United States, or the military or naval forces of the United States, or the uniform of the Army or Navy," or anything to bring those into "into contempt, scorn, contumely, or disrepute." Yet another provision banned anything that interfered with war production. There was little resistance to the legislation as it was debated, although one senator termed the bill "a peculiar sort of mental hysteria."[39]

The CPI in Washington was not alone in inflaming fanatical patriots. Some of the worst rhetoric about war opponents came out of the capital from administration officials and congressmen. Attorney General Gregory, speaking of dissenters said, "May God have mercy upon them for they need expect none from an outraged people and an avenging Government."[40]

In the communities east of St. Louis, both patriotism and imaginations ran high, in contrast to any actual German spy activity. Locals suspected a German plot when a steam yacht of the Alton Naval Militia exploded in the Alton Harbor.[41] A man accused of having pro-German allegiances was released by a deputy U.S. marshal after the man pledged to keep the flag flying outside his home at all times; that gesture seemed to satisfy the locals.[42] No threat was too implausible. Guards were posted twenty-four hours a day around a Belleville flour mill, lest German spies have an opportunity to poison the flour.[43] There had been gratuitous reports from East St. Louis of spies mixing ground glass in the flour at one mill to injure U.S. soldiers.[44] Staunton school officials had the Secret Service interrogate a boy and his father after the boy refused to salute the flag at school.[45] He was allowed to return after he promised to pay proper respect in the future. An East St. Louis man of German descent was arrested at his boardinghouse after he got into a parlor discussion about the war and said he wished he had one of the new airplanes with bombs so that he might "drop a few on the White House." Three fellow boarders signed the criminal complaint against him.[46]

By far the greatest number of victims of wartime persecution were those who did little more than express some support for Germany or lack of full support for U.S. efforts. As far as organized groups, none suffered as badly as Socialists and IWW members. Both groups openly expressed the commonly held view that U.S. involvement was a rich man's affair being fought by common men. But thanks to the tough talk from government officials and the polished efforts of CPI propaganda, most Americans did not want to hear that message in 1917 and 1918.

One of the first major patriotic hysteria incidents against Socialists was an attack on a Peace Parade in Boston in July 1917.[47] Civilians and soldiers beat those in the parade and twice ransacked the Socialists' office. Ironically, one of the signs destroyed read: "First War Victims—Freedom of Assembly, Freedom of Speech." Perhaps no single Socialist was persecuted more than Eugene Debs, the party's leader. After a 1918 antiwar speech in Canton, Ohio, he was arrested, tried, and imprisoned until 1921.[48]

Attorney General Gregory left wide discretion to the local district U.S. attorneys as to how vigorously they would prosecute sedition and treason cases. Antiwar speakers were prosecuted in some districts and left alone in others. By war's end nearly half of the prosecutions took place in just thirteen of the eighty-seven federal districts.[49] Most of those thirteen districts were in the western states where the IWW was active. Nationwide 1,956 cases were brought with a 45 percent conviction rate. Many of the cases had been as minor as expressing skepticism about the nation's leaders or complaining about the draft. In Illinois a McLean County woman was charged after she dared criticize the near-constant solicitation of money for the Red Cross.[50]

Perhaps the most egregious example of erroneous arrest involved a midwesterner who traveled to Florida, where he found the weather to be unseasonably cold for that time of year. Upon returning from a very chilly fishing trip, he was overheard to say: "Damn such a country as this."[51] He was reported, arrested, and charged with violating the Espionage Act and had to obtain the services of a lawyer to be released from jail.

In the eastern Missouri federal district, which covered the St. Louis area, the U.S. prosecutor appeared to let many of the cases die quietly. In the first year of the Treason Act, the district attorney obtained seventy indictments and got just eight convictions. But fifty-two complaints were *nolle prosequi*, with the local federal attorney advising the court that he would not proceed further with the case.[52]

Prosecutions in Illinois varied greatly too between the Northern District, which handled Chicago, and the Southern District, due to the numerous IWW cases in Chicago. Most of the 315 cases brought in the southern Illinois district court at Springfield were minor and more likely to have involved a flippant statement made by a first- or second-generation German immigrant. Only 17 of the 43 cases actually prosecuted in the Southern District resulted in convictions; most were simply dismissed. A guilty plea typically resulted in a $100 to $500 fine or three to four months in jail, with juries tending to be more heavy-handed than judges. There were 9 cases prosecuted from Madison County. The most severe local sentence went to a Granite City man who said that Germany and Hungary "were all right" and that he liked the kaiser and would fight for him. His candor to the jury would earn him two years in the federal penitentiary in Leavenworth, Kansas.[53]

A unique case from Madison County involved a farmer who complained of the new airplanes from the recently completed Scott Airfield, which started training pilots in September 1917 in adjacent St. Clair County. Henry Moehle believed the planes overhead were scaring his dairy cows and livestock, and in 1918 he threatened to shoot down any aircraft over his property. Eleven days later a warrant was issued for his arrest for violating the Espionage Act by "threatening to injure war material." Moehle, the native-born son of a German immigrant, was fined $500.[54]

Just being accused of violating the Espionage or Sedition Acts caused much suffering. While the majority of suspects were simply interrogated and released, others were indicted and sent to trial. Many would be held in jail or sentenced to prison time. Friends and acquaintances might shun the accused. Some suspects would lose their jobs; most all would lose at least some wages. And there was the cost of a legal defense, no problem for the rich, but crippling for the poor or working class. Trials were often a farce.[55] Many courts operated on a presumption of guilt rather than innocence. "To be an alien, radical or labor agitator is to go to jail," one congressman said.[56]

In the spring of 1918, at least some local courts and law officers were not inclined to give Germans aliens or German sympathizers any protection under the law, the Fourteenth Amendment Equal Protection Clause be damned. In Madison County Judge J. F. Gilham set aside a decision that awarded a $250 payment for a personal injury case after he learned the complainant was a German alien.[57] In East St. Louis police would not allow a Romanian immigrant to file charges against three men who beat him at the Aluminum Ore Company plant because he reportedly made disloyal statements.[58]

Infractions by the U.S. government against civil liberties became so common that a new organization, the National Civil Liberties Bureau (NCLB), began tracking them in 1917. It found 214 cases where the federal government prosecuted on espionage, treason, or draft-obstruction charges and 13 cases where people were prosecuted under state or local laws.[59] It was noted that each case might include numerous defendants. The NCLB also collected its information from newspaper clippings and noted the great disparity between what it had found and the numbers offered by the U.S. attorney general, which indicated that the federal prosecutions were greatly underreported in the press. The NCLB cited 23 cases where officials interfered with peaceful assembly, 47 cases of improper search and seizure, and 30 cases where teachers, professors, or other workers were dismissed for their political beliefs. The NCLB would reorganize in 1920 under the name it carries today, the American Civil Liberties Union.

Those suspected of disloyalty who were not arrested by federal authorities may have been better off at the hands of the government considering the treatment they received from delirious local patriots. From the start of U.S. involvement in the war, thousands of Americans and aliens were harassed in their local communities by nationalistic zealots. It would be impossible to count the number of incidents or victims; most were likely never reported to either police or local newspapers. As with the tracking of federal persecutions, the NCLB attempted to list incidents of mob violence from the beginning of the Great War until its end. These incidents too were greatly underreported since only major newspaper clippings were used to collect information. From the start of the war in 1917 through the first four months of 1918, the NCLB reported just 125 mob incidents.[60] The list did not include a number of incidents in southern Illinois, nor did it note any riots, including those in East St. Louis. Many of the reported incidents involved multiple victims.

The list also did not include instances where smaller groups intimidated or exacted their justice for the cause. Most of those incidents were likewise never reported to police. As with the other cases of harassment, words were often twisted or fabricated to make the suspect appear even more heinous.[61] These confrontations could happen in workplaces, stores, on public streets, or, perhaps most frequently, in saloons. Most often the mobs were composed of men. Women were sometimes involved, however, and in least two incidents led the attack. In another case fifty drafted men hired a black man to lash the back of a farmer whom they had already tarred and feathered.[62]

German immigrants and people with German names naturally drew the most scrutiny. The cited infraction could have been nearly any comment or action that might be construed as un-American. Unpatriotic "utterances" or negative comments about the country's leaders or military were sufficient. So was any comment that might be considered as supporting the Germans. A person's opposition to the draft or Liberty Bond sales or even the Red Cross or YMCA could be enough. Perhaps the person gave to those causes but hadn't given enough. Failing to stand for the national anthem would work. Likewise if someone was a Socialist, a member of IWW, a pacifist, a Mennonite, a Jehovah's Witness, or favored an early peace accord. With mobs, as with drunks in a saloon, there was no due process and limited rational thought. The allegation might have been true—or far from it. By the time a mob had formed and decided to take action, guilt or innocence became irrelevant. A sixty-eight-year-old man in Louisiana was beaten for not buying Liberty Bonds, for example, although he was later found to have purchased $5,000 worth.[63]

Punishment might have been as simple as being forced to kiss the flag or swear allegiance to the president or the country. But it was always under the threat of beating, doses administered as needed. Some victims were thrown into bodies of water, others "dunked" to the point of near-drowning. Some were painted yellow, to ironically show their cowardice, in retribution administered by a mob of people. Houses and businesses were painted yellow. Victims were driven from town; heads were shaved. A Utah man was thrown into a dough bin, where he nearly suffocated; another in Pennsylvania was forced to walk on the street with a dog chain around his neck.[64] All victims were intimidated, including a ninety-year-old bedridden man in Kansas who was forced to kiss the flag.[65] The mobs may have thought their actions amusing, but in the end they just provided some of the most ignominious examples of how civil liberties were defiled in the era.

Tar and feathering, or some variant thereof, was often prescribed. One prisoner was even tarred and feathered within the walls of a New Mexico prison, presumably with assistance from prison staff in obtaining the necessary materials.[66] Many were horsewhipped, at least one victim in Nevada with an iron cat-o'-nine-tails.[67] In San Francisco a man was induced to leave town, after a rope was tied around his neck as an extra incentive, by the ironically named Knights of Liberty.[68] Three other men were in the process of being lynched when they were rescued. Two more were threatened with lynching. Robert Prager, in Collinsville, was the only German immigrant lynched during World War I. Rev. W. T. Sims, a black preacher in York, South Carolina, was lynched on August 23, 1917, for voicing his opposition to the draft, but race no doubt was a factor.[69]

One pattern was clear: mob violence ramped up markedly in the spring of 1918, particularly in March and April.[70] The National Civil Liberties Bureau documented 17 incidents in March, 51 in April. The incidents in April would constitute more than 40 percent of the 125 it reported for the year.[71]

Another group that tracked mob violence was the National Association for the Advancement of Colored People. Lynching and mob killings of blacks were depressingly common in the era, with sixty-one reported in 1917 and the first four months of 1918, excluding those from the East St. Louis riots.[72] All the mob actions, save one, were below the Mason-Dixon Line. No reason could be given for some of the killings, other than insolence or perhaps to reinforce the South's social pecking order. Southern mobs had no second thoughts about taking the legal process into their own hands, particularly if the alleged crime had been committed against a woman. Of the sixty-one lynchings and mob killings of blacks in that period, forty-nine involved alleged crimes, but most victims would not see a fair trial in a court of law. Two of the victims were killed after being found guilty.

The mobs hung forty-one blacks; drowned, shot and killed, or beat to death sixteen others; and dispatched four by burning. The December 1917 burning at the stake of Lation Scott in Dyersburg, Tennessee, followed his admission that he had bound and gagged a white woman but not otherwise harmed her. Extended torture with hot irons preceded the immolation while thousands of men, women, and children watched just after church on a

Sunday afternoon in the town square. Children were lifted onto shoulders so they might have a better view. Others watched from nearby rooftops and second-story windows. Scott was somehow still partially conscious when the fire was finally lit about his mutilated body. The whole process took three and a half hours, much longer than the lynching in Dyersburg nine months earlier of a black man accused of shooting a police officer. Many prominent citizens of Dyersburg thought the torture and burning of Scott a disgrace to the community and said he should have been given a "decent lynching." The NAACP magazine explained, "By this is meant a quick, quiet hanging, with no display or torture."[73]

There had been limited anti-German violence in the Collinsville area early on. Just days after the U.S. declaration of war in 1917, interurban car conductor Joel Zumald got into an argument with other employees at an East St. Louis and Suburban Railway car shed in Maryville. A newspaper gleefully reported, under the headline "A Lesson in Patriotism," that Zumald had his left eye made into the colors of the American flag by an interurban motorman. "It was also reported that had not bystanders interfered, the job of decorating would have been more thorough. Too bad!" the newspaper stated.[74]

In Granite City a man of German extraction reportedly made derogatory comments to another man who had two sons in the army. He responded by hitting the pro-German in the jaw and sending him through a plate-glass window, severing a tendon in his left wrist. "Peter King was not arrested. He was applauded," a newspaper reported. "No more attacks on the flag are expected in Granite City."[75]

On January 20 one of the first 1918 incidents in southern Illinois occurred in Glen Carbon, a village just eight miles north of Collinsville. On that Sunday night in a saloon, six locals reportedly refused to sing or take off their hats when "The Star-Spangled Banner" was played. Newspapers reported that their choice of music was "Deutschland, Deutschland über Alles." This, of course, did not sit well with a dozen or more local boys. Fists flew and barroom chairs were thrown, and when the dust settled, there were a number of blackened eyes but no one was arrested. The pro-German boys fled for their homes, and it was reported that "the patriots were victorious."[76]

About sixty miles north of Collinsville, a series of patriotic demonstrations took place in February in Macoupin and Montgomery Counties, another area rich in coal mines and coal miners. Over 350 men celebrated Lincoln's Birthday, February 12, in Staunton by tar and feathering two men and forcing 100 others to kiss the flag or otherwise show their patriotism.[77]

The purge continued the next day in Staunton and had the effect of igniting a patriotic firestorm across Macoupin and Montgomery Counties. A mob of about two hundred on February 17 went after three labor organizers in Hillsboro, two of whom had also reportedly registered as conscientious objectors to the draft. The vigilantes made preparations for another tar and feather party and went in search of the trio, but they were frustrated when they were unable to find them.[78] Due to an erroneous tip, the mob went to the farm of Henry Donaldson in pursuit of the three men around 1:00 a.m. Donaldson's son, Clifford, who had no connection with the labor organizers and did not understand why the mob was at his door, fired warning shots.[79] At least three men were shot in the ensuing melee, twenty-year-old Clifford Donaldson among them; he died three days later. Donaldson had joined the navy in St. Louis the day before he was shot, and his name would absurdly be listed as a navy casualty of World War I. Dismayed at not finding the labor organizers at the Donaldson home, the mob went to the men's unoccupied apartment and brought all the trio's belongings out into the street, where they were burned "*in the name of freedom.*"[80]

In Collinsville on February 23, a group of men got into an argument with Jake Kremmer Sr. and questioned his loyalty.[81] A flag was produced, and Kremmer was made to kiss it; like most of those accosted, he had little choice in the matter. Two nights later patriotic passions were again inflamed in Maryville after twenty-six men were sent off that day to Camp Taylor and another loyalty program was conducted in Edwardsville at the

Wildey Theater.[82] Someone suggested that a loyalty parade would be a good thing for Maryville. Braced with a twenty-one-foot-wide flag and marchers full of beer, the procession made its way to at least three local saloons. One draftee who was encountered, Robert Kunze, expressed what some thought were disloyal sentiments. Kunze went into a saloon to avoid a fight, but the entourage followed. Inside they found Theodore Schuster, who had been to an army camp but was discharged when it was learned that he was a German alien. The crowd also thought Schuster displayed a disloyal attitude, and the flag was brought forward for him to kiss, which he knelt and did.

Maryville mayor Fred Neubauer, the saloon owner, stepped up to defend Schuster, and he was asked to kiss the flag too, which he did "good naturedly."[83] But the miners in the parade were not done with Schuster, and they asked the mine managers to dismiss the German alien for fear he would sabotage Donk Mine No. 2 at Maryville. Without a job Schuster left town two days later. Miner's Local 1802 president James Fornero thought the demonstration a good thing. "Maryville is all right. It is a loyal community and the few people who are not outspoken for Uncle Sam are keeping mighty quiet," Fornero said. "The boys only rounded up three, but the idea is to have everybody loyal. We're for Uncle Sam all the way through."[84]

The local press offered no rebuke of the miners, far from it. J. O. Monroe of the *Collinsville Herald* again expressed dismay that anyone would make a disloyal comment and suggested taking things to the next level. The column, titled "A Little Tar Might Help," cited typical complaints heard from the antiwar crowd, such as high corporate profits and postwar taxes, and Monroe said none of the talk should be tolerated.[85]

Now we're not worried about anybody being convinced by this sort of argument handed out as it was by this blabbering babbler, but just for his own benefit and to show him that the people are fighting for something and are not to be mocked by idlers of his sort, we suggest that a tarring party such as the several which took place in Macoupin County recently might be efficacious at least in stilling his silly tongue. Perhaps the information that such a thing might happen to him will be sufficient to quiet him. If not, we're satisfied we know a lot of folks who would be glad to join the party. And there'll be a lot of tar and feathers when the ceremonies begin.[86]

The uptick in violence against Germans and others in downstate Illinois did not go unnoticed in Springfield, the state capital. On February 25 Governor Frank Lowden declared: "Mob rule will not be tolerated in any part of the state, even though such mob rule acts in the name of loyalty to the Government. . . . Those who take the law into their own hands at such a time are helping not our own cause, but that of the enemy."[87]

Two days later Lowden shifted his focus to the federal government. Like many Americans he, at least privately, bought into the premise that people were taking the law into their own hands because the federal government was not doing enough to squelch treasonous activity. On February 28 he sent a telegram to Attorney General Thomas Gregory in Washington and asked that a special representative be detailed to him at Springfield, so he could work directly with state officials investigating treasonous and seditious acts. Lowden wanted more than was being done by the various U.S. district attorneys in the state. "A situation is developing out here which gives me great alarm," Lowden said. "Persons outrageously seditious have been reported to Federal authorities who have taken position that they are powerless to act. This has resulted in deep indignation in these communities, followed by some instances of mob action."[88]

Lowden explained that he had just investigated in one county and noted, "The most patriotic and orderly people in that county are fearful that nothing can prevent violence unless prosecution is at once instituted against a few notorious offenders." He said that if he had to declare martial law it would be "playing into the hands of those who are opposing the war. Could you not detail me some representative of your Department in whose discretion you have full confidence and who would assist me in seeing that these objectionable persons are brought to justice? Nothing would so allay the popular excitement I have described as if I were able to say to the people of the State that a representative of yours was on the ground cooperating with me and that all complaints of treasonable or seditious conduct would be promptly investigated."[89] Lowden would later dispatch Lieutenant Governor John Oglesby to Washington, carrying the same plea for federal assistance.[90] But the governor would not get his U.S. Department of Justice representative in Springfield until April 25, after much of the vigilante fury in Illinois had already been spent.[91]

The miners surely were not done with their work of intimidating Germans in the Collinsville area. Pleasant Ridge Evangelical Lutheran Church was situated in a farming area west of Maryville and north of Collinsville and Donk Mine No. 1. The minister at the church, Rev. Hans von Gemmingen, heard from several people that he could be the next victim of the mob of miners because he was an enemy alien. Gemmingen, forty-four years old, had been with the small church for six years and had no known disputes with townspeople. Now he, his wife, and their children felt very threatened.

He sought help from Sheriff Jenkin Jenkins on February 28.[92] Two deputies investigated and found no reason to believe that the minister or his family was in danger. The assurances, such as they were from Jenkins's men, did little to assuage the pastor's concerns. The next day Gemmingen and a neighbor went to Springfield and sought protection from Governor Lowden. With no state highway patrol yet, Lowden sent Colonel Claude Ryman of the Illinois National Guard to investigate. Ryman met with Jenkins and one of his deputies and found "no alarming condition," but he tried to verify that Jenkins and his men would do all they could to protect the minister and his family.

The main complaint against the minister was his failure to become a naturalized U.S. citizen. There were reports that the minister would not relinquish his German citizenship because doing so would preclude any inheritance to which his family would be entitled. Gemmingen had spent the first twenty years of his life in Germany, including a mandatory one-year stint in the German military.[93] Such information put the minister atop the local patriots' hit list. Sheriff Jenkins also decided it an opportune time to publicly divulge that federal officials had recently searched Gemmingen's home and property for a wireless radio, but nothing had been found. All such radios were to be dismantled by government order, but someone had reported that a wireless device was still operating north of Collinsville. Shortly after the federal search of the Gemmingen home and property, it was rumored that the radio use had suddenly stopped.

Gemmingen would be subjected to one more investigation, this one conducted by the ubiquitous UMW board member Mose Johnson. He said that he felt compelled to investigate the matter on behalf of the miners and took umbrage at the minister's plea for protection from the governor. "I deemed it my duty to make a thorough investigation in the Village of Maryville and I find there has been no demonstration of any unpatriotic remarks. . . . Therefore for the loyal citizens of Maryville and Pleasant Ridge, I can see no reason to appeal to the Governor or any other source for protection," Johnson said, "unless being guilty of some unpatriotic remark or action that is unfriendly to our country." In his statement Johnson questioned Gemmingen's failure to renounce his German citizenship. "Which is dearest to this country," Johnson asked, "the wealth that his children would inherit or our sons we freely give to this country?"[94]

Ten weeks later Gemmingen would give his last sermon at the Pleasant Ridge Lutheran Church before fleeing the local threats and intimidation.[95]

On March 8 J. O. Monroe backed away from his inflammatory statements of the prior week—sort of. In his column the editor-publisher said that some of the fairer sex, members of the Red Cross, thought his suggestion of tar and feathers for some in the community "might lead to very unwise action on the part of hot headed persons." As an alternative perhaps more men could take up knitting. The women showed Monroe a soldier's sweater that had been knitted by R. Guy Kneedler, president of the Red Cross and city council attorney. Tongue firmly planted in cheek, the editor played along: "And it is a handsome piece of workmanship as far as we can judge." But he reissued the warning to those who spoke in a disloyal manner: "For if Uncle Sam gets hold of them they might long for a smear of tar and a rub of feathers in preference."[96]

The hunt continued in northern Madison County for IWW supporters on March 16, when a group of men in New Douglas went in search of Joseph Mitchell. It was said that he had spoken in favor of the Wobblies. With reinforcements also coming from Staunton and Sorento, Mitchell reportedly called for his son to take him out of town by automobile post haste. A newspaper said that his son drove, "forgetting the speed laws and burning gasoline at a lively rate to get the parent to a place of safety."[97]

Over-the-top patriotism flared again a week later, this time ninety miles southeast of Collinsville. In the Franklin County coal-mining town of Christopher, four men were tarred and feathered on March 22, including a Polish Catholic priest, for allegedly saying, "God is with the Kaiser" and "the Kaiser will win the war."[98] The priest denied the accusation. Charges against the others were unknown.

Three days after the Christopher affair, a mob composed of about 1,500 coal miners ran rampant in nearby DuQuoin all day and conducted its own kangaroo court for four men accused of disloyalty.[99] The mob formed to celebrate the rumored capture of Germany's Crown Prince Wilhelm. The capture rumor ended up being untrue, but the authority of the mob was without question. It ordered all storekeepers in town to hang out a flag and close their doors for the celebration.[100]

All the accused men were made to kiss the flag for the crowd. One of them was said to have pulled a gun on a mine superintendent and state that Germany would win the war. When he pleaded guilty, he was promptly knocked to the ground. A restaurateur was convicted after he had recently aroused the displeasure of the visiting Jackie Band.[101] At least some members of the band, from the Great Lakes Naval Training Center, felt that the man had not fed them properly, which in 1918 DuQuoin was considered suspicious. For his culinary transgressions, the restaurant owner was tarred and feathered by the mob.

The same day a mob in the mining town of Benton in nearby Franklin County took issue with Mrs. Frances Pergen, a Bohemian, who reportedly said at the local post office that she hoped every American soldier sent to France would be killed and that the United States would starve to death if Germany didn't win the war.[102] Her statements were challenged by Henry Baker. The two ended up in some form of physical altercation, a scene that would have been memorable to witness, given that Baker had but one leg. Both were arrested by police and brought before a justice of the peace, who fined each of them $210. Word spread in Benton of the tussle and subsequent arrests. While Pergen was unable to find a lawyer willing to take her case, citizens anted up and paid Baker's fine.

The crowd of five hundred, many of them women, gave Pergen the "loyalty treatment," which in her case included being ridden out of town on a rail. That process involved the object of derision being lifted onto a fence rail or similar lumber and paraded around, in this case, up and down Main Street, and eventually out of town, while being forced to carry a flag in each hand and shout her approval of President Wilson and the United States.[103]

The mob actions in and near Franklin County did not amuse federal attorney Charles Karch, of the Southern District in East St. Louis. As despicable as they were, Karch knew the outcomes could have been worse. "The reason these did not end up in murder is more due to accident than to intention and design," he remarked.[104] Karch summoned more than fifty women to appear in federal court in Cairo after the Benton incident, but he acknowledged that it would be difficult to obtain convictions in any of the cases.[105]

Karch's office also became involved in the community of Steeleville, about sixty miles south of Collinsville, when the town board passed an ordinance prohibiting German from being spoken within its confines.[106] No violence was reported, but a group of citizens called on a church pastor and informed him of the new law. The majority of his congregants were Germans who did not speak or understand English, and they were required to attend another church or worship at home. The suspect church was also ordered to display an American flag outside. The U.S. attorney was reported to have explained that the local law was illegal and against the wishes of the federal government.

One might ask, where were the police during the World War I–era mob incidents? The best answer would probably be in the crowd, not necessarily leading the mob but certainly not making any significant move to restrain it. In a few instances police officers did intervene, but by and large the policemen of that era were neither professional nor ethical enough to perform their sworn duties. Two of those among the mob who were shot and injured by the Hillsboro farmer whose home was under siege were police officers.[107] Police actions in the East St. Louis riots of 1917 could more often be described as participating and watching rather than intervening. At least three East St. Louis policemen and one former policeman were indicted after the riots there.[108] Even without the war hysteria, police in the era were heavy-handed, and most complaints of brutality fell on deaf ears. A Milwaukee newspaper probably spoke of conditions in much of the nation when it said that mobs were "riding roughshod over law and order to punish instances of alleged disloyalty."[109]

Two men in Oklahoma were shot and killed by persons investigating their reported disloyalty in the spring of 1918. In the first case an allegedly disloyal Bulgarian was shot by a policeman after the victim reportedly fired first. The officer was acquitted, and the judge for the case gave a patriotic talk and warned pro-Germans not to speak against the United States. The second case also turned into a debate over patriotism rather than the facts of the shooting, when a member of a local council of defense shot a restaurant waiter. He too was acquitted.[110]

In the tumultuous spring of 1918, southern Illinois would infamously become a national leader in mob violence in the United

States. The series of mob incidents that occurred in Franklin, Macoupin, Madison, and Perry Counties would have at least one important shared characteristic: In all of them, coal mining was a major part of the local economy and along with that came subservience to UMW coal miners.

The mob actions in early 1918 could not be tied to any specific events on European battlefields. The Bolshevik Revolution had taken the Russians out of the fight with the Germans, and Italy had been nearly vanquished. This allowed Germany to consolidate forces and try to make all the gains it could on the western front before massive numbers of U.S. troops and massive amounts of U.S. matèriel flooded the field. The Germans mounted their offensive March 21 with 207 divisions compared to the Allies 173. In their assault on British lines between Arras and La Fere, the Germans had driven the Entente troops back as much as forty miles. But the word that hit the St. Louis–area newspapers didn't seem much different from what had been reported in prior months. Besides, the lion's share of U.S. troops were nowhere near the front and wouldn't be until later in 1918.

The first of April 1918 brought more of the same mob activity on the national level, but it started as a quiet week locally. On April 2 in LaSalle, Illinois, some two hundred miles north of Collinsville, a doctor was made to kiss the flag and "dunked" in a canal while the stores of two businessmen were painted yellow.[111] The physician's alleged crime was calling Secretary of War Newton Baker a "fathead."[112] On the same day, a man in Emerson, Nebraska was tarred and feathered for not giving to the Red Cross.[113] On April 3 the windows of the *Deutscher Herold* were painted yellow by a mob in Sioux Falls, South Dakota. A man in Sulphur, Oklahoma, had his head shaved on April 4 by a mob for allegedly being pro-German. He got off easier that day than a man in Boyce, Louisiana, who received one hundred lashes administered by prominent citizens, along with a coat of tar and feathers while he was made to shout, "To hell with the Kaiser," and, "Hurrah for Wilson."[114]

6

I Am Heart and Soul for the Good Old USA

Steel bars have never yet kept out a mob; it takes something a good deal stronger: human courage backed up by the consciousness of being right.

—Ray Stannard Baker, *Following the Color Line*

eading into the first week of April 1918, Collinsville was awash in over-the-top patriotism—and paranoia. This situation was helped no doubt by the first meeting of the Collinsville Neighborhood Committee of the Illinois State Council of Defense on March 27 at the Orpheum Theater. The purpose of the local committees was to "promote loyalty and suppress disloyalists," and membership of every true American would be sought. School Superintendent C. H. Dorris and other community leaders would head the group, but the featured speaker that night was Thomas Williamson, regarded as perhaps the best public orator in southern Illinois.

Williamson, tall and stately, would not disappoint that evening, whipping the large audience into "intense enthusiasm and stirring patriotic fervor." The Edwardsville attorney told the crowd that the United States was "large enough for all patriots, but too small for any traitor or a disloyal citizen." He praised union leaders and told the audience to remain alert. Williamson said the country's principle threat at home was defeating the spy system that was trying to work its way through churches, lodges, and labor unions. "Mr. Williamson concluded with a gem of eloquence and delivery and the audience rose to his flights with the most intense flattery, in that a pin could be heard to fall while he was soaring into the realms of imagery," one newspaper reported.[1]

After the meeting membership cards were distributed and turned in by the hundreds. One of the objectives of the state council of defense membership program was not just to get members but to ferret out those refusing to join—those who might not be loyal. A few Collinsville residents took umbrage at being asked to sign the card to prove their loyalty. A newspaper columnist urged signing the card: "Sign it without question and your loyalty will not be brought under suspicion. If you haggle and quibble about it, you lay yourself open at once to suspicion and no matter how much you protest later, the government will be watching your movements. The way to show yourself loyal is to join the rest of the loyalists."[2]

Another patriotic meeting took place a week later, on April 4, this one conducted by the Liberty Bond Sales Committee, which was determined that Collinsville would make a better showing for itself in the third Liberty Bond campaign that would kick off on April 6.[3] The city had underperformed in the first two drives, and the plan was to get the coal miners' unions more involved and push for each miner to buy a bond. One local had already agreed, and the others were expected to do so after the union officers and miners' pit committees from the miners' unions met with the bond-drive officials that evening. For the third drive, bond salesmen across the country were given appropriately colored yellow cards to document those who made disparaging statements about Liberty Bonds.[4] Completed cards were to be sent to the Treasury Department in Washington, where Secret Service agents would have access to files on all financial slackers.

After nearly a year of bombardment by government propaganda, much of the nation was paranoid about German spies and sabotage, and Collinsville was not an exception. And it would be difficult to find workingmen anywhere as preoccupied with spy hysteria as the coal miners of southern Illinois. In the last two weeks of March 1918, anxiety about coal mine sabotage in the region had increased. The heightened concern could be somewhat understandable given that miners were two hundred feet below the surface, with very limited means of egress. Yet two reported explosion incidents in the region seemed structured more to gain labor or management attention than to do any real damage to mines or kill miners. In both instances initial reports said that the socialist ıww union was responsible. But neither incident was ever connected to the Wobblies, and both appeared to have been done by people highly familiar with the local operations— people such as miners who had access to explosives.

The first incident was reported at the Shoal Creek Mine in Panama on March 19, not far from the earlier ıww troubles in Hillsboro and Mount Olive. The United Mine Workers local president there reported finding twenty-five sticks of dynamite at the bottom of an air shaft.[5] The attached fuse reportedly had been lit at the surface and was partly burned but had gone out. Locals quickly placed blame on six Italian immigrants in the area who were said to be ıww organizers and socialists.[6] uмw local officials also said that they had received threats of harm if they continued to work the mines. There had also been a recent unexplained arson attempt at a local church. But even in the witch-hunt environment of the spring of 1918, the arrested Italian men were released after a brief investigation by a federal Southern District attorney.[7]

On March 23 two kegs of powder exploded outside the Prairie Mine in nearby Fairview. The 8:00 a.m. blast occurred at an abandoned entrance to the mine, about a half mile from the main shaft and air shaft. The powder had been covered with heavy rocks and had a fifteen-foot fuse. It was suggested that if it had exploded a few minutes earlier, it could have injured or killed men on the topside. All but sixty of the Prairie miners returned to work after the blast, as it had done no real damage. The blast was investigated by a representative of the state fire marshal, but initially it was not believed to be connected with ıww members, several of whom reportedly worked at the mine. Nevertheless, an early newspaper report said, "It has the strong appearance of pro-Germanism and is the result of propaganda directed against American manufacturers of war materials."[8]

Further investigation did not uncover any link to pro-Germans but did determine that the explosion was probably intended just to send a message to the mining company.[9] The Prairie miners didn't think that way, however, and they passed a resolution calling for all miners to prove they were naturalized U.S. citizens before being allowed to descend into the mine shaft. They also threatened violence against all alien miners working the Prairie Mine. After the union passed the no-alien resolution, about 25 percent of the 380-miner workforce got the message and did not report for work. On April 15 a state deputy fire marshal arrested a miner from Fairview in connection with the explosion; he was reportedly the first man to reach the top of the mine after the blast.[10]

On March 28, the day after the big meeting of the Collinsville Neighborhood Committee of the state council of defense, a rumor circulated that powder kegs were found in an inappropriate location at Lumaghi Mine No. 2 in Collinsville. The mine superintendent quickly said that the report was entirely without foundation. Nonetheless, the mine was making arrangements to guard against "pro-German plots."[11]

The next day miners found a bottle they thought to be filled with a liquid explosive at the Black Eagle Mine in Fairview.[12] It was quickly discovered that the bottle contained some form of lantern oil, but the incident served to remind the jittery miners of how easily an item could make its way into the mine shaft. To increase security a guard was posted at the mine shaft entrance to make sure everyone entering saluted the American flag.

It didn't take much to sway the miners to scuttle work for the day, even with the federal wage agreement in place. The week before miners began using a flag salute at the Black Eagle Mine as a security measure, wildcat strikes shut down two Belleville mines when the companies failed to post the Stars and Stripes at mine entrances. The Eldnar Mine was struck on March 23 and the Muren Mine on March 25 because the colors weren't flying.[13] The wildcat strikes were in violation of the contract, and the miners were threatened with fines from the UMW. Union officials believed that the job action was simply an effort to incite trouble prior to election of District 12 union officers. The miners had effectively conducted one-day strikes against their elected union leadership.

The reason for miners not working didn't need to have much basis in fact either. About one hundred miners would fail to work one day in April because they feared an explosion would occur at the Taylor Mine in O'Fallon.[14] Upon investigation it was learned that the rumor of impending catastrophe came from one miner's mother, a self-proclaimed spiritualist. She learned of the threatened explosion from her deceased grandfather in a séance and dutifully spread the warning.

• • •

Most European immigrants in the late nineteenth and early twentieth centuries came to America for better economic opportunity. Arriving in 1905 Robert Paul Prager was among them, and in his drifting, largely unremarkable thirteen-year, two-day presence on U.S. soil, there is nothing to indicate that he ever found anything close to prosperity.

Little is known of Prager's background. He was born in the Saxony state capital of Dresden in February 1888 to baker Karl Heinrich Prager and his wife, Augusta Maria Louisa Prager.[15] He had six brothers and a sister, all of whom apparently remained in Germany. For unknown reasons Prager left home at age thirteen. Four years later, on March 19, 1905, he boarded Norddeutscher Lloyd's s s *Breslau* at Bremen, in northwest Germany, setting out alone for the thirteen-day trip to Baltimore.[16] The seventeen-year-old listed his occupation as baker and denied he had ever been in prison or any other institution, or that he was an anarchist or polygamist. He declared himself able to read and write and in good health, denying any disability. At the entry port, Prager stated his intention to live with his namesake uncle in Chicago, who at forty-four years old was a married wagon and carriage maker. Like so many from his homeland, Prager moved into the so-called German Triangle, an area between the midwestern cities of Cincinnati, Milwaukee, and St. Louis, which saw heavy immigration during the era.

Prager's whereabouts and activities are unknown until 1912, when he was arrested in Lake County, Indiana, in the Chicago area, for stealing a suit of clothes.[17] He was charged with grand larceny, and at age twenty-four pleaded guilty and was sentenced to one to eight years in prison, with time to be served at the Indiana Reformatory at Jeffersonville beginning December 28.[18] Prager was involved in a couple of dustups in the reformatory and ended up losing his left eye, which he had replaced with a glass prosthesis. He was paroled February 27, 1914, after serving about fourteen months of his sentence. Prager was released to the custody of the Central Howard Association in Chicago, which provided him a job and financial assistance.[19] He reported to the association for just one month, however, before once again striking out on his own.

By January 1915 Prager had somehow come to settle in the small community of Niobrara in northwest Nebraska, where he baked for Joseph Stejskal. His employer later described Prager as a "radical pro-German."[20] When the *Lusitania* was sunk on May 7, Prager reportedly said that President Wilson was nothing but an "English cur." Another report surfaced that Prager either left the tent or refused to stand when the National Anthem was played and the flag unfurled at a local Chautauqua circuit event, raising the ire of most people in the crowd. By September Prager had been fired from his job, but he stayed in Niobrara long enough to incur a few more debts before suddenly fleeing town.[21] Whatever occurred in Niobrara, it provided a glimpse into Prager's opinionated and argumentative personality, traits that ill served a man who spoke so impulsively. Sometimes he would rethink, regret, and apologize, but by that time the damage usually had already been done.

In late 1915 Prager traveled some two hundred miles south to Omaha, where he again found work as a baker.[22] By 1916 he had drifted, penniless and hungry, into St. Louis and the home of John and Elizabeth Pohl at 1105 South Thirteenth Street. Pohl, a Hungarian baker, provided Prager with food and clothing and helped him find work.[23] Prager joined Baker's Union Local 4, preferring to do extra work at various shops rather than stay with one bakery. He also joined the Odd Fellows, Harmonie Lodge 353, which had many German members and met Tuesday evenings on nearby Chouteau Avenue. Like most immigrants living in big cities, he no doubt found comfort in connecting with others from his homeland. But the immigrant neighborhoods could be rough and tumble too, as Prager would learn one day in January 1917 when he was robbed of his money, $9.40, near his home.[24]

When Prager arrived in St. Louis, others in the boardinghouse said that he had radical political views but that his opinion wholeheartedly changed about the time the United States entered the Great War. Prager suddenly became a crank on American patriotism.[25] He applied for his first citizenship papers the day after President Wilson's speech asking Congress to declare war.[26]

When Prager hung an American flag from a window each day after war was declared in April 1917, his friend John Pohl suggested it was too inflammatory for the south city area, which was home to many immigrants.[27] Prager became incensed with Pohl and complained of his being un-American. Shortly thereafter Prager moved to 1809 LaSalle Street, just a few blocks down Chouteau. But the matter was not over for Pohl, as he was arrested on suspicion of disloyalty by federal Secret Service agents and placed in the city jail for thirty-two days. No charges were ever filed, as Prager evidently declined to testify against the friend who had taken him in off the streets one year earlier.

Prager lived for about six weeks on LaSalle Street, using that address to register for the draft on National Registration Day, June 5, 1917, and later that month as a German alien. Prager also obtained a permit that allowed him to apply for work in zones that were normally barred to German aliens. He had tried to enlist in the navy in May but was rejected for physical reasons, presumably his eyesight. Perhaps to head off harassment, Prager was issued a letter by a naval officer explaining his rejection. "You have been patriotic enough, and no one will have the right to call you a slacker," the letter stated.[28]

Prager again moved several blocks away, this time to 1011 Dillon Street.[29] Like all registered German aliens, he was required to inform the U.S. marshal of any address change, but the Dillon Street home would be the last address he provided to the government. Prager moved briefly to Columbia, Missouri, and Gillespie, Illinois, before landing in Collinsville in the late summer of 1917.[30]

In Collinsville Prager took a job working for Italian bakery owner Lorenzo Bruno.[31] He rented a small house—some called it a shack—behind a larger brick home at 208 Vandalia Street. It was a literal stone's throw from the Y in the interurban tracks at Vandalia and Clay Streets and the busy saloons of Martin Fulton, Adam Boneski, and John Baltrasat. Across the street stood the imposing Gothic Saints Peter and Paul Catholic Church and equally commanding Parish School.

Prager shared the two-room home with Battiste Vallissa, a forty-six-year-old Italian coal miner. Prager mostly kept to himself. His most frequent visitors were neighborhood children, whom he often indulged with cookies and candies.[32] He would also let them come in occasionally to listen and dance to his Victrola, the one luxury in his otherwise spartan abode.[33] There were other visits too from a man and a woman, probably friends from St. Louis, who always appeared well dressed.[34] Their conversations were often loud but in German, so few knew what was being said. The visits would sometimes end in argument.[35]

Bruno said Prager was a good baker, but he also found him to be argumentative and have a violent temper. The most trivial things seemed to anger him; in November Prager wanted to fight Bruno over a frivolous baking concern.[36] As tempers wore thin at Bruno's Bakery, Prager decided he would try his hand at coal mining, no doubt hearing of the great money miners were earning in the spring of 1918.

In March Prager was able to get a nighttime laborer's position at Donk Mine No. 2, in Maryville.[37] It did not pay what the miners were earning, but it was a decent wage and would provide experience he needed to become a full-fledged miner. State regulations required that miners have two years of experience laboring at the mine prior to taking a simple practical exam that allowed them to become full-fledged miners.[38] But Prager didn't intend to wait that long. He applied to President James Fornero to join Maryville umw Local 1802 as a miner.[39] His first application was rejected because no other miners had signed it to vouch for Prager's claim of four years' mining experience. He said he had not been a miner per se but had worked as a timberman in mines. He resubmitted the application to Fornero, this time signed by three immigrant miners, indicating that Prager was experienced. One report claimed that Prager had asked for a umw membership transfer, which would have cost just $10 as opposed to a first membership application costing $50.[40]

The miners at Maryville were a suspicious lot, however. Many were Italian, Russian, or Bohemian immigrants, and they were leery of the German Prager.[41] It was later reported that mine manager John Lobenat, a naturalized Russian, thought Prager suspect when he stated his intention to try to also become a mine manager.[42] Prager, who at the time had worked in Maryville as a laborer for just a week, reportedly asked Lobenat about the responsibilities of managers, mine air controls, and damage that could be done by explosions.

In the coming weeks, Prager's opinionated and argumentative nature made him few friends but a number of enemies at Donk Mine No. 2. Being an immigrant with a heavy accent didn't help, and rumors of Prager being pro-German became rampant. A few pro-Socialist rants by Prager didn't help matters either. The miner's rejection of Socialist talk by Prager is curious, given that Socialists in Collinsville and Maryville were not viewed negatively at the time. There were Socialist candidates for four of the six open elected positions in the city in 1917, when highly respected Miners Local 685 president Robert Bertolero ran as party candidate for mayor. And Socialist concepts proudly played out on Main Street too: the Collinsville Cooperative Store opened in January 1918 and quickly sold out its $8,000 in stocks to 180 families.[43] The store promised that members of all income classes would be treated the same, and that profit margins would remain low.[44]

By Wednesday, April 3, union president Fornero had rejected Prager's application to join the local as a miner on the grounds that he had lied about his work experience and was a German spy.[45] A miners' meeting that evening at Hrubetz Saloon and Hall in Maryville turned into a patriotic circus, with Prager as the star attraction. Prager was taken out to the street and made to parade about, all while kissing the flag.[46] Rumor more than fact built the miners' case against Prager. He may or may not have made Socialist comments, but miner hearsay alone marked him as a German spy. Given the recent explosions at other area mines, it was not unexpected that someone would fabricate a story that Prager was hoarding blasting powder at his home, with the intent of blowing up the Maryville mine.[47]

Earlier in the day, Prager had complained of being rejected by the union to Mine Superintendent Walter Clark, a Donk's Coal Company man rather than a union member.[48] Clark said that he had talked with Prager and thought he was "all right," and he denied rumors of any missing powder at the mine.[49]

What had started as a relatively tame patriotic demonstration in Maryville became more inflamed, and threats against Prager grew more intense. Fornero and umw district board member Mose Johnson intervened and took custody of Prager. The union officials told Prager to stay away from Maryville, and they escorted him without delay to a streetcar bound for Collinsville. Before Prager and his two union escorts left Maryville just before 8:00 p.m., Johnson phoned Collinsville police chief Tony Staten and requested that an officer search Prager's home for pro-German material and hoarded gunpowder.[50] Chief Staten thought Prager was being brought to town on a later car, so no police officer was waiting for the party when the streetcar arrived about ten minutes later at the Y interurban stop.

Johnson and Fornero had two miners take Prager to the back room at Fulton's Y Saloon, where they could keep an eye on him.[51] Meanwhile, they walked three blocks to the Collinsville Police Station and asked that Prager be arrested as a German spy. The officers declined, however, citing a lack of proof. The police chief would later deny that his men had been asked to take Prager into custody. Johnson and Fornero returned to the saloon, where Johnson and Prager apparently agreed to meet again at 3:00 p.m. Thursday at the office of Sheriff Jenkin Jenkins in Edwardsville. Johnson told Prager that the meetings with police were to arrange for his protection from mobs. In fact Johnson intended to have him jailed as a spy, and Prager knew it. With the affair calming down for the evening, Prager was escorted to his home just a few hundred steps away.

After being threatened by an angry mob, warned to leave the area, and at risk of incarceration by the police, most men would have packed their bags and fled. But that would have been out of character for Robert Prager. Obstinate, unyielding—and used to doing battle on his own—Prager would make his voice heard. And it would be his undoing.

Later that night Prager would in his mind begin drafting a letter to the miners of Local 1802, telling them how he had been treated unfairly by their union president, James Fornero, and proclaiming his loyalty to the United States. On the morning of Thursday, April 4, Prager wrote out his four-paragraph proclamation. A few blocks away on East Main Street, Prager found the Holzweg and Thomas Agency, an insurance and realty firm that offered typing services.[52] There stenographer Thetis Thompson made Prager's thoughts intelligible and clear in English and provided enough carbon copies to help him get his message out to the miners in Maryville.

In the proclamation Prager said Fornero's actions "take away my daily bread," which he said was not the will of a workingman's union. He said he would obey union regulations, asserting, "I have been a union man at all times and never once a scab." Prager said he was entitled to a fair hearing regarding the allegations against him: "I ask in the name of humanity to examine me to find out what is the reason I am kept out of work." He said he had declared his intention to become a naturalized American citizen and awaited his second naturalization papers. Prager stated, "I am heart and soul for the good old USA. I am of German birth, of which accident I cannot help."[53]

Prager closed the proclamation with a postscript stating that he had been unfairly branded a liar and a German spy by Fornero, who had tried to have him arrested in Maryville, Collinsville, and Edwardsville. Prager said Fornero "tried hard to have an angry mob deal with me"; he claimed that Fornero had told him to leave his home and not come to Maryville again if he knew what was good for his health. On the first allegation, Fornero was probably right. In Prager's effort to get a miner's job, at minimum he had grossly exaggerated his experience. Although it was possible that he had four years of mining experience, it was not at all likely. Since entering the United States he had worked mostly as a baker, and it is doubtful he could have worked much in the mines in Germany before he emigrated at age seventeen. Most certainly Prager had not known his three sponsoring miners for four years.

Prager was determined, however. After reading his proclamation, the miners would no doubt reject the opinion of their popular union president and allow the German immigrant to work in the mines—at least that was Prager's thinking. That afternoon he took the interurban to Maryville, with one copy of the proclamation tucked in his pocket, the others in hand.[54] He posted the notices about the village, in saloons and other places where the miners might see them. When the men began to come out of the mine around 4:00 p.m., they saw his posts and became enraged. They ripped them down and went in search of Prager. He hid out in the village until dark, then made his way to the interurban line for the ten-minute trip back to Collinsville. He would be ominously followed by a half dozen or so Maryville miners taking a later interurban car.[55]

As Prager made his postings in Maryville, another interurban car passed through the village headed north to Edwardsville. It carried UMW board member Mose Johnson, accompanied by miner Alfred Bailey, who were to meet Sheriff Jenkins at 3:00 p.m. at the county jail. But the subject of their meeting, Robert Prager, would be a no show. He would not be jailed in Edwardsville that night as a possible spy. Nor would he be jailed there for his own protection.

When the Maryville miners arrived in Collinsville, they went first to Fulton's Y Saloon, the hub of all activity, to begin their search for Prager.[56] They told the Collinsville miners of their intention to hold Prager accountable for his proclamation and said that he was a Socialist spy who planned to blow up Donk Mine No. 2. In no time Prager's ever-worsening transgressions were the talk of the saloon. After another drink, and energized by the even less-enlightened Collinsville miners, a contingent of the seventy-five or so men at Fulton's went the short distance to Prager's home. They would be followed by others just wanting to see the Maryville men deal with the German spy.

Louis Fellhauer, a Lead Works employee, lived in the home in front of Prager's shanty. He was reading around 9:45 p.m. when he heard a handful of miners rap on the door of the darkened shack that was home to Vallissa and Prager.[57] A light from inside came on, and Fellhauer watched as the men ordered Prager to leave town within ten minutes. "All right brothers, I'll go," he said and started packing. The miners reassembled on the sidewalk across the street, in front of the Saints Peter and Paul Catholic Church. But simply forcing the German to leave town wouldn't quite appease the group of waiting men, some no doubt well on their way to yet another drunken evening. It was not humiliating enough, not patriotic enough. "Let's get him now," one of them said.

A few men went back and kicked and beat on his door, yelling for Prager to come out of his home now and join them across the street. A flag had been brought for him to kiss. "All right, brothers, I'll go," Prager said, "if you don't hurt me."[58] They assured the German immigrant that they just wanted him to kiss the flag to show his allegiance to Uncle Sam. Prager, wearing his jacket and hat, joined the men on the sidewalk and was ordered to cheer for the United States. He again told them he would do anything they wanted, as long as they would not harm him. Prager told them, "Brothers, I am a loyal USA workingman." After a few moments the miners marched Prager to the front of Fulton's, where everyone could see him sing of his patriotism and kiss the flag. He did not protest when he was told to remove his shoes and hang them around his neck and was wrapped in the large American flag.

The impromptu patriotic show at Fulton's caused even more men to gather round the diminutive German. The crowd swelled to over one hundred as it moved just south, where the miners decided to show off their captive to the men collected in the Main Street saloons. By this time very few in the crowd knew anything directly about Prager, but rumor and hearsay only were sufficient. The group turned west on Main, where their loyalty demonstration could be seen by the men at the fourteen saloons west of Vandalia Street. Somewhere along the way, two boys of nine or ten years old began marching in front of the procession carrying small flags.[59] With men coming out of the bars to join in the festivities, the mob continued to force Prager to sing and make patriotic statements. He could not manage "The Star-Spangled Banner" but was able to sing "We'll Fight for the Red, White and Blue" to the tune of "Columbia, the Gem of the Ocean."[60]

Mayor John Siegel saw the men as he left the planning meeting for the third Liberty Loan drive at the Orpheum and thought the group was for the most part orderly as it paraded Prager down the middle of Main Street. Nonetheless, Siegel encouraged the men to disband. One of the mob leaders stepped up to the mayor and warned him not to interfere. Pointing to the young boys carrying the two flags, he said, "Mr. Mayor, we dare you to defy that flag."[61] Wanting no part of being considered disloyal, the mayor continued on to his medical office across the street.

The temperament of the crowd was rapidly transforming, however; it had become meaner. Men in the crowd were now striking Prager. Bystanders got into the act by cursing the German. Other young boys, out past bedtime, threw down handfuls of tacks in the barefoot Prager's path. After he was forced to walk over them by his escorts, the boys scooped up the tacks with their hands and threw them in his path again.[62] When Siegel returned to the street a few minutes later, he saw how unruly the crowd had become. And the mob had grown markedly, now perhaps three hundred strong.[63] Loud threats were hurled at Prager, and men were clamoring that he deserved a coat of tar and feathers. Siegel went back into his office and phoned motorcycle patrolmen Fred Frost, who was acting as desk sergeant at the police station, to report the mob.[64] It was now about 10:00 p.m. The police station was housed in city Hall on Center Street, a short distance from Main, and three officers took off on foot.

The mob had just passed the last two bars on Main Street at Seminary Street and was preparing to turn back east again by the time Patrolman Frost arrived "in a dogtrot." Patrolmen John Tobnick and Martin Futcheck were behind him. Frost asked a Maryville miner on the sidewalk, John Hallworth, who was in the center of the mob.[65] Hallworth said it was a supposed pro-German and asked Frost to take him into custody.

Hallworth was a voice of reason among the Maryville miners. At age forty-three, he was mature, married, and settled in Collinsville with five children. He had worked at the Maryville mine for six years and was uptown that night for the same Liberty Bond meeting that the mayor had attended.[66] With dark hair, a full mustache, and piercing eyes, Hallworth appeared the archetype immigrant. He had come from the mines in Pontefract, England, just eight years earlier but was now a naturalized citizen and well-respected among the men. Earlier a group of fifteen or twenty miners had asked him what he thought they should do with the immigrant who had cursed the president and threatened to blow up the mine. Hallworth urged them to let the police and the state council of defense deal with Prager, discouraging their talk of tar and feathers.[67] The others seemed to agree and went into Fulton's for a drink. But Hallworth would follow and watch a short while later from the sidewalk when other miners first took Prager from his home.

After speaking with Hallworth, Patrolman Frost promptly ran into the crowd and pushed Prager free from behind and out of the grasp of his two captors. Frost yelled back that he would lock the man up. There were protests from the swarm of miners, but Hallworth yelled, "Let the officers have him, boys."[68]

With perhaps a dozen men from the mob staying on their heels, the policemen ran with Prager down Seminary and Church Streets to the police station.[69] As they ran, Frost noted Prager was barefoot and said, "Good Lord, man, where are your shoes?" Prager pointed to the pair hanging around his neck. Asked if his feet were cold, Prager replied, "They're numb."

From a distance Mayor Siegel watched as the officers took the immigrant from the mob and then also made haste to city hall and the police station. Arriving before Prager and the officers, Siegel tried to phone Sheriff Jenkins to alert him to the brewing storm in Collinsville, but he was unable to make contact.[70] The Collinsville police would have to weather this mob on their own. The officers arrived with Prager and locked him in one of the basement cells. The mayor went to the front lawn of city hall and spoke for about five minutes with the men who had run after the officers. He told them that Prager would be turned over to federal authorities and that the legal system should be allowed to run its course. Siegel encouraged the men to go home.[71] The men were displeased, but most of the crowd walked back to Main Street to meet up with the main contingent of the mob. Quite a number had already gone home or back to the saloons.

After speaking with the men in front of city hall, Siegel went to the basement cells and met with Prager to ask him a few questions. The immigrant showed the mayor his alien registration card and permit to work in restricted areas. Though most of the remaining men had moved a half block north to the Main and Center intersection, a few still lingered outside city hall.

The remnants of the mob that collected at Main and Center Streets felt cheated. They wanted to have their fun with Prager but had been denied that by the mayor and police. Most of the one hundred or more men ignored requests to disperse, many walking between the crowd and the corner saloons of Fred Neubauer and William Horstman to have yet another drink. Leery of the drunken group just a stone's throw from city hall, Mayor Siegel ordered the police officers to tell the uptown saloon operators to close.[72] Dispersing the crowd of mostly inebriated men was no doubt the correct strategic decision, but Siegel failed miserably in his tactic of closing the saloons. The order came about 10:30 p.m. and had the effect of sending intoxicated men from the nineteen saloons uptown into the street to meet up with the men still upset that Prager had been taken from them.[73] To make matters worse, in closing the bars the policemen announced it was because a German spy was being held in jail. Many of those who might otherwise have gone straight home elected to join the crowd at Main and Center, not wanting to miss the action. "The boys had no place to go except home," one witness said, "and they weren't quite ready to go home."[74] A crowd of more than two hundred had now collected in the intersection.

One of them was Joe Riegel. He had been three blocks east at Jules Schiller's Saloon, working on his umpteenth drink of the night, when a policeman arrived to close the bar and announce that a big crowd had collected because of the jailed spy.[75] Riegel had been a miner at Donk Mine No. 2 mine, but in October 1917 he had transferred to Lumaghi Mine No. 2.[76] Perhaps due to his earlier dustup with UMW board member Mose Johnson, he was now working—no doubt at lesser pay—as a shoe cobbler. At twenty-eight years old, he was discharged in 1914 after serving a three-year army stint. But in 1918 Riegel could rightfully be called a draft dodger and a deadbeat dad. He had been classified 4A, as a father who provided for a wife and child. Yet he had not lived with his wife or paid any form of child support for months.[77] When he did live with his wife, he was often gone a week at a time. Riegel was an impetuous troublemaker and a drunk. When not sleeping or working, he spent his time in saloons and had been drinking heavily that day.[78] He carried on into the night with a regimen of beer and whiskey. After finishing his beer, he walked up to where the mob had assembled with a coworker from Union Shoe Company, Frank Pelczor. Riegel hoped of perhaps getting a look at the alleged spy to see if he knew him.

No doubt many of the men in the saloons did go home or otherwise disperse. After their first patriotic parade with Prager, most of the handful of miners who had come from Maryville reassembled at Fulton's Y Saloon along with Mose Johnson and Local 1802 president James Fornero. Johnson urged the men to go home, and they did about 10:20 p.m. on a northbound interurban.[79] The Maryville contingent had gotten what it was after: Prager had been humiliated and made to show his patriotism and then sent away. Johnson too began to walk home, along the way meeting up with John Hallworth, who had gotten a bite to eat at Leavitt's Restaurant on Main Street.[80] The two men, among very few in town who had some power to assuage and calm the crowd, walked together on the way to their homes along the St. Louis Road.

As word quickly spread about the spy being held at the police station, no one bothered to use the word *alleged*. Few even knew his name. But the German was variously reported to have planned to blow up Donk Mine No. 2, to have hoarded explosive powder at his home, to be a Socialist, and to have made slurs against President Wilson. Wafting in thick mob mentality, it was all fact. Yet the crowd didn't know quite what to do and argued among themselves at the intersection. The debate raged as cooler heads said they should let federal authorities deal with Prager and others thought he should first be tarred and feathered.[81]

Any hope of coherent reasoning was lost when one man started singing "The Star Spangled Banner" and then many others joined in, "singing lustily."[82] One of the men brought forward the flag that had been used to cloak Prager earlier, and more cheers rose from the crowd. Wesley Beaver, a twenty-six-year-old saloon porter who had left his job at Fulton's to join the festivities, grabbed one side of the flag while another man grabbed the other to fully display its forty-eight stars and thirteen stripes. Held out in front for everyone to see, it was the only license this mob needed to have its way with the German spy. One man finally yelled, "Shall we go home or get him?" Calls for the latter resonated from the crowd. Then a cheer went up to "follow the flag" as the mob stormed back toward city hall, falling in behind the colors. It was about 10:45 p.m.[83]

Mayor Siegel saw the men coming and walked onto the front

landing of the sturdy Italianate building. Constructed in 1885, its red brick and limestone walls housed city offices and meeting rooms, with the police station occupying one-half of the first floor and jail cells in the rear of the basement. Dr. John Siegel was himself a pillar of the community, and not just due to his being elected to a second term as mayor. As a popular physician and surgeon, he had literally cared for city residents—and no doubt a number of the men in the mob before him—for over twenty years.

Siegel tried to calm the mob, urging the men to let justice run its course, to let the federal authorities deal with Prager.[84] But they would not follow the doctor's advice this evening. Beaver and the other man carrying the flag walked up the steps, followed immediately by a mob that filled the stoop and overflowed the front lawn of City Hall. "We're going to follow the flag," the men said. Beaver yelled for the crowd to go in and get the German, but Siegel stood firm.

The police officers mostly remained inside, none daring to venture into the crowd. Siegel was helped by other community leaders who worked the crowd from the sides and the rear, trying to calm the men and get them to listen to reason. They included men of standing, like Alderman Tim Kane, a blacksmith, and former mayor R. Guy Kneedler, an attorney who now served as the City of Collinsville's legal counsel.[85] Let the man get a fair trial, they urged. If he is a spy, he can provide valuable information to the government. Don't do something that will be a stain on Collinsville. Go peaceably to your homes.[86]

But the mob would not be placated. Men yelled back that Siegel and the others were just as pro-German as the man they protected. Dick Dukes, a twenty-two-year-old miner, stood at the steps and told the mayor that he'd take care of the spy all by himself. "If they let me in there with him I guarantee he won't last 15 minutes," said the tall, rugged Dukes.[87] William Brockmeier, the former president of Miners Local 826 from Lumaghi Mine No. 3, protested about the police interference in their patriotic parade of Prager.

August Schimpff, the publisher of the *Collinsville Advertiser*, analyzed the crowd:

> A number of radicals and agitators howled loudly for violence and made many threats of rioting and insisted that the advice of the cooler heads be over ruled. These bloodthirsty agitators were of no real standing, not recognized as good citizens or even men of sound principles, but as with the case of excited men, they were given applause which led them to even greater lengths of lawlessness. Puffed up with the sense of their importance to which they were strangers, some of them advocated that the jail be rushed and even that duly appointed officers be overpowered in their desire to commit a violent act. But one thing was conspicuous as usual, and that was the loudest talking agitators wanted somebody else to do the fighting.[88]

One of those whose sense of importance was inflated that Thursday night was Joe Riegel. A veteran of the U.S. Army Coast Artillery Corps, which defended the nation's shoreline from invading ships between 1911 and 1914, Riegel carried his discharge papers with him to prove it. At twenty-eight Riegel was about ten years older than many of the other drunken men who made up the crowd—but not so old as to be burdened with mature wisdom or responsibility. Tall and cocky he also had a reputation as a roughneck, a tough—someone not to be trifled with.

While the mayor and others tried to calm the mob, the police officers felt Prager's best chance was to get him out of town, and they planned to do so. They just didn't plan very well, and that would lead to the second tactical error of the night. After closing the saloons, Patrolman Frost pulled his car into the alley behind city hall, and Patrolman Futcheck planned to bring Prager out; together they would take him to either Belleville or East St. Louis. But the policemen got cold feet after Frost was accosted outside. "Where did you take him you ——?" the patrolman was asked.[89] "I believe they would have done violence to me if I had told them I had taken him away, so I told them I had been to close up a saloon," Frost said later. Instead of removing the immigrant from the building, Futcheck helped Prager hide in a clay sewer pipe in the city hall basement, in the event that the crowd got its hands on the key to the jail cells. It apparently had not occurred to the policemen to simply hide the cell keys.

In front of city hall, the scene became more threatening as additional men straggled in to join the mob, once again about three hundred strong. The longer the mayor talked, the more agitated the inebriated men seemed to get. One of the policemen whispered to Siegel, who had been holding firm on the front steps, that Prager had been taken from the building by federal authorities.[90] Siegel didn't believe it and went to check the cells himself. Not seeing Prager in the cells, the mayor announced to the men that they might as well go home since the suspected pro-German had already been taken away by federal men. A chorus of boos and catcalls was directed at Siegel and the others. They were disloyalists and as traitorous as the spy, the crowd told them. But some in the mob thought Prager was still inside; Joe Riegel was among them.[91]

Relishing his leadership role, Riegel charged up the city hall steps to speak with the mayor. He showed Siegel his army discharge papers and announced, "I'm an American soldier and we're going to get this man."[92] The mayor again said that Prager had been taken away, but Riegel didn't believe him and said he should be allowed to check inside because he was a "United States man." Believing that Prager was gone, Siegel consented to the building being searched.

Led by Riegel nearly one hundred men entered the building to check. Police officers unlocked a supervisor's room to show that Prager was not there. One jailed prisoner in the basement cells was asked to stand and present himself so that the mob could be sure he was not Prager.[93] The basement doors had purposely been left unlocked to avoid arousing suspicion.

Those searching did not find Prager after checking the building. They walked out to find most of the mob already leaving, accepting that the alleged spy had been taken from their grasp. The police officers were quietly optimistic that their ruse would be successful. What was left of the mob continued to curse the mayor and the policemen, wondering how Prager could have been taken. It didn't make sense since the building's entrances had been watched the entire time, someone said. Prager must still be in the building. A smaller group redoubled their efforts in searching the building again. Riegel and Beaver would be among a score of men who would search once more in the basement. Again most found nothing.

Riegel and Beaver were the last two men in the basement. Riegel was headed out when he heard Beaver say that he had found the man. "What are you trying to give me, you damn fool?"[94] Riegel asked as he walked toward Beaver in the basement. But Beaver had found Prager, crouched in a four-foot-long piece of clay tile. Prager, at only five feet four inches and 145 pounds, could just fit inside. "Come on out of there and let us get a look at you," Riegel said.[95]

Beaver and Riegel lifted the immigrant up and out of the tile. They marched him through the city offices before leading him out to the street, one on each arm. It was about 11:30 p.m. Others in front of city hall joined in as Prager was brought out, and by the time they arrived at Main and Center Streets with their man, the mob was rapidly re-forming. Calls of "they got him" rang out. Now the men were even crueler, giving no quarter to the immigrant, taking out their frustration that their party had been interrupted. As soon as Riegel and Beaver brought Prager back to Main Street, he was struck on the head hard enough to knock him down.[96] Held so he could not defend himself or escape, the beatings would continue until he was no more.

For Beaver it was a chance to stand out for once, to be a big man. The least consequential of three men sharing the name Wesley Beaver in 1918 Collinsville, as a saloon porter he emptied spittoons and trash, swept floors and stocked beer at Fulton's. His bulging blue eyes had earned him the sobriquet of Popeye. But he was blind in one of those eyes and impaired in the other; unable neither to read nor to write, he signed his name with an *X*.[97] But Beaver was a happy-go-lucky sort, and he would be happiest tonight carrying the flag in front of the procession once again, this time with James DeMatties, an eighteen-year-old coal miner from Donk Mine No. 1.[98] Beaver relinquished his hold on Prager's right arm to another man in the mob. Several men would take turns holding the undersized immigrant's right arm for the next fifty minutes. But the man holding the left arm, Joe Riegel, would maintain his grip on Prager until they reached the hanging tree.

Beaver carried the flag in front for just another two blocks, before deciding it was time to get back and clean up at Fulton's. Another man took his place. Meanwhile Prager had been told to resume his patriotic show, which included intoning the national anthem, cheering for the red, white, and blue and President Wilson, and kissing the flag on demand. Instead of remaining uptown, the men now continued marching west on Main Street.[99] Somehow word had reached the mob leaders that police would not interfere if they happened to conduct their business outside the city limits. So the mob headed west on Main and turned onto the St. Louis Road, along the interurban tracks. Twice it stopped streetcars and entertained the occupants with its victim. There was some confusion about what to do with the man, but a general consensus was that the pro-German should be tarred and feathered once they were outside the city.[100] Yet the mob was too wound up, having too much fun, to think of how it would get, or prepare, the necessary materials.

Back near city hall, a number of angry men had assembled in the adjacent fire department engine house after the first search of the building came up empty. Still venting their anger at the mayor and the police for releasing Prager to federal authorities, the men discussed dealing with others in Collinsville who they felt were traitorous. Mayor Siegel went to the engine house to try to calm the men.[101] The group named four or five residents they considered unpatriotic or with pro-German sympathies—perhaps the mob should deal with them tonight too.

While the mayor tried to diffuse the group in the engine house, William Brockmeier arrived and told Siegel that Prager had been found in the basement and taken back to Main Street. Although Brockmeier had earlier complained about Prager being protected and was among the men to search city hall, Siegel asked for his help. The mayor requested that the former miners' local president keep the mob from harming Prager: "Save him if you can." Brockmeier, hobbled by a recent leg injury at the mine, took off to try to catch up with the reconstituted mob, which by now was three blocks west on Main Street.[102] Siegel went back to city hall, where he asked the officers to follow the mob and try to persuade the men not to harm Prager. The mayor apparently did not mention retrieving him from the mob.[103]

No explanation was ever given for what the city's four police officers on duty were doing when Riegel and Beaver took Prager from the basement. The crowd outside city hall had been very small when Prager was brought out; retaking him from the two men should have been an easy task for the four officers, all armed with revolvers. Inside the station was an array of long guns for even greater persuasive ability. Even when the mob was at its largest, there was never an indication that any of its members were armed.[104] But the police did not use their weapons that evening. After hiding him in the basement, they would apparently never get close to Prager or the mob again.

As impressive as Patrolman Fred Frost's actions were in taking Prager from the crowd earlier, the efforts of the four officers later ranged from disinterested to simply inept. When alerted that Prager had literally been taken from under their noses, Frost and officers Martin Futcheck, Harry Stephens, and John Tobnick ran toward Main Street. In a scene worthy of a Keystone Cops silent film, all the officers ran east on Main, while the loud and unruly mob went west. Several blocks later, upon discovering their error, the officers also went west. By this time the mob was out of sight, so they sent Officer Stephens back for an automobile and waited for him while catching their breath at Guernsey Street. The officers' story from that point was that even with the automobile, they could not catch up with the mob of two hundred men on foot before it was outside the city limits.[105] The mob had stopped several times to show off its prize to passing automobiles and streetcars, but there was never any rescue attempt nor any effort to dissuade violence against Prager, as the four officers contentedly followed in a car.

Also tagging along behind the group was Bernhardt Mueller, a thirty-five-year-old barber who had just opened his shop on Main Street next to the new McLanahan Ford dealership. He had watched the goings-on at city hall and earlier, applauding when the flag was brought forward.[106] He was native born, but his father was from Germany. Mueller was spirited and outspoken, opinionated, and unashamed of his German heritage, even in the xenophobic era of the Great War. He had signed his 1918 draft registration card with his full given name, Bernhardt Gotfried Berthold Mueller. The barber didn't know anything about the alleged spy and would not judge him, but he had followed along, like many others, just out of curiosity.

In fact the mob at times may have been outnumbered by those just watching to see what would happen to the alleged spy. Whether their curiosity was based on patriotism or fascination with the macabre, a number of businessmen and community leaders besides Mueller would follow the procession. They included Notley Shoulders, twenty-eight, a city alderman and electrical construction foreman; William Horstman, thirty-six, owner of the ABC Saloon at Main and Center Streets; and George Coukoulis, thirty-eight, the Greek immigrant owner of the Collinsville Candy Kitchen.[107]

At least four other businessmen would also end up at the scene of the lynching. Two of them published Collinsville's weekly newspapers. Both were present for the patriotic parading of the immigrant and the commotion at city hall. August Schimpff, fifty-three, was a former miner, but with a background as a printer he had purchased the *Advertiser* newspaper. James O. Monroe, twenty-nine, was relatively new to town, having purchased the *Herald* less than a year earlier. While Schimpff probably walked to the top of Bluff Hill, Monroe was taken there in the automobile of Louis Blumberg, thirty-three, the owner of the dry goods store Silverblooms. Also accompanying Monroe and Blumberg was Earle Bitzer, twenty-one, the manager of Bitzer Garage, his father's business. On a night when civic responsibility should have trumped journalistic integrity, Schimpff and Monroe, like the other businessmen, simply watched when the cruel affair turned into a lynching.

The police, merchants, workingmen, and others who failed to intercede all had a hand in sealing Robert Prager's fate that evening. The eighteenth-century English statesman Edmund Burke is widely credited with having said, "All that is necessary for the triumph of evil is that good men do nothing." In April 1918 it would be difficult to find a more appropriate illustration than the one provided on the streets of Collinsville.

As the excited men in the mob went to and fro uptown and out the St. Louis Road, German immigrants and those who had been criticized for being pro-German were justifiably concerned. Word of the mob spread rapidly to those who were awake and some who were not. For all they knew, the mob would be after them too. They stayed indoors and quiet, hoping that they were out of sight, and out of consideration, of any of the drunken men who might harass them. Nineteen-year-old Louis Johann, an employee at Bitzer Garage, took refuge in the closed rumble seat of a new car, fearing the mob was after everyone of German lineage in the city.[108]

After the reinvigorated mob left the uptown area with Prager, Mayor Siegel also feared it would try to harm other suspected pro-Germans in the city. During the East St. Louis riots the previous summer, Siegel had set up a vigilance committee of twenty leading citizens who agreed to help enforce the law in Collinsville should the need arise.[109] The mayor was especially concerned with protecting three or four people whose names were mentioned earlier at the fire station, but he was anxious about other prominent German families too. Ironically the armed vigilance committee members, who he hoped would be able to protect Collinsville residents, were contacted by phone by the police officers, now back from following the mob. After midnight about ten of the committee members appeared at city hall and were dispatched to protect the families that were believed to be at greatest risk. Phone service problems prevented them from reaching the other members of the committee. Siegel stayed at City Hall the remainder of the night, fearful that the mob would strike again but hoping that it had spent its fury.

• • •

By half past midnight on April 5, the mob atop Bluff Hill had finished the business that would shame Collinsville for generations to come. That Robert Prager would be the only German immigrant lynched in the United States during the Great War would make the event all the more ignominious.

Most witnesses left the lynching scene rattled by what they had just observed, some undoubtedly feeling the guilt of having made no effort to stop it. But the men most responsible for the murder congratulated one another on the effort. "We'll, I've done my part in putting one German out of the world," Riegel said. Another man in the group felt relief, knowing his actions that night might end the rumors and challenges that he was pro-German.[110] The men slowly made their way back uptown, about a thirty-minute walk.

As the men peeled away to go to their homes, the two-mile jaunt brought some clarity for Riegel. The thrill of leadership was beginning to wear off, as was the alcohol. It had been more than two hours since his last drink. He began to think that the whole affair had been imprudent, that he didn't even know the man whom he—more than anyone—had helped lynch, and he certainly wasn't aware of any harm Prager had done.

It was near 1:00 a.m. when Riegel, walking home on Main Street, saw the lights burning late at the *Herald* newspaper office. Inside editor J. O. Monroe was typing out what would be the biggest story of his journalism career for publication in the next day's newspaper.[111] The lighted office reminded Riegel that he had Prager's last note in his coat pocket. He didn't really know how to get it to Germany or even Washington, for that matter.

"Here is a little ad for you," Riegel said as he entered and passed the note to Monroe.[112] The editor looked over the thirty-word message as Riegel watched. Monroe knew a little German, thanks to his immigrant mother-in-law, who lived with his young family, and he roughly translated the note while Riegel listened and confirmed that it was more or less what Prager had said about forty-five minutes ago.

Riegel continued on home, but he was restless and had trouble falling asleep. He told himself he had not done anything wrong and that he shouldn't feel guilty, but he conceded that the lynching was "kind of foolish, that was all."[113]

At about the same time, Madison County coroner Roy Lowe got a telephone call in Edwardsville reporting the incident. The case was his by about 350 feet, the distance of the lynching tree from the St. Clair County line to the south. Lowe ordered Collinsville undertaker Vincent Herr to remove the body, saying he would visit the city in the morning to begin the investigation. Herr called a local livery service and asked it to prepare a horse team and driver for the "dead wagon," as opposed to the ambulance used for those still on the earthly side. Herr went to the scene with the driver, and the undertaker used his five-inch Case pocketknife to cut down Robert Prager's body.[114]

1. Robert Prager, his name
apparently written on the
photograph he intended to send
to prospective mail-order brides.
Courtesy of the author.

2. Lumaghi Coal Company Mine No. 2 was one of five large mines operating in the Collinsville area in 1918. All told more than two thousand men worked as miners in the area, more than half the male workforce. Collinsville Historical Museum.

3. Men at Consolidated Mine No. 17 prepare to take the steam hoist into the mine. Collinsville Historical Museum.

4. U.S. Committee on Public
Information chairman George Creel.
Library of Congress.

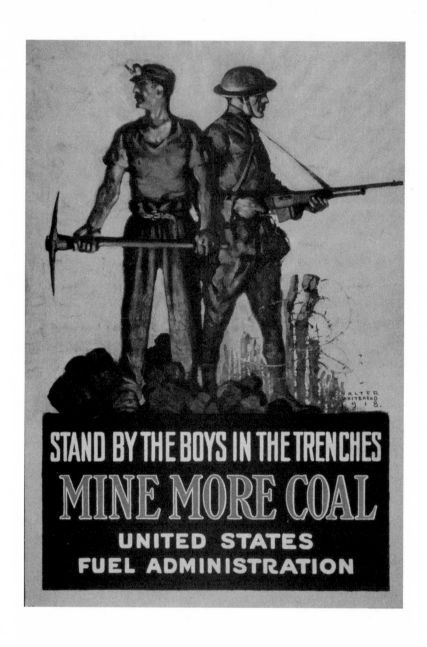

5. Posters were created that targeted
workers in all critical occupations.
Library of Congress.

ONLY THE NAVY CAN STOP THIS

6. Many CPI posters demonized Germans,
represented here in a likeness of Kaiser Wilhelm II
wielding his bloody sword over prostrate women
and children. Library of Congress.

7. (*opposite top*) Collinsville women of the Red Cross knitted clothing items, made comfort kits for soldiers, and turned linen into bandages. The group had over 1,800 members by late 1917. Collinsville Historical Museum.

8. (*opposite bottom*) Men working at the St. Louis Smelting and Refining Company in Collinsville. Blacks were hired to work at the smelter but were not allowed to work in the better-paying coal mines. Collinsville Historical Museum.

9. (*above*) The Collinsville works of the St. Louis Smelting and Refining Company, where a unionization battle in 1917 handed Collinsville coal miners one of their few defeats. The managers' homes appear in the upper right corner. Collinsville Historical Museum.

10. Madison County sheriff Jenkin Jenkins,
a former Collinsville coal miner turned
politician. *Edwardsville Intelligencer*.

11. The federal government blamed most
Great War–era labor strife on German
sympathizers. Library of Congress.

Collinsville, Illinois, December 29, 1917

AMERICAN DEFENSE SOCIETY WARNING.

Every German or Austrian in the United States, unless known by years of association to be absolutely loyal, should be treated as a potential spy.

Be on the alert. Keep your eyes and ears open. Take nothing for granted. Energy and alertness may save the life of your son, your husband or your brother.

The enemy is engaged in making war upon this country, in transmitting news to Berlin and in spreading peace propaganda as well as lies about the condition and morale of American military forces.

Whenever any suspicious act or disloyal word comes to your notice communicate at once with the police department or with the local office of the Department of Justice.

Police Headquarters,
Telephone Kinloch 162; Bell 100.

12. A notice in the *Collinsville Advertiser* from December 1917 warns residents to remain leery of Germans and Austrians. *Collinsville Advertiser*.

13. CPI posters directed at new immigrants
urged them to show their patriotism by
purchasing war bonds. Library of Congress.

14. A *St. Louis Post-Dispatch* cartoon depicting Kaiser Wilhelm II and Uncle Sam from March 30, 1918, six days before the lynching. *St. Louis Post-Dispatch.*

"VARE ISS THE NEAREST MUNITION FACTORY?"

15. The ABC Bar at Main and Center Streets and owner William Horstman, one of at least nineteen saloons in uptown Collinsville in 1918. Collinsville Historical Museum.

16. Main Street near Center Street in Collinsville, an intersection that would be jammed with a mob of more than two hundred drunken men before Robert Prager was taken from city hall late on April 4, 1918. Collinsville Historical Museum.

WATER TOWER, FIRE DEPT. AND CITY HALL COLLINSVILLE ILL. H H.BREGSTONE ST LOUIS

17. Collinsville's city hall and fire station. Courtesy of the author.

18. Collinsville mayor J. H. Siegel.
City of Collinsville.

Robert Paul Prager
Father
Carl Henry Prager
York Street
Tresten
Germany

Linbe Eltern!
Ich mus heute den 4-4-18
sterben bitte betet füvems
mine leiben Eltern
das ist mein letzter Brief
oder lebenzeiqen von miier
Eun leiber Sohn
und Bruder
Robt Paul

19. Dear Parents! I must this day 4-4-18 die. Please pray for us, my dear parents. That is my last letter or sign of life of mine. Your dear son and brother, Robert Paul. *St. Louis Star*. Translated by Carmen Freeman.

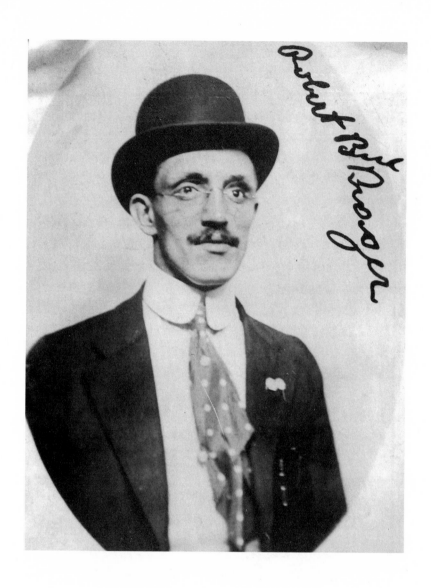

20. Robert Prager.
St. Louis Post-Dispatch.

German Whom Mob Hanged and Tree That Was Used

21. The hanging tree atop Bluff Hill as it appeared the morning after the lynching. It was removed to make way for power lines in 1962. The land is now part of St. John Cemetery. *St. Louis Star.*

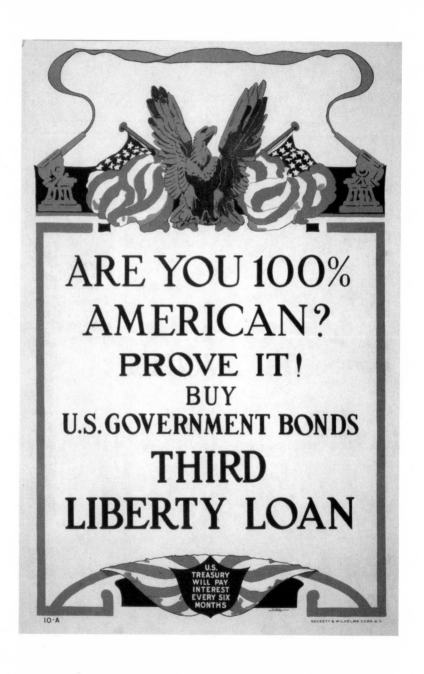

22. The third Liberty Loan campaign officially began one day after Prager's lynching, and in Collinsville suspected pro-Germans were challenged on the street about whether they had bought war bonds. Library of Congress.

23. *Collinsville Herald* editor and publisher J. O. Monroe and one of his sons at the newspaper office. Collinsville Historical Museum.

SLACKER!

Thousands of you who read this page have been filled with loathing and contempt for those shirkers and cowards to whom we apply the epithet, *"slacker."*

But there are *others*, in addition to those who are too cowardly to shoulder a gun, to whom that term of black disgrace applies.

Any man or woman in this town---I don't care whether that man or woman is rich or poor---who does not take all the Liberty Bonds that he or she possibly can, *is in exactly the same class with those wretched creatures of feeble brain and feeble spine, those cowards we call "SLACKERS."*

The Right Hand of Patriotism

The advertising for the Third Liberty Loan in this city has been made possible through the patriotism of the following firms, who have generously contributed the space in which the advertising will appear:

Alligator Oil Clothing Company.
American Bakery Company.
Anheuser-Busch.
Brauls Bros. Bag Company.
Brown Shoe Company, Inc.
Campbell Glass & Paint Company.
Central States Life Insurance Company.
Certainteed Products Corporation.
Charter Oak Stove & Range Company.
Chase Bag Company.
Wm. H. Cumpton Company.
Elsenstadt Manufacturing Company.
Ely & Walker Dry Goods Company.
Famous & Barr Company.
Garland's.
Hettig Statler, Inc.
Hydraulic Press Brick Company.
International Fur Exchange.
International Shoe Company.
Kinloch Telephone Company.
Kline's.
Laclede-Christy Clay Products Company
Laclede Steel Company.
Lesser Goldman Cotton Company.
Levis-Zukoski Mercantile Company.
The A. H. Lewis Medicine Company.
Liggett & Myers Tobacco Company.
McKinley-Sloan Shoe Company.
McKay-Norris Shoe Company.
Missouri State Life Insurance Company.
National Candy Company.
National Coin Lockers.
N. O. Nelson Manufacturing Company.
Nowell Motor Car Company.
R. Nugent & Bro. Dry Goods Company.
Paris Medicine Company.
Ralston-Purina Mills.
Rice-Stix Dry Goods Company.
St. Louis Brass Manufacturing Company
St. Louis Brewing Association.
St. Louis Clearing House and Associated Banks.
St. Louis Globe-Democrat.
St. Louis Post-Dispatch.
St. Louis Republic.
St. Louis Star.
St. Louis Times.
Scruggs-Vandervoort-Barney Dry Goods Company.
Shapleigh Hardware Company.
Smith, Myers & Company.
Stannard's.
Southwestern Bell Telephone Company.
Mark C. Steinberg & Co.
Wm. Barr & Fuller Dry Goods Company.
Cupples-Smith Soda Company.
Wagner Electric Manufacturing Company.

Such a man or woman isn't worthy to *blacken the shoes* of an American soldier who goes across to give his life on the blood-soaked soil of France.

Such men and women, no matter whether they live in cottages or mansions, are not *fit to associate with REAL AMERICANS.* Such men and women are not fit to live in this community, or *anywhere else in America.* They are not fit to *live at all.*

For such men and women are perfectly satisfied to continue their selfish pleasures and go along in their selfish, narrow ruts, while the *best young men in America* go across the sea to place their bodies as a barrier of human flesh and blood between us and our enemies.

Such men and women are *yellow to the core.* By neglecting to take all the Liberty Bonds they can, they're helping the Kaiser, they're *making the war last longer,* they're helping to drive *cold bayonet steel into American soldiers'* breasts.

If you can't pay cash for your bonds, you can borrow a part of the money at your bank, using the bonds as security; or, you can buy them at your bank on easy partial payment plan. It is no trouble to buy Liberty Bonds---it is no trouble to pay for them. See your banker today.

24. This advertisement to promote the purchase of war bonds ran in both the *Collinsville Herald* and the *St. Louis Times* in April 1918, with the cost underwritten by local businesses. The tone and tenor of the ad reflect the intolerant mood of the era. *St. Louis Times.*

25. The defendants from top row left: William Brockmeier, Joe Riegel, John Hallworth, Charles Cranmer, Richard Dukes Jr., and their single guard, Deputy Sheriff Vernon Coons. Front row: Wesley Beaver, Frank Flannery, Cecil Larremore, James DeMatties, Enid Elmore, and Calvin Gilmore. *St. Louis Post-Dispatch*.

The Eleven Defendants in Prager Lynching Trial and Their Custodian

Top row, left to right: William Brockmeier, Joseph Riegel, confessed leader of the mob; John L. Hallsworth, Charles Cranmer, Richard Dukes Jr., Deputy Sheriff Vernon D. Coons.
Bottom row, left to right: Wesley Beaver, Frank Flannery, Cecil Larremore, James De Matties, Enid "Peanuts" Elmore, Calvin Gilmore.

26. The same photograph as it appeared in the May 15, 1918, *St. Louis Post-Dispatch*, with flags cut from the picture. *St. Louis Post-Dispatch*.

27. Madison County state's attorney Joseph Streuber. *Edwardsville Intelligencer*.

28. Illinois assistant attorney general C. W. Middlekauff, who assisted State's Attorney Streuber with the prosecution. Library of Congress.

29. Judge Louis Bernreuter.
Edwardsville Intelligencer.

30. Defense attorneys
James Bandy, his son
Harold Bandy, and
Thomas Williamson.
St. Louis Times.

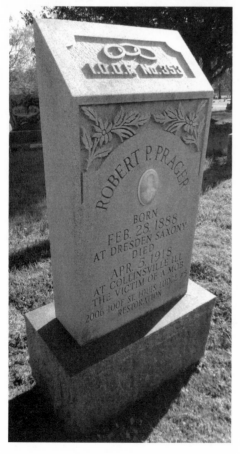

31. During the last week of the trial, ninety-seven "selected" Collinsville men would depart for army training, including this group of nineteen posing with draft board member C. H. Maurer, top right, on May 29, 1918. Collinsville Historical Museum.

32. Robert Prager's headstone in St. Matthew Cemetery in St. Louis. It was replaced in 2006 by St. Louis Odd Fellows. Courtesy of the author.

7

I Want to Tell and Get It off My Mind

Robert P. Prager Foully Murdered in Collinsville—This Crime Must Not Go Unpunished—
Get the Guilty Men—Let No Guilty Man Escape—The Fair Name of Illinois Has Been Dragged into Disgrace

—*Belleville News-Democrat* editorial headline, April 5, 1918

When daylight broke in Collinsville and people started moving about on Friday, April 5, 1918, there was little indication of the chaos that had reigned in the city just six hours earlier. Few knew of the lynching upon waking, but word spread like wildfire.[1] When businesses opened, those involved in the lynching, witnesses, and others spoke candidly of what they had seen, heard, or done. No effort was made early in the day to conceal anyone's identity. One observer noted that people were discussing the hanging "as though it had been a picnic."[2]

As the lynching had occurred outside the city limits, the Collinsville police would have no part in the investigation. Madison County coroner Roy Lowe arrived from Edwardsville and met with county sheriff Jenkin Jenkins. They spoke with city officials and other witnesses of the events of the prior sixteen hours. By Illinois statute the coroner was compelled to investigate every death. Lowe, at thirty-two years old the county's youngest-ever coroner, had been elected two years prior and was aggressive and determined to see justice done. Before coming to Collinsville that morning, he had conferred with Madison County state's attorney Joseph Streuber and then by telephone with Illinois attorney general Edward Brundage. Sheriff Jenkins's involvement in the investigation seemed minimal, which was good given his close ties with Collinsville's miners.

Many knew nothing of the incident until reading the first news account in the *Collinsville Herald*. Publisher J. O. Monroe had been up until 4:00 a.m. finishing the stories for inclusion in the regular weekly edition, published on Fridays. Monroe wrote what he had witnessed and heard, stark and raw with all the dramatic details. And he wanted the story to be accurate, knowing it would be picked up by the "news wires of the world." Years later Monroe said that this first story was "free from the reactions, the intimidations, the dissembling and the revisions of stories rationalized later."[3] People would rush to buy an extra edition the *Herald* printed later that evening, which included the day's events.

The lynching was quickly denounced by State's Attorney Streuber, who called it a disgrace. "Public acts and utterances disloyal to the American flag are as vicious and atrocious a crime as the acts of persons who form a mob and take human life. One is treason, the other is murder. The penalty is the same for both. This is a moment when loyalty and law alike must be supreme, and loyalty does not require lawlessness."[4]

Sheriff Jenkins and Coroner Lowe searched Prager's shack, and Lowe quickly announced they had found nothing to indicate that the victim was disloyal in any way, nor had he been hoarding powder to blow up the mine. Newspapermen, arriving from St. Louis and places all over the Midwest, then took it upon themselves to conduct their own search of the home and found Prager had hung three American flags on the walls.[5] He also had pictures of American battleships and maps, the type of items sought by a military enthusiast but of no value to any spy or agent. At least one report later surfaced that investigators also found Liberty Bonds that Prager purchased, but no official statement was ever made to that effect.[6] One letter to Prager said that the U.S. Navy was seeking bakers, the sender apparently unaware that Prager had previously been rejected for service.

The newspapers did note the significant amount of mail Prager received or intended to mail. Most were letters, in both English and German, for matrimonial advertisements found in magazines. One reporter said the letters showed that Prager had a good command of written English and was "quite intelligent." They painted a picture of a lonely man, desperately seeking someone to become his wife. In one letter he told of living in the extreme northwest, where there were few women, and said he moved back to the central states to find a wife. He said he made $25 a week as a baker, had "means of his own," and was a man of high character. Prager had received a number of replies to his letters. Along with the letters, the newsmen found two different photographs of Prager with his name written on each, apparently so respondents could keep their prospective suitors straight. Those two photos provide the only known visual depictions of the lynching victim.[7]

Herald publisher Monroe had a field day with some of the letters. After the other newspapermen had gone over those in English, Monroe took the letters in German for translation. Some letters discuss the initiation of two friends of Prager into some type of organization, presumably a lodge or club. The writer also discusses Prager bringing a St. Louis man some Collinsville "chickens," presumably girls. The letter implied that Prager should not bring the man such young women and that his coworkers thought someone as old as he should not be with girls that young. The writer said that Prager should bring him "a nice fat hen" next time.[8]

Monroe said the letters "may have been references to perfectly innocent lodge ceremony or may have been other allusions to hidden practices of the vilest sort." The editor further stated that if Prager went out with young girls and took them to friends and wrote letters to women he had not met, "it would look as if he might have been immoral possibly to the extent of being in regular business in young womenhood" and "white slave trade." Monroe's active imagination regarding Prager's social life reflected the efforts by the local publishers to sully the victim's reputation, in an apparent attempt to somehow rationalize the lynching.[9] They were alone in their efforts, however, as other newspapers continued to criticize the feeble motivations for the hanging.

Those closest to Prager were shocked to learn of his death. Tears rolled down the cheeks of roommate Battiste Vallissa as he talked to reporters, saying that Prager was loyal to the United States.[10] John Pohl, whom Prager had caused to be jailed in St. Louis, even rallied to his defense, as did his wife. "I became sick . . . as I read of his terrible end," Elizabeth Pohl said. "He always talked of his great love for this country." Lorenzo Bruno said he had never heard Prager make a disloyal remark.[11] His friends at the Odd Fellows lodges, in both St. Louis and Collinsville, said Prager was a loyal American. The St. Louis Harmonie Lodge 353 later passed a resolution condemning the lynching; it said, "No man can stay an Odd Fellow in spirit and in fact unless he is and stays faithful to our country."[12]

Illinois governor Frank Lowden issued a statement condemning the lynching and threatened to declare martial law in Collinsville if local police could not preserve order. A day later in Rock Island, the governor spoke at length about the affair. "There is no place in all the world where news of this mob action at Collinsville, in this state—I say it with shame—will be so welcomed as at the court of Berlin," Lowden said. "Patriotism will not be permitted to be used as a cloak for crime in Illinois if I can help it."[13]

In East St. Louis on Friday, pieces of the half-inch manila lynching rope were eagerly sought as souvenirs. Left behind atop Bluff Hill by undertaker Vincent Herr, the rope had been retrieved from the tree and taken to East St. Louis, where police officers and others cut it up for mementos of the affair. One man was reported to have the entire noose portion.[14]

Collinsville officials were still on edge Friday about the safety of other residents who were suspected of being pro-German. At least three of the people who were named by the mob Thursday night left town on Friday.[15] A businessman was told, nonetheless, that three more men were going to be lynched by the mob.[16] Mayor Siegel continued to use his vigilance committee to help protect the city. "I have made very thorough preparations to prevent any further trouble. There are armed guards all around and anybody who starts anything won't last three minutes," the mayor said. It was reported that twenty-eight German aliens were registered with the Collinsville police, and some of them had also left town. One newspaper noted the high percentage of city residents who were foreign born and could not "speak English intelligently."[17]

Of German lineage or not, most Collinsville residents felt that the lynching was wrong, but they kept their opinions to themselves, not wanting to suffer the same fate. Yet many defended the mob's actions and criticized Prager based on what they had heard about him.[18] A. C. Gauen, president of the chamber of commerce, no doubt exaggerated when he said, "It is condemned from one end of town to the other, by 99 1/2 percent of the people. It was done by a bunch of roughnecks." He went further to try to displace the blame. "The fact is that it was due to outside influence. It started in Maryville. We don't have that kind of people here. Notwithstanding that there are many nationalities in Collinsville, there is remarkably little lawlessness. The police records show that."[19]

Whether simply coincidence or the result of a greater plan, membership cards printed by the state council of defense began to surface again in Collinsville that Friday. Ostensibly they were applications to join the scd Collinsville Neighborhood Committee, which had held its impassioned organizing meeting nine days earlier. Those signing the card pledged to "wage war against the military rulers of Germany to make the world safe for democracy and to aid in the successful prosecution of the war."[20] The prior week some residents had said that they felt the cards unnecessary to show their loyalty. But fewer than twelve hours after a mob had lynched Robert Prager, the cards served an additional purpose.

Groups of men with handfuls of loyalty cards swarmed the city, seeking the signatures of those they suspected of being pro-German or those who might cooperate with investigating authorities. The message was clear: Sign the card to show your loyalty—and your agreement not to assist in the investigation of the lynching. Many men were confronted on the streets and in businesses and compelled to sign the cards.

By midday rumors were rampant that arrests would soon be made. And they would have been, if Coroner Lowe had his way. He had heard five names repeatedly mentioned as having played active roles in the crime, at either city hall or the scene of the lynching. By law Lowe still had to conduct an inquest, but he thought the evidence compelling enough that those five should swiftly be taken off the streets. He sought out one of Collinsville's justices of the peace and asked that warrants be issued for the men.[21] But there were two problems with the request. The first was that in Illinois in 1918 justices of the peace could handle only minor criminal and civil cases and were not authorized to be in any way involved in felony proceedings. The second was that the justice approached by Lowe wanted no part in the lynching affair.

Why the justices of the peace didn't want to get involved became clearer after one of them, Adam Schroeppel, was surrounded by a crowd of men in Fulton's Y Saloon just after lunchtime and ordered to sign a loyalty card.[22] Schroeppel, sixty-eight, was native born and had lived his whole life in Collinsville, where he had raised thirteen children. He was first asked if he had purchased Liberty Bonds or Saving Stamps. Schroeppel said he had not but his children had. The men who surrounded him questioned his loyalty and said he was pro-German. He started to leave when he was held back and forced to sign a loyalty card. Schroeppel said he was "just a plain, ordinary old Dutchman" but loyal to the United States.

By 5:00 p.m. Friday Lowe had empaneled his coroner's jury, and it had viewed Prager's body. He also announced that the inquest and interviewing of witnesses would begin Monday at 10:00 a.m. at city hall. The jury would include a retiree and five businessmen, one of whom was a justice of the peace. Another would be J. O. Monroe, one of the newspaper publishers who had witnessed the lynching.

The loyalty cards blanketed the town on Saturday too, some distributed house by house.[23] A local council of defense officer denied the cards had any connection with the lynching, but he did note the upswing in the number of them distributed and turned in. Also on Saturday many men inexplicably marched up and down city streets carrying American flags, delivering a silent message of patriotic intimidation.[24]

There had been threats on the street Friday afternoon that another vigilance committee, this one composed of miners, would spring into action if any of the mob leaders were arrested and "rescue them from the hands of the law."[25] This news, coupled with Lowe getting no cooperation from the justice of the peace, prompted a second warning from Governor Lowden that he would send in the state militia and invoke martial law if any mob tried to "stay justice by intimidation."[26]

Assistance from the state would arrive Saturday, April 6, in the form of Assistant Attorney General William Trautmann and Colonel Claude Ryman of the Illinois National Guard. They had reached Edwardsville the prior evening and met with State's Attorney Streuber and Sheriff Jenkins. By 10:00 a.m. they were in Collinsville, where they met with local officials; they also assessed the situation in Maryville.[27] Trautmann, Ryman, Streuber, and Mayor Siegel would confer for an hour that afternoon before deciding that martial law would not be declared unless there was further trouble. Trautmann also conferred with Coroner Roy Lowe and announced that there would be no immediate arrests, at least until after the coroner's inquest was complete. The arrival of the state officials served to calm the community. The state also assigned undercover men to investigate, a task they would not entrust to local officers.

As the full story of the lynching was told, no agency was as roundly criticized as the Collinsville Police Department. Save for Officer Frost's initial rescue of Prager, there was little good to say about its efforts. The decision to only follow the mob out of the city limits looked nearly as bad as allowing Prager to be taken from the city hall basement in the first place. Most police officers in that era were political appointees with little professionalism and even less training. The four officers who had been on duty in Collinsville were former coal miners and no doubt knew many of the men in the mob. But the single most important reason for their inaction might have been the common belief at city hall that night that the mob intended only to tar and feather Prager—*to have a little fun with him.*[28] It would be criminal, yes, but decidedly less than murder. "I didn't think they intended to harm him," Mayor Siegel said. "But if the police had fired one shot into the crowd, the whole town would have been on top of them and the police would have been hanging around here too."[29]

Siegel's portrayal of the risk to police was overstated. No police weapon was ever drawn, and no one in the mob was believed to be armed. The officers had easy access to enough firepower to quell the insurrection but not enough resolve to use it. Frost later portrayed the mob as so crazed that it would have taken its anger out on others if not Prager. "I never saw men more bloodthirsty," Frost said. "I saw how enraged they were and feared they would sate their lust on someone, either an officer or some other citizen toward whom they might have felt animosity."[30] Police Chief Tony Staten used the same flawed logic when speaking with a reporter, no doubt to try to lessen the criticism. "In one way, I believe it is a good thing they got Prager. If he had been spirited away by the police I believe the mob would have vented its rage by hanging two or three Collinsville persons who have been suspected of disloyalty."[31]

The editor of the *Belleville News-Democrat*, Fred Kern, would take Staten to task for the comments. "He puts it on the ground that Prager was a kind of vicarious sacrifice," Kern said in an editorial. "Brave Chief? Big Chief? Mighty Chief?" Kern wrote, "Let them rob and loot the store in order that they let the bank alone. There's some philosophy for you. It takes a wise head indeed to think that out."[32]

Chief Staten got his information about the incident secondhand, for he apparently had never bothered to appear at the police station during the anarchy, and no one had bothered to call him either, although he lived just six blocks away.[33] He had been in telephone contact with Frost earlier but apparently played no role, and provided no leadership, in handling the incident that evening. He finally went to city hall after Prager had been taken away but, like his officers, would not go to the lynching scene.

The heavy involvement of coal miners in Prager's demise also prompted UMW state board member Mose Johnson and Local 1802 president James Fornero to issue a statement that Prager was indeed a spy.[34] They claimed that the miners had been investigating the immigrant for some time and he was someone who would harm the mining industry. They said that Prager told others Germany was fighting for a righteous cause and the United States went out of its way to join the war. The union men also spelled out the measures they had taken to have Prager arrested or placed in protective custody.

Mayor Siegel took the time Friday to telegram U.S. senator Lee Overman, chair of the Senate Judiciary Committee, asking for tougher federal disloyalty legislation. He told Overman that the lynching of Prager "was the direct result of a widespread feeling in this community that the government will not punish disloyalty and, although I deprecate the existence of this feeling, it is nevertheless not without some foundation." The mayor said numerous complaints had been made about disloyal persons in the city, but that no action had been taken by the federal government, perhaps due to the inadequacy of current laws.[35] The Prager case would become one of the reasons cited for passage of the Sedition Act, which became law in May 1918 and effectively made 1917's Treason Act even more oppressive.

In discussing the Sedition Bill the following week, Senator Lawrence Sherman, fifty-nine years old and cranky, unloaded on Collinsville, never mind that it was in his home state. He said the hanging was not justification for the Sedition Bill, but that the drunken miners who did the lynching were simply murderers who should themselves hang.[36] Sherman said Siegel's telegram to Overman was a disgrace to Collinsville and "an indication of abject cowardice and stamp[ed] him as a poltroon in office and a renegade in public life." He charged that the mayor "did not lift his hand" to stop the mob. "Evidently the mob was filled with the patriotism which made St. Louis famous," he said. "Evidently it came from a brewery or Peoria." Sherman castigated the Collinsville police for their performance and also warned that elected officials must not kowtow to union labor. "The thing that is necessary is that we elect sheriffs and mayors who will enforce the laws," Sherman said in the Senate chamber.[37]

Two miles away at 1600 Pennsylvania Avenue, there was official silence on the Prager affair. The cabinet had discussed the matter Friday afternoon after the U.S. attorney from East St. Louis alerted Attorney General Thomas Gregory. Cabinet members described it as a "deplorable incident," and likewise used it to call for passage of the Sedition Bill.[38] President Wilson had been concerned enough about vigilante mobs in November 1917 to remark that any man who joined a mob and took the law into his own hands was "not worthy of the free institutions of the United States." Yet when that very thing happened five months later in Collinsville, Wilson would not utter one word of condemnation. Two former presidents, Teddy Roosevelt and William Howard Taft, did condemn the mob action, however.[39]

Condemnation was also swift in coming from the editorial writers of the nation's newspapers and magazines. Most placed some blame on the lack of stronger disloyalty laws, as did the *Adrian (MI) Telegram*: "The body of a poor fool hanging on a tree and a dark spot of blood-guilt on the State of Illinois are the first fruits of our imbecile policy toward disloyalists." Others cited fear of what the German army would do to captured U.S. soldiers. The *New York Sun* said it was preposterous to blame the lynching on the lack of better sedition laws: "He was lynched because the State of Illinois, the County of Madison, and the Town of Collinsville failed to provide the protection it is their duty to furnish to every citizen, honest or dishonest, well behaved or criminal." Along those lines, the *Albany (NY) Knickerbocker Press* said one honest, determined officer is a match for any mob, and "where lynchings happen it is because the officers of the law are whiter-livered curs than the crowd they ought to suppress."[40]

A handful of papers, including the *Washington Post*, took the opposite wartime view: "It is a healthful and wholesome awakening in the interior part of the country. Enemy propaganda must be stopped, even if a few lynchings may occur."[41] The *Post* had weighed in earlier when Overman suggested that a myriad of German operatives were at work in America: "The more one ponders Senator Overman's estimate of 400,000 German spies, the harder it is to grow righteously indignant over the Illinois lynching."[42]

The *New Republic* magazine attacked the 1918 American mindset, which seemingly turned its back on the lynching of blacks and those in Collinsville who failed to stand up for Prager's rights, saying the lynching occurred "while the more decent members of the community expostulated mildly or averted their eyes." For the United States to be regarded as a "clean and honorable nation," men had to be strong enough to act, the magazine said. "If there were in the community men with any sense of humanity and fair play and courage to take personal risks in the defense of the weak, the silence of the press does them grave injustice."[43]

The *St. Louis Argus*, a weekly "published in the interest of colored people," also queried why the daily papers were suddenly in an uproar about lynching in an editorial under the heading, "Depends on Whose Ox Is Gored."[44] Editors of the *Westliche Post*, St. Louis's German-language daily newspaper, urged calm in the German community but feared where such violence could lead: "The hanging in Collinsville the day before the anniversary of the war should open the eyes of anyone to the disaster which threatens this country when blind racial hate gains the upper hand. . . . What happened yesterday to the [blacks] and happens today to the Germans will happen tomorrow to someone else. The mob, once incited, does not discriminate."[45]

Perhaps one of the most impassioned editorials was written by Kern of the *Belleville News-Democrat*. Kern had fifteen years earlier seen a black man lynched while serving as mayor of that city, twelve miles south of Collinsville.

Mobs are always brutal, always cowardly, always fiendish, never fair, never just, never decent, and seldom sober and never honorable. As a rule they are soaked with whiskey from the soles of their feet to the crowns of their wooden heads. Besides that, patriotism is oftentimes the last resort of scoundrels. They use it to

get even with somebody, to vent their spleen, to get their enemies, or to take advantage of those they dislike for some reason
or other. They only too often get the wrong fellow. They are the
invention of the very devil, and are entirely out of place and keeping on American soil.[46]

When the story of Prager's lynching in Illinois was reported
in the *Collinsville (OK) Star*, it was displayed under the headline
"Warning." It no doubt proved inspirational to the men in that
region, some of whom were about as intolerant as the coal miners in southern Illinois. The men in Collinsville, Oklahoma, were
agitated with a Mennonite Brethren farmer who they felt did not
support the war. Not to be outdone by Collinsvillians two states
to the east, they took Henry Reimer from a jail cell on April 19
and first made him kiss all forty-eight stars on the flag. A mob of
fifty had nearly hung Reimer from a basketball goal until a cou-
rageous assistant chief of police grabbed his swinging body after
he had passed out. In Oklahoma, as elsewhere, the Mennonites'
war opposition was based purely on religious pacifism, not support of Germany or lack of support for the United States.[47]

Back in Illinois undertaker Vincent Herr was still waiting on
Saturday for Prager's body to be claimed by family or friends.
The wait would be yet another reminder of how alone Prager
was in the United States. Herr had found a lapel pin on his jacket
from the Independent Order of Odd Fellows. In Prager's pockets
Herr had found a small notebook and a copy of his proclamation
to the members of Local 1802. The notebook contained a message to contact a Mrs. McAichion in Chattanooga, Tennessee,
in case of an accident.[48] Herr had attempted to do so but learned
she rejected the telegram, perhaps after reading the nationwide
headlines about the Collinsville lynching and wanting no connection to it.

The city's morbid curiosity of the affair exceeded its desire to
provide any eternal resting place for Prager's body.[49] Herr was
besieged with requests to see the corpse and obliged by putting
it on display Friday for the public, at a time when wakes were

typically conducted at a family home. A long line formed along the 300 block of East Main Street as people flocked to view the body. A thirteen-year-old schoolboy joined the line of curious spectators as it slowly moved inside. He had heard to look on the neck for red, white, and blue marks left by the hanging rope but reported seeing no such discoloration.[50] The display was mercifully ended after the Harmonie Independent Order of Odd Fellows (IOOF) Lodge 353 agreed to pay for Prager's funeral and sent a carriage from a St. Louis undertaker at noon Sunday, but not before thousands of Collinsville residents had viewed the body.

The events of the preceding seventy-two hours no doubt played a major part in the Holy Cross Lutheran Church deciding to purchase two $100 Liberty Bonds in a congregational vote April 7, so that it might show the strong patriotism of the Germans in its congregation.[51] Every church in Collinsville, save for one, allowed Liberty Loan Committee speakers to participate in services and seek individual support for the bond drive. In fact many in the predominantly German congregation at Holy Cross had already made large war bond purchases. Over the course of five bond drives, members would purchase $35,000 in Liberty Bonds.[52] What was most unusual—perhaps unheard of—was that the church itself would buy the two bonds, as if it were purchasing a form of protection for its congregation. And the measure was approved one week before the Liberty Loan speaker was even scheduled to make his appeal before them. At a time when Jehovah's Witnesses, Mennonites, and other Christian church leaders were being scorned or jailed for their opposition to the conflict, Collinsville's largest Lutheran church voted to directly help fund the war effort.

Trautmann, of the attorney general's office, would stay in town to provide badly needed assistance to Lowe at the coroner's inquest, and his first recommendation would jolt the community. Trautmann suggested the inquest be closed to the public so that witnesses would speak freely and the impact of intimidation might be minimized, and Lowe agreed. Trautmann, raised just outside Collinsville on a farm that bordered Consolidated Mine No. 17, knew the area and the people, and he felt it was the best chance of bringing charges. "From all I hear and read, there must have been plenty of men nearby who could not have failed to see the actual act," Trautmann said. He reminded reporters of the governor's determination to see prosecution. "The State will spend every dollar it has to bring the guilty ones to justice."[53]

The closed inquest didn't sit well with the crowd of two hundred that had collected on the city hall lawn waiting to get in Monday morning.[54] Even Mayor Siegel thought it a bad idea because he believed city residents wanted the facts made public. Others claimed there would be a whitewash by county authorities. Most indignant at being left out of the preceding was UMW board member Mose Johnson, who seemingly tried to incite the various disgruntled groups on the city hall lawn after the decision was announced.[55] City police, county deputies, and five deputy coroners provided security.

Closing the inquest would also exclude the press, with the exception of the *Herald*'s Monroe, who was on the coroner's jury. Reporters were invited to sit in on the sessions if they agreed to print nothing of the testimony; as a group they declined.[56] Allowed to sit in as a courtesy were Mayor Siegel and Postmaster James Simpson, serving as a representative of the federal government. Madison County state's attorney Streuber was also on hand for Monday's proceedings. The three days of the inquest provided the apogee in honest testimony about what actually happened the night of April 4 and the first minutes of April 5, and the coroner's jury was impressed with the candor of most of the witnesses. "Hardly a thing which transpired was kept hidden from the jury," Monroe said. "There undoubtedly would have been more reservation had there been a crowd present."[57]

Seven public officials testified Monday. The inquest then recessed until Wednesday morning due to a Tuesday trial in Edwardsville that required the attendance of both Lowe and Streuber. The police did little to improve their image at the inquest on Monday. When asked why he did not try to learn the names of those in the mob, one officer said he was waiting for orders.

Patrolman Frost, twenty-eight, a lifelong resident of the city and a policeman for three years, said he could identify only one man in the mob. Perhaps he recognized some faces, he added, but he didn't know the men's names. "Then you don't know anyone in town," Trautmann said. Asked why the police did not immediately follow when they learned that Prager had been taken from the basement, Frost said he had to stop and answer a ringing telephone because he thought the caller might be the chief. He also acknowledged several missed opportunities for the officers to get Prager out of town, or at least more convincingly make the mob believe that Prager had been taken away. Asked pointedly by Trautmann if the officers had been content with just following the mob and not helping Prager, Frost said: "No, you've got the wrong idea about that. We tried to catch up with them and couldn't."[58]

The second meeting of the Collinsville Neighborhood of the Illinois Council of Defense at the Orpheum Theater was held the night of Tuesday, April 9. Mayor Siegel told the packed house of four hundred that the mob would have gotten to Prager only "over [his] dead body" had he known the immigrant was actually still inside the building.[59] The key speaker that evening was Ben Weidel, the grand master of the Missouri Odd Fellows. He spoke of the unfairness of mobs and encouraged going to authorities to report disloyal remarks and then having the courage to testify at trial. Weidel said the focus of most patriotic parades of pro-Germans was wrong, that the U.S. flag was too good to be kissed by disloyalists. And the only hangings, Weidel said, should be in jail yards.

When the inquest resumed Wednesday, it was a time for the suspected mob leaders to tell their story, and no one seemed more forthright than Joe Riegel. Led by a guilty conscience, and certainly not any legal advice, he spoke for more than an hour and calmly laid out the evening as he remembered it. He said that he had no malice toward Prager and thoughtfully worked his way through what was a chaotic night, rubbing his head and puffing on a cigarette. He had a "shamed smile" on his face, but editor

Monroe noted that the confession was "without taint of criminal intent."[60] He laid his newsboy cap on the floor and leaned back in the chair as he spoke to the jurors in the city council chambers.

Whether purposely leaving out incriminating details or because he truly did not remember, Riegel said he was not sure who placed the noose on Prager's neck or the rope over the tree limb. He acknowledged that he was very drunk and tended to do whatever the crowd directed. He carefully thought before providing the names of at least six participants in the actual hanging. "I want to tell you officers all I know, but I don't want to complicate [*sic*] anybody in it I'm not sure of." Monroe said it seemed Riegel may have been in a drunken daze throughout the ordeal: "Listening to him, one was led to believe that if he had been asked to climb the tree he would have done it without question and would have adjusted the noose with the same automatic response. Had he been hypnotized he could not have responded more readily to immediate suggestion of circumstances. Had he not been so frank and honest through it all, one would have called it cold-blooded, so void was it of emotion of any sort."[61]

Riegel's remarkable candor caused Trautmann to warn the witness several times that statements he made could be used against him in court. "Well I don't care," Riegel said. "When I got home that night I got to thinking about how I helped kill that fellow who never did anything to me, and who I didn't even know, and I couldn't sleep. I want to tell and get it off my mind. I'm ready to take my medicine."[62]

The closed inquest, which had caused so much resentment Monday morning, ended up getting such heavy coverage in the newspapers that most observers believed a reporter, or perhaps several, had been able to sneak their way into the ventilation system of city hall and hear all the testimony they wanted.[63] Both the *St. Louis Star* and the *Collinsville Herald* ran nearly identical accounts of Riegel's confession.[64]

As if that were not enough, Riegel gave a full confession to reporter Paul Anderson of the *St. Louis Post-Dispatch* on Wednesday at city hall before testifying at the inquest. It was essentially the same version that he gave the coroner's jury, but speaking to the reporter Riegel showed more bravado and levity. His army experience had made him a leader, he believed: "The crowd kind of made me the big man in it and I was kind of swelled up about that." Riegel said Prager would not have been harmed if he had been found locked in a cell, stating, "It made us sore that the police had sneaked him away." He also implicated others: "I know lots of them that did pull [on the rope] and I will give their names to the Coroner. If I've done any wrong I am willing to take my punishment. If they convict me and send me up it will be alright, but I would rather serve my term in the Army."[65] Riegel's first confession to Anderson was on the street in the *Post*'s city and final editions not long after he had concluded his late afternoon session with the coroner's jury.

"If I had not been drunk, I would not have done what I did. Many of the other men in the mob were drunk too. I do not believe any sober men helped lynch Prager, but many young boys joined in who were not drunk. They got into the crowd and yelled and helped for the fun of the thing. The police could have stopped us if they would have wanted to," Riegel told Anderson in his first confession.[66]

It was a great scoop for Anderson, already an experienced and respected reporter at age twenty-four. Distinguished and fearless, his reporting of the East St. Louis riots had earned acclaim from a U.S. House committee that investigated the incident. With neat, center-parted hair and a well-trimmed pyramidal mustache, he would have fit as well in a corporate boardroom or society function as he had in the cramped entryway where he interviewed the lynch-mob leader. A decade later he would win the Pulitzer Prize for his reporting work.

After Riegel testified to the coroner's jury, his embittered wife came looking for him at the police station, hoping to find her estranged husband in jail. Told that he was not under arrest, at least not yet, she went to Union Shoe Repair and gloated over his legal predicament. Riegel tried to placate her and asked her to live with him again, but Emma Riegel would have none of it. "I hope the —— hangs," she said to others in the shop. "If he doesn't, I'll hang him myself." Since her husband left several months ago, she had worked as a waitress in St. Louis.[67] The two had married three years prior, she at sixteen and he at twenty-four; now their two-year-old son was being raised by her mother.

Wesley Beaver, William Brockmeier, Richard Dukes, Enid Elmore, and other suspected mob members and witnesses also testified Wednesday about their actions at city hall; all denied being at the lynching scene. Some other witnesses were less open, denying seeing anyone or that they were anywhere near the mob, city hall, or the lynching scene. Their inability or unwillingness to provide information, although they had been identified by others as being present, made them appear "absolutely ridiculous" to the coroner's jury, Monroe said. "They would have made a far better impression had they admitted having some little part to do in the mob, but either their judgement or their advice had been too bad for that. Other witnesses tore their attempts at alibis to shreds."[68]

Miner's union state board member Mose Johnson testified before the jury that Prager was disloyal and a spy, but he was unable to produce any evidence to back up his claim. He gave the jury a written statement from the mine manager accusing Prager of asking suspicious questions. He also provided two bulletins sent from the Department of Labor in 1917 warning to be on the lookout for spies. "One man in a mine can kill 600," Johnson said. "That's why the miner is afraid of spies." For all the rumors and allegations that miners had spread about Prager, Johnson could produce no proof that he had done anything illegal or planned to in the future. Nevertheless, Johnson said he was convinced the victim was disloyal.[69]

The inquest was not without its lighter moments. Frank Hogge testified that he was so intoxicated when the bars closed he could remember little of who or what he saw. He thought the mayor was speaking at some form of political rally in front of city hall that Thursday night. "You know there's always somebody cutting up around Collinsville with some foolishness," Hogge said. Gus Palecek spoke of Wesley Beaver being in the mob. He was asked if the happy-go-lucky porter still worked at Fulton's Y Saloon. "They fired him Sunday," Palecek said, "but they do that every week." Beaver testified as to his near blindness. He said he could play cards only by holding them to his face. Someone asked if he played pinochle. "No, no, not pinochle," Beaver said, smiling and shaking his head.[70]

By Thursday afternoon the coroner's jury had heard enough. It deliberated for four hours before deciding that five men should be held over for the grand jury on the charge of murder. They were:

Joe Riegel, twenty-eight, for actions with the mob at city hall, including removing Prager from the building, and for his leadership at the lynching scene;

Wesley Beaver, twenty-six, for actions with the mob at city hall, including removing Prager from the building;

Richard Dukes, twenty-two, for actions with the mob at city hall;

William Brockmeier, forty-one, for actions with the mob at city hall; and

Enid Elmore, twenty-one, for actions with the mob at city hall.

Lowe issued the arrest warrants, and two sheriff's deputies rounded up the men and took them to the county jail. Beaver was easy to find, as he had been detained in the police chief's office most of the day. Riegel likewise hung around city hall all day of his own volition, ready to be arrested. Facing a capital murder charge, they would all be held without bond.[71]

The coroner's jury had interviewed thirty-three witnesses and was pleased with what it had learned about the lynching, despite the lack of cooperation from a handful. The jurors had heard the names of forty other people involved in the crime and believed it possible that the grand jury would indict another two dozen or more. As a coroner's jury, it only had the authority to approve warrants for murder. Charges related to mob activity would have to come from the grand jury. Following advice from prosecutors, the jurors applied Illinois's conspiracy statute, which stated that all participants in the mob could be found guilty of murder, regardless of whether they had assisted in the actual lynching.[72]

At the same hour Riegel was baring his soul at the inquest, Prager's funeral service was conducted before an overflow crowd at the William Schumacher Undertaking Company, not far from Prager's old St. Louis neighborhood. Floral arrangements covered the room. Just before the casket was closed, Odd Fellows officers from Harmonie Lodge 353 pinned a small flag on the breast of his jacket, as Prager had requested.[73] The casket was then covered with the Stars and Stripes. The service was described as "probably the strangest ever held in St. Louis," for Prager was the first German immigrant to be killed in such a manner.

Rev. W. S. Simon delivered a sermon that brought tears to the eyes of most of those in the parlor. "When Prager's mother will be told of the unlawful death of her son in this land of the free, what do you think will be her feelings? It is true that she is a German and lives in Germany, but whether she is a German, English or French, what of her mother's heart? Will it not break? Has her son received justice?" The Jesus Evangelical Church minister criticized mob action in the United States: "The spirit which resulted in the death of Prager is as far from democracy as is the Kaiser's government. It is destructive and not the true spirit of American government. That was a great victory for Germany. It was cruel and barbaric."[74] Prager was buried among other German immigrants in St. Matthew Cemetery in a remote plot purchased by the Odd Fellows, appropriately near St. Louis's Dutchtown South neighborhood, two miles west of the Mississippi River.

The $197 bill for the funeral would eventually be paid by the State of Illinois, "believing that the authorities of the state in which Prager was lynched would consider it their moral obligation to give him proper burial at their own expense." Previously the Swedish ambassador had offered to pay reasonable charges, perhaps acting on behalf of the German government, but the state declined the offer.[75]

Miners Local 1802 wasted no time in having a judicial proceeding of its own, dealing with the immigrant miners who had vouched for Prager's experience. Union leaders investigated and found nothing to indicate that Prager had ever been a member of any UMW local and had only twenty-eight days' experience working in a mine, all of that as a laborer at Donk Mine No. 2. The local conducted a trial April 14 for the three members who had signed as references for Prager. Joseph Robino, Paul Schrieber, and John Tonso were all found guilty and fined $50, the maximum penalty short of expulsion from the union—and the ultimate loss of their jobs.[76]

When the Madison County Grand Jury began hearing witnesses in the Prager case four days later, the proceedings at the courthouse in Edwardsville were actually confidential, as the law intended. As Assistant Attorney General Trautmann and State's Attorney Streuber brought witnesses before the fifteen-man panel, each from a different township in the county, the grand jury developed its own understanding of what happened. Only one of the incarcerated men would be among the thirty-seven witnesses, but twelve of the witnesses had appeared before the coroner's jury. On the first day of the grand jury session, some of the called witnesses went to visit the men in the county jail and reported them to be "cheerful and fairly content."[77] Based on what he had heard from Trautmann, Illinois attorney general Edward Brundage was confident of successful prosecution. The case was not about any pro-German sympathies, Brundage said, but concerned a union dispute at the mine. "Absolutely nothing was developed by the investigation to show that Prager was in any way unpatriotic," the attorney general said. "I am certain of the indictments and I am certain we will obtain convictions."[78]

Late in the afternoon of April 25, the grand jury returned indictments for murder against twelve men, including the five already in custody.[79] Sheriff's deputies Vernon Coons and Hannah Jokerst brought the arrest warrants to Collinsville just before noon the following day, when the city was again in the midst of whipping itself into another patriotic frenzy, this time in support of the third Liberty Bond sale. The parade had been planned for the week prior but was postponed due to almost continual rainy conditions. A half-day holiday had been declared, and all businesses, schools, and industries were closed.[80] It was reported as the city's largest parade ever. With seemingly every business, union, school, and group in the parade, more than 6,000 marched, with just 1,000 watching on the sidewalks. An estimated 2,500 of the marchers were miners. Red Cross workers wore nurse uniforms, while knitting-mill employees wore flag helmets. Many of the schoolchildren wore Uncle Sam or nurse costumes, and all of them sang patriotic songs. Nearly everyone waved a flag; stores were sold out of flags and red, white, and blue bunting.

Just before the parade stepped off at 2:15 p.m., the city's new service flag was raised over Main and Center Streets, the same intersection that twenty-three days prior had been filled with the drunken, singing mob that would take Robert Prager from city hall. On this afternoon the service flag would be raised with 277 stars for each Collinsville man serving his country and 3 circled stars for the men who had died thus far from disease.[81] At the intersection three cheers were proposed for the boys serving their country, then for President Wilson, and then for America, with the crowd roaring each time. After the parade people jammed into every available seat at the Orpheum for patriotic speeches and music.

As the festivities died down, deputies started looking for the other seven indicted men. They were:

Charles Cranmer, twenty, for actions at the lynching scene;

James DeMatties, eighteen, for actions at the lynching scene;

Frank Flannery, nineteen, for actions at the lynching scene;

Calvin Gilmore, forty-four, for being part of the mob on the St. Louis Road;

John Hallworth, forty-three, for being with the group of men who removed Prager from his home on Vandalia Street;

Cecil Larremore, seventeen, for actions at the lynching scene; and

George Davis, a man who would never be further identified or even located, for that matter.

None of the indictments was as surprising to the community as Hallworth's. He was mature and level headed and had walked home along St. Louis Road with Mose Johnson well before Prager was taken from city hall. Hallworth had watched from across the street when Prager was called from his home, but he later encouraged the mob to turn him over to police. Hallworth was a good citizen, active in the Liberty Bond Drives, and by some accounts held the local record for getting the most people to join the Red Cross.[82] Hallworth turned himself in at city hall after first confirming the charge by calling Chief Staten.

Taken in their totality, the indictments seemed scattershot. The actions of Beaver and Riegel at city hall were significant, but why were Brockmeier, Dukes, and Elmore the only men charged from a mob of three hundred? Why were Riegel, Cranmer, and Larremore the only men indicted of the perhaps two dozen or more who had their hands on Prager—and the rope—at the hanging tree? Why was Hallworth the only one indicted of dozens who went to the front of Prager's home, although he reportedly stood on the sidewalk across the street and watched? How were the others involved at all?

The indicted men were first brought to the police station and then taken en masse to Edwardsville. Families came to see them, bringing food and cigarettes. Patrick Flannery, a miner, went into Chief Staten's office to see his son, Frank. "What is the charge against you son?" he asked. Told it was murder, Flannery looked at his son and said, "That is the worst charge against the law, but I want you to tell the truth. If you lie you have to shift, and maybe you can't. I want you to tell the truth, even if it hurts me." The everpresent Mose Johnson was there too, surprised about the charges. Seven of those indicted were coal miners or had previously worked the mines. "This is not a miner's fight, but I will help give them bond," Johnson said. "I know by the Eternal Gods that one fellow is not guilty. I went home with him." But as with the others charged with murder, there would be no bond for any of the men. Defendant George Davis was not located that day and would remain at large until charges against him were eventually dismissed.[83]

Five of the eleven arrested men were married. Elmore had a wife and a young child, as did Riegel. Brockmeier and Gilmore had wives and four children each. Including Hallworth's wife and five children, the jailed men would leave behind twenty dependents, at least temporarily.

The grand jury indicted no one for mob violence, although an Illinois statute provided broad powers for dealing with such assemblies in 1918.[84] When five or more people assembled with the intent to form a mob bent on doing serious injury, the law set a fine of up to $1,000 and one year in jail upon conviction. The same statute allowed police to justifiably kill or injure even those in a small crowd if it failed to disperse upon command. The governor was authorized to immediately remove from office any county sheriff who allowed a mob to take a prisoner from custody and subsequently be lynched, but there was as yet no provision for removal of a city police chief.

The grand jury also indicted the four Collinsville police officers working that night for omission of duty and nonfeasance. The officers were accused of failing to stop or disperse the mob or make arrests, although they had seen Prager assaulted. Nor did the officers request or command any assistance in an effort to control the mob.[85] One of the officers, John Tobnick, had resigned and was working one of his last shifts as a police officer the night of the lynching. Not surprisingly Tobnick would become a miner. Fred Frost, Martin Futcheck, Harry Stephens, and Tobnick were each required to post $1,200 bond but were not jailed. The charge against the police officers carried a maximum fine of $10,000 and removal from office.

Chief Staten defended his officers' actions and doubted they would be convicted. Staten said he felt much of the criticism directed at Collinsville officials and officers was done to encourage officers elsewhere to suppress violence in their own jurisdictions.[86] The officers were allowed to work while on bond because Mayor Siegel felt that to remove the officers while charged would be tantamount to agreeing that they were guilty.[87]

The eleven men charged with murder were arraigned by Judge

John Gilham on May 2, and all pleaded not guilty. As they had been since their arrest, the men were confident and cheerful.[88] They talked and joked with a newspaper reporter while waiting to be returned to jail.

Governor Lowden cited the Collinsville affair in continuing his pressure on federal officials to provide more investigators. When the federal agent finally arrived in late April to help state investigators, it was claimed that Lowden had assembled in Illinois "one of the most far-reaching intelligence and espionage organizations to beat down sedition and prevent mob assaults upon pacifists, pro-Germans and Bolsheviks."[89]

8

A Farcical Patriotic Orgy

In times of war, the law falls silent.

—Cicero, *Pro Milone*

The trial began just thirty-eight days after Prager had been killed, unprecedented speed for such a complicated and sensational case. Never before had Madison County seen so many defendants on trial together on such a serious charge. The prosecution's challenge was daunting. By its very nature, lynching was a remarkably public crime, much of its worth intended to serve as a warning to those who dared challenge common beliefs or standards in the community. But as conspicuous as lynching was, charges against lynch mobs were remarkably rare, with convictions scarcer still. If the case did go to trial, the burden of finding members of the mob guilty would fall largely to people who may even have been in the crowd themselves. And discerning who was *most* guilty among scores of people in a mob usually proved yet another overwhelming task. All those challenges and more faced prosecutors in Madison County on the first day of the trial, May 13.

The eleven defendants' chairs stretched around the tables of both the defense council and the prosecution in Third Judicial Circuit judge Louis Bernreuter's courtroom the first day of the trial. The fifty-five-year-old Bernreuter was the best choice of circuit judges to hear the case as he was the only one who didn't live in the collar of Illinois communities east of St. Louis. His home was in Nashville, Illinois, some fifty miles east in Washington County. But Bernreuter had lived in Madison County the first nine years of his life. His father, a physician, was forced to move his practice there after he had shown sympathy to blacks in his hometown during the Civil War. His father's compassion didn't sit well with many of the town's residents who had relocated, along with their pro-slavery sentiment, from Nashville, Tennessee.

Bernreuter had worked in labor jobs and taught school before reading law and passing the bar in 1894.[1] By 1918 the balding but dignified jurist had served as a Third Circuit judge for fifteen years and would serve fifteen more before being voted out in the Democratic landslide of 1932. Principled and religious, Bernreuter was widely respected in Nashville and on the circuit. He and his wife, Wilhelmina, had raised a son and a daughter in Nashville, where he served as a Sunday school teacher for fifty years. For a hobby Bernreuter practiced his hand at drawing.

Save for Charles Cranmer, the defendants were all in high spirits, almost carefree, on the first day. Cranmer appeared somewhat nervous.[2] But they were all nicely dressed, as they would be throughout the trial, wearing suits, ties, and polished shoes. Sheriff Jenkins housed the accused men in rooms on the second floor of the county jail, not in the bleak, poorly ventilated cells with common prisoners.[3] And they were well fed, reportedly enjoying steak and other first-rate fare.

The men walked across the street from the county jail to the Courthouse each day without any handcuffs or shackles to restrain them. At times the eleven murder defendants were escorted by a single, indifferent sheriff's deputy. Each of the men wore a thick red, white, and blue ribbon pin on his left lapel, lest the judge or jurors wonder about their allegiance. They joked with bystanders and whistled on their way to court and bantered with spectators and newspapermen when Bernreuter was not in the courtroom.[4]

Regrettable or not the trial would provide Madison County a national stage to show off its pride-and-joy courthouse, under three years old at the time. The Classical Revival–style building of white Georgian marble dominated downtown Edwardsville, with grand double-door entrances on each of its four sides. A great skylight and chandeliers illuminated the open rotunda and the oak and wrought-iron balustrades and ornate cornices out-side the second- and third-floor courtrooms.

The day started off with UMW official Mose Johnson and others once again taking law enforcement into their own hands and bring-ing Gil Davis to the sheriff's office, believing him to be George Davis, the twelfth indicted man, who had yet to be located.[5] Davis, a former lead smelter worker, presumably went back home after being informed by the sheriff and the state's attorney that he wasn't the wanted man.

Once Bernreuter opened the trial at 9:00 a.m., the first order of business was a defense motion to quash the indictment of Cran-mer because he had been called as a witness before the grand jury, and his name had somehow been left off some indictment documents.[6] The prosecution argued that Cranmer was charged based on the testimony of others, not his own statements. It also stated that the lack of defendants' names on indictments was not an issue in cases following the riots in East St. Louis, which had resulted in more than forty convictions. After a delay of several hours, Bernreuter overruled the motion.

The longest phase of the trial began when prosecuting attor-neys started interviewing prospective jurors Monday afternoon and found that only three of the twenty-five had not already formed an opinion about the widely publicized case. And those three approved by the prosecution still had to pass muster with the defense, as jurors would be presented to the attorneys for the accused only in groups of four. In Madison County jurors were normally chosen from a jurors' box, but it became clear that the trial would quickly exhaust that resource.[7] Sheriff Jenkin Jenkins was ordered to bring in one hundred more prospective jurors after counsel from both sides saw the scope of their need.

Finding jurors who had not already formed an opinion was just one problem. Both the defense and the prosecution were allowed twenty peremptory challenges per defendant, allowing for up to 440 potential jurors to be disqualified with no reason whatsoever.[8] There was no limit on the number of talesmen who could be rejected for cause by either counsel. Alien immigrants were allowed to serve as long as they were county residents and understood English, but attorneys could dismiss any prospective juror who opposed the death penalty, was over sixty-five, or was caring for a disabled relative. The county's pool of eligible jurors was also already greatly reduced because miners and Collinsville residents were passed over and farmers generally were not chosen due to the crop-planting season.

About one hundred Collinsville residents attended the early days of the trial, including union leaders Mose Johnson and James Fornero. Some thirty area lawyers turned out the first day just to see the spectacle. Newspaper reporters, from both local and national publications, were out in full force. Also in the crowd were family members or friends of those charged. Fifteen women mingled with the defendants over the front rail, speaking of random matters back in town, laughing and joking.[9]

It was reported that the Odd Fellows organizations in Collinsville and St. Louis were watching the trial progress and were ready to prove that Prager was loyal to the United States, if needed. But there was no indication any IOOF members ever attended the trial.[10] With none of the victim's family or friends to watch the proceeding, the only people in the courtroom seeking justice for Robert Prager would be the attorneys seated at the prosecution table.

When proceedings kicked off the second day, the trial was moved to another, larger courtroom on the third floor where the defendants would not have to be lined up behind both the defense and the prosecution tables. The new courtroom allowed the eleven accused to sit in front of and behind the defense table with the most youthful and best-looking men, newspapers noted, now positioned in the front row and closest to jurors.[11]

One reporter was taken by the appearance of the defendants: "The men, most of them but youths, were listless and cared not to converse with one another when opportunity was offered. Yet their attitude betokened little worry and they left their chairs sprightly when court adjourned." He was struck by how young most of the accused appeared: "They are not of the type one sees in City Jail, but rather of the typical small-town pool hall loafer sort. Even so, it is hard to imagine from their appearances that they were the leaders of a drunken mob, as has been charged, which relentlessly dragged a man to his death. All looked well-dressed and wore linen collars."[12]

A photographer from the *St. Louis Post-Dispatch* asked the defendants if he might take their picture as they entered the courthouse on the second day. All agreed except Calvin Gilmore, who said he would be photographed only if he could hold an American flag in his hand.[13] The others joined in the request. Given the era the flags were not hard to come by and the accused were photographed on the steps of the courthouse, along with Deputy Vernon Coons, all dutifully hoisting twelve-inch flags.

But the flags were all cut out of the photo, no small feat in 1918, before it was printed in the next day's *Post-Dispatch*.[14] Editor and publisher Joseph Pulitzer II, perhaps in deference to his father's Hungarian lineage, would not help the defendants establish their patriotic defense on the front page of his newspaper.

The photo itself seems a study in dissimilarity, certainly not of a group you would expect to find together in public. The three older men were about twice the age of the six younger defendants. William Brockmeier, forty-one, and John Hallworth, forty-three, appeared hard-edged and all business in the back row. Calvin Gilmore, the oldest of the group at forty-four, looked cool and calm in the front. Wesley Beaver and Joe Riegel, twenty-six and twenty-eight respectively, blended easily with the younger men. Beaver was wide-eyed, as if in over his head, and Riegel's expression could almost be called a smirk.

The younger men ranged from the tall and rugged twenty-two-year-old Richard Dukes, with his fedora strategically cocked on his head, to the youngest, seventeen-year-old Cecil Larremore, whose youthful face showed no sign of tenderness. Charles Cranmer, twenty, and James DeMatties, eighteen, showed some concern for the gravity of the situation they had found themselves in. Enid Elmore, twenty-two, was baby-faced and seemed unaware, while Frank Flannery, nineteen, was clearly the shortest of the bunch, though his scowl and menacing stare did everything to belie that fact.

Leading the prosecution team would be Charles Middlekauff, the gray-haired, gruff and tough looking Illinois assistant attorney general who had some success in the prosecutions following the riots in East St. Louis. He was an 1891 graduate from the University of Michigan Law School and would later serve as a U.S. assistant attorney general. He lived with his wife and daughter in Freeport, near the Illinois border with Wisconsin.

Madison County's state's attorney Joseph Streuber, forty-six, would work alongside Middlekauff. Streuber, a Republican, had beaten lead defense counsel James Bandy, a Democrat, for the state's attorney position in the 1916 election after serving as probate judge and city attorney in his hometown of Highland. He presented as both upstanding and sincere, a man whom county voters would want as their top law enforcement officer. At age seventeen Streuber had begun studying law whenever he was not working at his father's sawmill or farm, and he passed the bar five years later.[15] He and his wife, Katherine, had a son, William, who at twenty years old was near the age of most of the defendants.

Given Sheriff Jenkins's cozy history with union men in general and miners in particular, it's hard to know what level of expectation the judge and prosecutors had before giving him the assignment of finding unbiased jurors. Perhaps it was of little surprise when the potential jurors he brought forth Tuesday were even more opinionated than those who had come before the court Monday; all were strongly inclined to support the defendants. On the third day of the trial, Middlekauff and Streuber filed a motion with Bernreuter to relieve Jenkins and his deputies from the job of finding and overseeing jurors.

The prosecuting attorneys unloaded on Sheriff Jenkins's performance since his election two years prior, saying he had "not exercised sound discretion" in performing his duties and that his office was negligent.[16] They said that the sheriff allowed sentenced prisoners to roam at large instead of being incarcerated in the county jail; that he had been fined $1,000 in federal court related to the Lead Works case; and that he regularly failed to properly subpoena witnesses and find adequate jurors. In the Prager case specifically, they said Jenkins had only brought fourth those who favored the defendants or had shown other prejudice benefiting the accused. It was further noted that one of Jenkins's deputies, Hannah Jokerst, was the uncle of defendant Richard Dukes.

After a session in the judge's chambers, Bernreuter agreed with the motion and stripped Jenkins of the duties of getting talesmen and providing security for chosen jurors. The judge said that he needed to appoint men of the "highest standing and ability" who could step in immediately to find potential jurors, despite other jobs or responsibilities they might have. For that inconvenience Bernreuter said that the special bailiffs should be paid $10 per day. So began a process of trying to find special bailiffs. Despite the pay the men most desirable for the job were generally too busy to want it. Sheriff Jenkins told a reporter he didn't mind being relieved of the juror duties. "I'm not a pro-German," Jenkins said. "If they want another officer it's all right with me."[17]

The court could have sought jurors from another Illinois county, but transportation being what it was in 1918, it would not have been very practical. The state was not permitted to ask for a change of venue, and it was about the last thing the defense wanted. Two of the prospective jurors were typical of those interviewed. Asked his feelings about German immigrants, an Alton resident with an Anglo surname said, "I am pretty much anti-German."[18] Later, when asked his feelings particularly about Prager, the man said, "I still think he [Prager] was pretty far from home." An Edwardsville clerk with a German surname was asked if he had formed an opinion on the case. "I think they are all guilty," he said.[19] The normally cool and considerate Bernreuter slammed his gavel down, causing many in the soporific courtroom to jump up straight in their chairs. The judge leaned forward from the raised wood-paneled bench and admonished the man for his gratuitous remark.

Also on Wednesday Judge Bernreuter dealt with Bernhardt Mueller, the Main Street barber who had followed the mob out the St. Louis Road and witnessed the hanging. The previous day

Mueller was visiting an Edwardsville barbershop and discussed what he had seen the night of the lynching. Another man in the shop was a prospective juror and reportedly told Mueller that he could not discuss the case. Mueller was said to have told the man it didn't matter as the lynching was the "most cold-blooded murder ever committed" and that the defendants deserved what Prager got.[20] When sheriff's deputy Vernon Coons heard of the conversation, he brought Mueller before the judge. In his chambers with the attorneys present, Bernreuter reprimanded Mueller and told him to refrain from any such conversations with possible jurors in the future. Mueller, stout and stern in appearance, with thick, round glasses, could only listen when the judge said that he might take up charges against Mueller later. But Bernreuter never did.

The five miners' locals in the Collinsville area each contributed $100 toward defending the eleven accused men. The team of defense attorneys included James Bandy, fifty-two, the former circuit court judge and state's attorney who lost his reelection bid in 1916 to Streuber. Bandy would be assisted by his twenty-seven-year-old son, Harold. The Bandys, arriving at court each day in their boater hats, seemed the embodiment of small-town attorneys. James exuded quiet confidence, while Harold, though competent, just seemed glad to be there. Both lived with their wives in Granite City.

The star of the defense team was Thomas Williamson, the tall and distinguished—some might say arrogant—Edwardsville attorney. One of the best public orators in southern Illinois, he had been the speaker at the Collinsville Neighborhood Committee meeting of the Illinois Council of Defense that had stirred the local crowd into such a patriotic fervor just nine days before Prager's death.[21] He served without charge to the defendants and played just a minimal part in day-to-day proceedings, but his stirring deliveries and probing interrogations late in the trial made him the star in the courtroom.

Prominent in the Edwardsville community, Williamson and his wife, Mattie, had four children. Then fifty years old, he began teaching at age seventeen, then attended Valparaiso University followed by Washington University Law School in St. Louis.[22] He was a Presbyterian Church trustee and president of the Edwardsville School Board, but he was perhaps best known for the stirring Memorial Day speech he gave to the Grand Army of the Republic veterans in 1910. Copies of the address were widely distributed.

The three defense attorneys represented all eleven defendants. That they were tried together probably worked in their favor. In the modern criminal prosecution setting, there probably would have been multiple trials, with perhaps each defendant having a different counselor to represent his interests.

James Bandy's questions to prospective jurors in the first week showed his hand in the planned defense. Bandy said Prager was a German spy and likened him to a burglar killed by a homeowner because he was not "in the peace of the people," as stated in Illinois homicide statutes. Streuber, the state's attorney, said that he would challenge that concept. He noted that Illinois Supreme Court decisions made clear that protections of the law extended to all. "The law protects foreigners, criminals and all others without question," Streuber said.[23]

The process of finding impartial jurors seemingly took forever, although the pool of candidates had surely improved. The third floor of the courthouse was crowded with talesmen, who were being summoned in groups of one hundred to await their turn. The first groups collected by the special bailiffs were primarily businessmen who worked in the area of the courthouse in Edwardsville; the bailiffs would branch out farther in the county as time passed. Illinois's attorney general had also sent six investigators to help check the backgrounds of the prospective jurors.[24] But five days into the process, on Friday, May 17, just four jurors had been selected from the 279 men interviewed. "The Prager case is moving at a rate of speed which makes the snail, tortoise and other deliberately-geared mechanisms look like Saturday night speed demons," one newspaper reported.[25]

As the tedious jury selection continued, Judge Bernreuter tried to relieve some of the stress Thursday evening by fishing in the

Cahokia Creek Bottoms Area, below the bluffs overlooking the Mississippi River Valley. The judge came back with no fish but covered in mosquito bites; he claimed that the local variety of mosquitos was a much tougher lot than those found in his home-town.[26] Bernreuter told the selected jurors they could fish if they so choose, but that the fish were the only things at Cahokia Creek not biting. "If you know where there is a pond out on the prairie in the open, it might be alright," the judge said. He cautioned the four men not to go where others might interfere with their work as jurors.[27] They were allowed to read newspapers and magazines if the objectionable items had been censored by the clerk or bailiff. He encouraged them to exercise, take automobile rides, and play cards, but directed them not to discuss the case among themselves.

The four jurymen relaxed over the weekend, not electing to fish or take an automobile ride. They did see a Red Cross parade in downtown Edwardsville and took several long walks, however.[28] It was quickly back to reality as fireworks erupted between the two legal teams Monday morning, earning both sides admonishment from Bernreuter to be more "peaceable." The attorneys continued to toy with each other throughout the jury-selection process. If an objection for cause was contested and overruled by the judge, a peremptory objection would be used. The defense went to great lengths to get a drafted soldier on the panel, only to have to use a peremptory challenge to have him dismissed when it didn't like his opinions.[29]

Newspapers noted that people in the county seat seemingly remained detached from the murder trial. "Despite the fact that its wires lead to the corners of an interested and critical world, the town of Edwardsville maintains, thus far, in comparative indifference to the important trial."[30] During the long jury-selection process, the crowd in the courtroom had dwindled down to an average of about forty per day.

The Edwardsville community, however, was doing what it could to avoid its own civic embarrassments, the most recent case involving Rev. J. D. Metzler of St. Boniface Catholic Church. The priest had raised the ire of the local committee of the state council of defense, including Thomas Williamson, by allegedly making pro-German statements. He had also drawn criticism for not observing the Great War's version of daylight savings time, causing the Angelus bells to be sounded one hour late.[31] Repeatedly advised by congregation members that his life was in danger, Metzler finally agreed to leave town. The last straw reportedly was Metzler's not allowing women of the church to loan out parish dishes to feed servicemen who had come for the Red Cross parade.[32] Just after Prager's lynching, Edwardsville's mayor had sworn in fifty deputies to help city police maintain order when suspected pro-Germans in the community were threatened with tar and feathers.[33]

The defense strategy citing Prager's alleged disloyalty was seemingly shut down by Judge Bernreuter on Wednesday, May 22, when he said disloyal talk would not be justification for taking a man's life. The subject came to a head when Middlekauff said such testimony did not prove Prager wasn't "at peace with the people." The Illinois assistant attorney general told a prospective juror, "This is the law, and if selected as a juryman you will follow the law."[34]

Middlekauff's statement brought an explosive protest from the defense. Jurors and prospective jurors were cleared from the courtroom as they argued the point. James Bandy said it was not Middlekauff's place to interpret the law. State's Attorney Streuber shouted out in agreement with Middlekauff and said, "We do not represent that Prager was not disloyal," but added that it did not mean that the immigrant wasn't at peace with the people. He criticized defense attorneys for constantly keeping the war before prospective jurors in an effort to justify the killing, and said, "No law justifies lynching."[35]

Bernreuter said that taking a life might be justified only if the accused was committing an act that was an immediate threat to life. "If you see a man laying ties on a railroad track to wreck a troop train or carrying a bomb to destroy public property, or setting fire to a factory or mine where munitions are manufactured, or government supplies produced then, if you cannot well cope with him yourself, you can kill him and it will be alright," the judge said.[36] If the man was merely making disloyal statements, however, he should be dealt with through the legal system, Bernreuter said. By noon that Wednesday, eight of the twelve needed jurors had been chosen from 525 men questioned.

After the closing out of ten days of jury selection on May 24, the eight chosen jurors and three jurors who were tentatively selected did go fishing that Saturday. They were accompanied by two bailiffs. Before he dismissed them Friday, Bernreuter thanked the men. "I know you are tired. I want to make it as comfortable for you as I can," the judge said. "I want to compliment you men. Others were either afraid of the job or afraid of their duty."[37] The new courthouse allowed the men to be truly sequestered in the somewhat concealed fourth-floor jurors' quarters on the west side, a dormitory-like area, complete with a lounge, bathrooms and showers.

One newspaper noted how evading jury duty had become a "popular pastime" in Madison County.[38] For as many people in the county who had strong opinions about the guilt or innocence of the accused, just as many seemed to be doing everything they could to avoid serving on the panel. Friday afternoon the judge reprimanded five prospective jurors for "deliberately and willfully" disqualifying themselves.[39] The men worked at the same store and, under questioning, gave the exact same answers although they had not been in the courtroom together. It was later learned that the store owner had directed the men to stay off the jury because the store was busy.

The drawn-out jury selection process did provide some moments of comic relief. Due to language barriers, communication with an Italian immigrant took extensive effort from the clerk and court just to get answers to the relatively simple screening questions; his term was short lived.[40] Another prospective juror put his left hand in the air to be sworn in. "Other hand, other hand," Middlekauff barked. The man's response was to wildly wave just the stump of a right arm, which was concealed in his coat sleeve. Another talesman's attitude toward the questions was described as "an exasperating smile and loud chewing of gum." His rapid-fire answers to the attorneys' questions were both far from the point and hard to understand, and they drew Bernreuter's rebuke: "This is most serious and not to be made light of. Quit that smiling and don't let me see you chewing gum anymore." The man obeyed, then said he was very hard of hearing; he was finally excused. "He's a good gum chewer," Bernreuter said after the man left, "but I don't believe he should serve."[41]

Choosing the last group of four jurors took nearly four days, despite Judge Bernreuter's offer to buy dinner for the attorneys if they could finish by the end of court hours one day. Both sides eventually agreed to stop questioning jurors on loyalty and international affairs, which helped greatly.[42] The jury battle ended suddenly Monday afternoon, May 27, after 725 talesmen had been called. The monotonous juror selection had nearly emptied the courtroom, but when the defense saw no reason to reject Frank Weeks as the twelfth juror, defense attorney James Bandy called for the clerk to "swear the jury" at about 4:00 p.m.[43] The eleven defendants, who had to watch for nearly eleven days, cheered and clapped their hands. Of the twelve jurors, eight came from Edwardsville, three from Alton, and one from Worden. State's Attorney Streuber asked for evening recess before opening statements. The defense objected. Judge Bernreuter left the decision to the jurors. "We've had enough recess your honor," one juror said, and the judge agreed.[44]

Opening statements were relatively brief, under thirty minutes total for both sides, given the gravity of the case. But the quick start of the trial had caught both legal teams off guard. Streuber spoke first, making it clear that the prosecution didn't represent Prager or any pro-German sentiment, and that it had exerted considerable effort to keep anyone with pro-German sentiment off the panel. "We wanted only pure and loyal Americans on this jury. I hope there is not a man in the jury who has in him a drop of pro-German blood, for this is a question for true Americans to pass on."[45] Streuber said complaints against Prager should have been taken to authorities and he shouldn't have been tried and executed by a mob. "We represent the law and the orderly enforcement," Streuber said. "We ask that the majesty of the law be upheld." He also outlined particular roles that seven of the eleven men had played in the incident and said that all were guilty of murder under Illinois's conspiracy laws. That statute did not make it necessary for each man to have held the rope to be found guilty, Streuber noted.[46]

James Bandy fired the first shots for the defense. "We hardly know what these boys are accused of, but I want to say to you, I don't have to tell you we are patriotic, you know that. A statement to a jury is not supposed to be a speech to show you wherein is patriotism. They claim the defendants, a great crowd, did lots of things that night, yet they have only 11 here before you." He said the defendants were innocent and could not be connected to the actual hanging of Prager. Bandy would chip away at Prager's loyalty, saying Prager was un-American and had referred to President Wilson as "a damn dog" who should be killed. He said the defense could prove that Prager had stated Germany would win the war and that America had no business in the conflict. "We don't know who lynched him, but there was cause for it," Bandy said. "When the evidence is over, you will find many things the state has not shown." Bandy said he believed the jury, in its verdict, would not blame the Collinsville community for what it had done.[47]

As much as State's Attorney Streuber was caught off guard by the quick trial start, it was not nearly as abrupt as his encounter that evening with Sheriff Jenkins. There had been bad blood between the two previously; they were both Republicans but led rival factions of the party in Madison County. After the trial closed for the day, Streuber went to May Brothers Café and Saloon, across from the courthouse on Edwardsville's Main Street, to wait for the streetcar bringing his wife from St. Louis. When she arrived, they planned to drive to their home in Highland. In walking to the saloon, Streuber and Jenkins passed on the street. Streuber reportedly smiled and spoke to the sheriff. Jenkins responded that he didn't want to speak to the state's attorney and called him a pro-German.[48]

Jenkins was infuriated with Streuber after the exchange, so much so that one man tried to find Streuber and warn him that the sheriff was on the warpath. The recent animus was said to be the result of the charges of incompetence that Streuber had made May 15, when he had the sheriff removed from bringing in potential jurors. Jenkins found Streuber at the saloon and said, "You've got to stop putting out this stuff about me. We must have an understanding." The sheriff didn't like the state's attorney's response and challenged him to fight. Streuber declined, saying he had just come out of the trial and was nervous and worn out and that Jenkins was angry. "We'll talk it over another time," he told Jenkins. Jenkins said that he would settle the matter now and landed a punch on Streuber's cheek. Friends stepped in to separate the men.[49]

Jenkins said he could prove that Streuber was pro-German and, in best schoolyard fashion, told the state's attorney he could also "whip any friend" of Streuber's too. The sheriff left May Brothers and so did the state's attorney, the latter seeking treatment for a laceration at the office of Dr. Edward Fiegenbaum. The timing of the attack was suspect. It had been twelve days since Streuber had requested Jenkins's removal from the duty of finding jurors. Since the trial had just started, Streuber could only speculate that Jenkins intended to injure him badly enough to prevent his participation in the proceedings.

Collinsville mayor John Siegel was the first of eleven prosecution witnesses called on Tuesday, May 28, and he told the story as he remembered the night of April 4, just fifty-four days earlier. He said he didn't know many of the people in the mob; he had learned Joe Riegel's name only that night. He also remembered Wesley Beaver, a character from a local saloon, and William Brockmeier, formerly a coal miner union president. The forty-six-year-old mayor, who had practiced medicine in town nearly twenty years, said he could identify only three men in the mob of about three hundred.[50]

Collinsville city attorney and former mayor R. Guy Kneedler followed Siegel on the stand. He had been among the community leaders who tried to calm the mob on Main Street and in front of city hall. He corroborated Siegel's account. He had recognized Richard Dukes and Joe Riegel in the crowd several blocks away but said he recognized no one in the mob at city hall. The forty-five-year-old former mayor said that he felt he knew everyone in town. Asked why he didn't recognize any faces in the mob at city hall, Kneedler replied, "Probably because I wasn't looking for anyone in particular."[51] The testimony of the mayor and the former mayor established a pattern that would continue with most witnesses throughout the trial. Men of standing, many of whom were born and raised in Collinsville, would name few, if any, of those they had seen the night of the lynching.

The defense challenged the prosecution's premise that anyone in the mob was as guilty as those who had held the hanging rope. When Mayor Siegel referred to the mob in generalities, defense attorneys objected. Who specifically, they wanted to know, was the mayor referring to? Which defendants could be specifically identified, and why were they singled out from hundreds of others in the mob? What was the difference between a bystander and a mob participant? Asked how he had seen the men in the mob, former mayor Kneedler said he had been speaking among them. "Oh, you were one of the crowd then?" a defense attorney asked. "Yes, I was one of the crowd," Kneedler said.[52] Bernreuter later allowed that witnesses could use the term *they* in describing the mob.

Despite the great interest in the case, there were a limited number of spectators Tuesday. At the start of testimony, once dozens of potential witnesses had been excluded from the courtroom, spectators numbered just seven women and twenty-five men.[53] With temperatures approaching ninety degrees outside, courthouse windows were open, and trains passing just south of the courthouse nearly drowned out the critical testimony of witnesses. Even the defendants who were seated next to the witness box had to be attentive to hear the testimony.

John Bruso, a lumber company owner and foreman of the coroner's jury in Collinsville, spent two hours on the stand that day.

With the prosecution knowing that witnesses and the accused would not be as forthright as they had been for the coroner's jury just a few days after the lynching, Bruso was asked to report what the jury had been told at the inquest. Defense attorneys objected that the inquest had been closed and said that the defendants were not advised of their rights and did not give statements voluntarily. Bernreuter overruled and allowed the testimony, but he criticized the closed inquest.[54] The defense then continually sought clarification of which pronoun the inquest witness used, *I, they,* or *we,* whenever Bruso mentioned specific actions. Defense attorneys also objected when Bruso admitted reviewing the inquest transcript to refresh his memory during the lunch recess. Bernreuter agreed this time, ruling Bruso could testify only to what he personally remembered. Bruso would end up implicating six of the defendants as being in the mob at city hall or the lynching scene.

Critical eyewitness testimony came from two young men who were in the Bitzer Garage service car the night of the lynching. The car was loaded down with eight riders already, boys who were curious to see what would happen to Prager, before three or four others jumped on the running boards and ordered driver Harry Linneman, eighteen, to take them to Schmidt's Mound Park for tar. Linneman told how he had followed the mob after seeing it head west on Main Street.[55] Along the way he picked up friends who likewise wanted to see what all the ruckus was about. After being unable to find tar at Schmidt's, Linneman was ordered to drive back to town and told to stop once again atop Bluff Hill. When the service car stopped, the hanging rope was removed from the car.

Linneman identified three of the defendants as being at the lynching scene. He had seen Joe Riegel grab the rope and place it over the tree limb, and he also identified James DeMatties and Charles Cranmer as involved. He had stayed in the car and did not see what was happening under the tree, but he did hear someone call out that everyone in the crowd must touch the rope.[56] One of the riders in Linneman's car, twenty-year-old Edmund Nagel, also testified that Riegel had placed the rope on the tree. He had also seen Wesley Beaver bring Prager out of city hall, where he noted that Richard Dukes was in the crowd. Nagel had seen defendant Cecil Larremore at the lynching scene, handling papers that he took from Prager's pocket. Defendant James DeMatties had ordered the service car to stop upon its return from Schmidt's, Nagel said. Clarence Nagel, Edmund's twenty-two-year-old brother, would be called to the stand the next day and name Frank Flannery as also being at the lynching scene.

Louis Gerding, twenty-two, had driven another car carrying young men who were following the mob that night. He and two friends had seen the crowd after leaving a moving picture show and followed it to city hall. The trio had then driven behind the mob out the St. Louis Road; eventually they were told to point the car's headlights on the lynching tree. Prager had used the left front fender of Gerding's automobile to write his last note because the car had a spotlight. Gerding provided the court its most graphic account of the incident. Despite being in the midst of all the activity at the lynching scene, Gerding said he could not identify anyone in the crowd. He was asked if he knew what would happen as Prager walked away after writing his note: "I had a suspicion," he said. Defense attorney James Bandy continued on the point: "Just sat and watched the entertainment—that's what it was to you, wasn't it?" Asked if he had been entertained, Gerding said: "I saw all I cared to see."[57]

Barber Bernhardt Mueller's appearance opened the trial Wednesday with the most damaging testimony yet against Joe Riegel and the others. He also withstood the most blistering attack from a defense team bent on impugning his patriotism. Mueller said that he had followed the mob after it had gotten Prager from city hall, as had so many others. He identified Beaver and DeMatties as carrying the flag in front of the procession in the early going and said he had seen Dukes in front of city hall. At this point lead defense counsel James Bandy objected, saying that Mueller was a testifying defendant and should be charged as the others. "Your theory is that anyone who saw the occurrence is guilty?" Bernreuter asked. Bandy said yes and was promptly overruled.[58]

Among those actively involved atop Bluff Hill, Mueller identified only Cranmer and Riegel. He had not seen who placed the rope on the tree or around Riegel's neck, but he would be the only witness who admitted seeing Riegel yank on the rope: "He pulled on the rope but he couldn't raise the man."[59] Riegel then called out to the crowd for help, and a good number rushed up to the rope, Mueller said. He had been unable to identify others on the rope. Prosecutors said Riegel's call for help was not just to help with the task of lifting but to establish a pledge of secrecy among everyone involved in the hanging. Mueller admitted that he had not objected or tried to stop the lynching, saying he was afraid to act.

Bandy accused Mueller of being pro-German, an allegation the witness fiercely denied. State's Attorney Streuber said Mueller was a member of the National Council of Defense. "Don't you know you can't get into a meeting of the Council?" Bandy asked.[60] Again Mueller angrily denied the charge. State's Attorney Streuber asked Mueller if he had received any form of notice that he was suspended from the group, and Mueller said no.

Paul Anderson, the *St. Louis Post-Dispatch* reporter who had gotten a full confession from Joe Riegel before he testified at the inquest, was covering the trial. Like Riegel's statement to the coroner's jury, the interview he granted to Anderson was damning, implicating him from the time Prager was taken from city hall to the point when his feet were lifted from the earth on Bluff Hill. The prosecution knew it was critical. Although Anderson had been subpoenaed as a witness for the trial, no one from the prosecution team thought to exclude the newsman from the courtroom when testimony began. When it came time for him to testify, the court quickly ruled that Anderson could not since he had heard other witness testimony.[61] It seemed a major blow to the state's case.

Patrolman Fred Frost again gave his version of the incident, noting John Hallworth's comments that Prager should be turned over to the officer. Officer Martin Futcheck told of his unsuccessful effort to get Prager out to Frost's car.

The trial pace seemed to pick up speed when the defense stopped its frequent challenges to prosecution questions, most all of which the judge overruled. Still there were sharp exchanges between the two legal teams, requiring Bernreuter to "hush wordy tiffs" between counsel.[62] Overall, however, the trial was less spectacular than many had expected.

Albert Kneedler, the nineteen-year-old nephew of the former mayor, testified in his U.S. Army uniform, having enlisted on May 17. Kneedler said that Cranmer, Beaver, and Enid Elmore were at city hall, but like so many other witnesses, he identified no one at the lynching scene. He reported seeing Prager struck so hard at the lynching scene that he was knocked flat on his face.[63]

The remainder of the fourteen prosecution witnesses called that second day mostly provided undisputed facts about what had occurred. Coroner Roy Lowe, like coroner's jury foreman John Bruso, was allowed to testify only from memory and could not use the inquest transcript. The general responses from witnesses named few participants at city hall and fewer still from the lynching scene. No one besides Mueller and the occupants of Linneman's car identified anyone who had touched the hanging rope.[64] And only Mueller identified Riegel as having pulled on the rope. The names of the perhaps two dozen men or boys who helped raise Prager to his death were never mentioned in court and were committed only to whisper and innuendo for generations to come in Collinsville.

Those with a very limited recollection of the lynching scene included Notley Shoulders, twenty-eight, a city alderman and construction foreman by trade. He was among a handful of witnesses who claimed to have heard an approaching streetcar and left to get on just before the hanging. A theatrical equivalent might have been watching a two-hour show and then departing just before the final act. Yet Bernhardt Mueller, who had ridden the same streetcar into town, said that he saw the whole lynching.[65]

At 3:00 p.m. Wednesday the prosecution provided the biggest surprise of the day when it said it would close its case within one hour on Friday. There would be no court on Thursday in observance of Decoration Day, May 30, the judge decided, and the prosecutors said they needed time to find one or two more witnesses. Defense attorneys objected to the delay, but Judge Bernreuter said it was reasonable given the protracted time it had taken to seat the jury. Little earthshaking information would be revealed by the last of those whom the prosecution called to the stand. The bigger story seemed to be the number of witnesses who would not appear.

Prosecutors had subpoenaed at least sixty-nine witnesses for the trial, but they would call just twenty-six to the stand. The six investigators from the attorney general's office had been delegated to help round up those expected to testify for the state. Some of the witnesses may have been redundant or otherwise unnecessary, but given the climate of intimidation in Collinsville, it's fair to assume that many weren't called because they wouldn't be very forthcoming about what—or more importantly whom—they had seen. Most of the witnesses already called had identified defendants only as being part of the mob and had not tied them to specific acts that were more incriminating. If prosecutors had indeed brought forth the strongest witnesses who gave them the best chance to win convictions, it had proven the state's case wasn't at all strong.

With the defense saying it would not take more than one day to present its side, there was some optimism that the trial could end Saturday, June 1. Judge Bernreuter wanted to pick up the extra day that week to make up for the holiday and extended time it had taken to find a jury. The eleven defendants seemed cheerful, and why not, with their attorneys already predicting acquittal.[66]

Jurors were making the best of their relative confinement, which for the first-chosen men was more than two weeks. The jurors got along well, and three of them played musical instruments, with David Fiegenbaum on guitar, William Dippold on mandolin, and the coronet appropriately being played by Frederick Horn. They entertained every night, usually followed by refreshments. The music of Sunday evening was entirely sacred, but other nights it was of the patriotic and popular variety.[67]

Back in Collinsville the city's largest contingent ever of "selected men" had been sent off that week, with seventy-eight departing on Monday and an additional nineteen on Wednesday. Stars for the new inductees helped fill the city's service flag at Main and Center Streets. Both groups were given the now-standard send-off celebration by city leaders, with one businessman telling the newly drafted soldiers, "Au revoir, but not goodbye."[68]

When the defense team got its turn Friday morning, its approach could be described in just two words: disloyalty and denial. The attorneys' plan was to paint Prager as a disloyalist and to have the defendants deny just about anything and everything that might be incriminating. The first witness brought to the stand Friday was Thomas Holt, a Maryville miner and justice of the peace in the village. Lead defense attorney James Bandy asked him, "Did Prager ever say the war was uncalled for and that the President ought to be shot?"[69] The prosecution quickly objected, stating that Prager's patriotism was not on trial. The jurors were taken from the room while counsel argued the issue.

Lead defense attorney James Bandy said the testimony should be admissible in that it showed provocation for the lynching and would perhaps provide for a lighter sentence for those who might be found guilty. For the prosecution Charles Middlekauff questioned Holt about his conversation with Prager, which took place the day before the hanging. Holt said that the victim had told him he was a Socialist and opposed to the war and that the United States had made a mistake in entering the war. Holt told Middlekauff that he had reported the conversation with Prager to others the day after the lynching.[70]

Judge Bernreuter ruled that the conversation could not have been provocative to the miners if they did not learn of it until after the lynching. The judge said that the defendants must have been aware of it before the lynching for it to have any impact on the case. "If any of these defendants had heard reports that Prager was disloyal, if as Prager walked down the street and cheered for Germany instead of for the United States and the Stars and Stripes, there would have been substantial provocation which would mitigate their punishment," Bernreuter said.[71] Holt was then dismissed as a witness. Worth noting is that Holt's discussion with Prager in Maryville was apparently unwitnessed and stood in sharp contrast to every other indication that the immigrant had become a fanatical American patriot.

In the afternoon session, defense attorneys made another attempt to slip in witnesses to prove Prager's disloyalty. They were residents of Niobrara, Nebraska, where Prager had a dustup with the locals in 1915. Some witnesses to that encounter came forward after reading about the lynching. But Judge Bernreuter disallowed the testimony, again since there was no proof that the defendants knew about the incident before the hanging.[72] (The Niobrara testimony may have been completely factual but still irrelevant since Prager apparently did not manifest patriotism for his new nation until 1917, when the United States entered the world war.)

When the eleven defendants took the stand in their own defense on Friday, jurors saw and heard everything from accurate recollections to outright lies and deceit. The state had failed to present any evidence implicating most of them for doing anything other than just being in the mob at various times. From the awkward introductions of evidence heard by the coroner's jury to the inadmissibility of Riegel's newspaper interview, the evidence linking a murder charge to most of the defendants was tenuous at best.[73]

John Hallworth spoke of watching Prager being taken from his home and of his own efforts to discourage violence and get the men to initially turn Prager over to the police. A witness confirmed his assistance to the police on Main Street, and no other part of Hallworth's testimony was refuted.

Enid "Peanuts" Elmore acknowledged being in the crowd at city hall and said he had followed the mob down to the start of the St. Louis Road and then gone home. His testimony was never refuted.

Frank Flannery acknowledged being at the lynching scene but denied involvement and said that he had left prior to the hanging. His testimony was apparently never refuted.

Wesley Beaver acknowledged being at city hall and said that he had carried the flag out on Main Street for two blocks before handing it off to another person and then returning to his job at Fulton's. But he had also been seen on the front steps of city hall earlier and had a hand in getting Prager out of the building. Between his account and those of witnesses were great discrepancies concerning Beaver's level of involvement.

William Brockmeier acknowledged being at city hall in the mob and speaking with the mayor, but he said he had been unable to catch up to the mob after it left city hall. Yet a church pastor reported seeing him get on the interurban at the Hardscrabble stop, where the mob had just stopped the streetcar.

Calvin Gilmore said that he had seen the mob at city hall and had gone home shortly thereafter. A witness, however, reported seeing his daughter yelling from the interurban at the Hardscrabble stop, trying to get her father to go home with her sometime later.

Richard Dukes admitted being at city hall and following the mob out the St. Louis Road. He also acknowledged walking nearly two miles from uptown to where the pavement ended on the St. Louis Road, but he said that he had not gone the one hundred or so steps farther to the lynching site and denied being within twenty feet of Prager at any time. He denied making any comment threatening Prager to Mayor Siegel at city hall; he said that he had merely stated Prager would not last fifteen minutes if the angry mob got to him. Dukes's version of the discussion also contradicted witness statements.

James DeMatties said that he had followed at the rear of the mob on Main Street and left the site of the lynching when he heard someone mention they had found a rope. He denied ordering the car to stop on Bluff Hill. But witnesses reported seeing him carry the flag in front of the procession and his ordering at least one car to stop at the hanging tree.

Cecil Larremore acknowledged being in the crowd at City Hall but said that he had not gone to the lynching scene but rather stopped a short distance away because of a foot injury suffered in the mines three months earlier. But a witness identified him as going through the papers found in Prager's pockets under the hanging tree.

Charles Cranmer admitted to being at city hall and going to the lynching scene, but said that he had not gotten within one hundred feet of the tree. He said that he had provided paper and pencil to Prager upon request and stood by Gerding's automobile when the note was written. To be standing by the car, Cranmer would most certainly have been much closer to the lynching tree than he admitted.

Joe Riegel basically denied everything incriminating. He said that he had showed his discharge papers to Mayor Siegel in an effort to help him protect Prager. He said he had followed the mob and urged the men several times to "be careful" of what they did to the immigrant. He denied ever being closer than twenty feet to Prager, except for when he wrote his farewell note. He acknowledged no part in removing Prager from city hall or his lynching. He said that a "big man" named Davis had put the rope on the tree, conveniently citing the name of the defendant who had never been located. Riegel said someone had given him Prager's last note and told him to send it to Prager's parents. He denied incriminating statements he had made to the coroner's jury and in the interview with Paul Anderson of the *Post-Dispatch*. Most all of Riegel's critical testimony was contradicted by witnesses or in his prior confessions.

Riegel said that a deputy sheriff had taken him to the coroner's inquest and that he was not properly sworn in and was "badly frightened" by the questioning. Dukes also implied that he was threatened at the inquest. Cranmer also said that Assistant Attorney General William Trautmann had threatened him when he testified before the grand jury.

In rebuttal the prosecution primarily attacked Riegel's sanitized version of the evening's events. It had been most repellent to hear testimony that directly contradicted the accounts of a number of reliable witnesses and Riegel's own confessions. Mayor Siegel was recalled to again describe Riegel's actions at city hall. Middlekauff also read incriminating paragraphs from the *Post-Dispatch* interview, after each one asking Riegel if he had not made the statement. "No sir," was the consistent reply. The defense made continual objections to this process, all of which were overruled by Bernreuter. But Riegel did manage a smile when Middlekauff read one portion of the interview: "I had a lot of liquor in me when I started, and because I had been in the Army the crowd kind of made me the big man in it," Riegel said. "I was kind of swelled up about that."[74]

During rebuttal the prosecutors were able to refute more of the defendants' testimony when they put the stenographer from the coroner's inquest on the witness stand. He confirmed from his shorthand notes critical portions of that testimony, which differed greatly from what the jury heard from some defendants in Judge Bernreuter's courtroom eight weeks later.[75] The prosecution also benefited by putting Paul Anderson of the *Post-Dispatch* on the stand, ostensibly to verify Riegel's virtual confession in the April 10 interview. Anderson had been barred from testifying earlier in the trial because he was in the courtroom when witnesses should have been excluded. But in rebuttal Anderson's testimony would allow the jury to hear the incriminating admissions of the man most responsible for Robert Prager's death.

The defense ended its case by parading ten character witnesses to the stand to speak of the positive qualities of the defendants, some vouching for several of the men on trial. Most were connected to the mining industry, but four spoke of Charles Cranmer's work at the East St. Louis stockyards. The defense portion of the trial took just six hours, no doubt shortened because Bernreuter would not allow most of the testimony about Prager's alleged disloyalty.[76]

When he rapped his gavel to adjourn at 4:30 Friday afternoon, the judge was pleased that the case would soon come to a close, a week earlier than he had once anticipated.[77] Despite its inability to introduce any significant testimony that would paint Prager as unpatriotic, the defense was content with its case. No doubt it was glad that most witnesses had done such a meager job of tying any of the defendants to the actual lynching. The state had made its strongest case against Joe Riegel at the lynching tree.

But even in that instance only one man in a crowd of one hundred, barber Bernhardt Mueller, had been brave enough to tell the jury about Riegel pulling on the rope two months earlier. Commenting privately, the prosecutors too acknowledged the fragile nature of their case and hinted they would be satisfied with just one or more convictions of the eleven charged.

Emotions were still running high, and they certainly weren't checked at the courthouse door that evening. Lead defense attorney James Bandy ended up taking the same interurban car home to Granite City that Paul Anderson of the *Post-Dispatch* took to the newspaper office. He shouted to other passengers on the streetcar that Anderson had been born in Germany, was not an American citizen, and was pro-German. None of that was true, but Bandy carried on: "That fellow has been up on the witness stand trying to protect a German spy, and trying to send a lot of American boys to the penitentiary."[78]

When closing arguments began at 8:00 a.m. Saturday, the first day of June, the courtroom's curved wooden benches filled for the first time, with most everyone expecting a verdict by day's end. And with one last chance to sway the jury, the facts of the Prager lynching again took a secondary role to the cause célèbre of 1918, patriotism. Both the prosecution and the defense told the jury that it could best show its patriotism by finding the defendants, respectively, guilty or innocent.

State's Attorney Joseph Streuber spoke first to the jurors, calling the case one of the most important in Madison County history, with implications reaching all over the United States. He reminded the jurors of their great responsibility and then played the loyalty card. "Love for our country is not the mere shouting and singing of patriotic songs and flying of flags, but includes love for that which the country stands. Can any loyal American say that America stands for mob law?" Streuber said.[79] "The man who justifies mob law is a disloyalist. Any man who says America stands for mob rule is a traitor to America."[80]

Streuber briefly touched on the testimony against each defendant before saying that the court had been fair in not allowing some allegations of Prager's disloyalty to be heard. He said the defense had been unable to prove that any of the defendants had knowledge of those allegations before Prager was lynched.

"The cause of this present war is Germany's lawlessness," the state's attorney said. "Can this jury approve of mob law?"[81] Streuber told the jurors that when Prager was hung, the happiest man in the world was Kaiser Wilhelm and the most displeased were President Woodrow Wilson and Governor Frank Lowden.

All three defense attorneys would take part in the closing arguments. Harold Bandy, the son of lead defense counsel James Bandy, was up first and challenged the charges that had been brought. "These defendants are charged with murder, not participation in a mob. They are indicted for murder and cannot be convicted for gathering at the City Hall and shouting against pro-Germanism. The most serious thing they did was disturb the peace," Harold Bandy said. "Unless you believe these men went out with malice in their hearts to hang Prager, it is your duty to acquit them."[82] He also attacked the credibility of two of the most damning witnesses, reporter Paul Anderson and Bernhardt Mueller.

James Bandy followed his son before the jurors and placed blame everywhere but with the defendants. "This has been a case of persecution since the day of the hanging," he said. "There are usually two sides to the case, but this is an exception. Detectives, the Attorney General's office and the newspapers have all been called upon to contribute," Bandy said.[83] "The State's Attorneys duty is not to persecute, and when he found out after investigation that these men were innocent he should have had the manhood to stand up and nolle the cases."[84]

"Loyalty should have been an issue in this trial," Bandy asserted. "We could have justified the action of the patriotic men of Collinsville, had not the court prevented the introduction of testimony to show what inspired the people of Madison County on the night of April 4 and the early morning of April 5."[85] He also accused State's Attorney Streuber of being deliberately unpatriotic by keeping Dukes and Riegel out of the army, as both were now subject to the draft.

Bandy challenged why others had not been charged in the crime since the mob comprised as many as three hundred people at times. He said that many of the witnesses brought before the court were just as guilty as the defendants: "There was the big editor Schimpff, who tried to get the death note, Horstman the saloonkeeper, Gerding who turned on the spotlight, the goggle-eyed barber, Mueller, Mayor Siegel and the policemen who were there, and the little two by four editor Monroe over there—why weren't they indicted. They are all old heads, all but Monroe, and this hanging was done by old heads, not boys. Cranmer is indicted because he furnished the paper and pencil. He was no more guilty than the others I have named."[86]

The lead defense counsel called *Herald* editor J. O. Monroe and *Post-Dispatch* reporter Paul Anderson "fixers" for their reporting on the lynching, the investigation, and the trial. (During a later court recess, James Bandy would laugh about the statement to the newspapermen: "You boys have enough sense to know how to take that.")[87]

Bandy continued to play on the age of most of the defendants when he said, "This hanging was done by old heads. The miners were afraid Prager would blow up the mine, and they put him out of the way.[88] The elder Bandy continued: "This man Prager was not loyal. He was a pro-German and the people of Collinsville knew it and others knew it. I know the jury will do its duty and that tonight these boys will be seated around the dinner table with their parents and this jury will find consolation in having done its duty."[89]

The defense team saved its biggest weapon for last. The great orator of the group, Thomas Williamson, provided the patriotic, nearly two-hour finale for the defense, just as he had provided the stirring finish to the first meeting of the Illinois Council of Defense in Collinsville days before the lynching. Tall and dashing, Williamson was both dramatic and engaging to the jurors, commanding the area in front of the jury box. He told the jurors that he was assisting in the defense pro bono because he felt the "persecution" had gone far enough. "I believe the highest duty any man can discharge is to defend men innocently charged with a crime such as this."[90]

Williamson referred to Streuber's closing comment about the kaiser being pleased with the lynching. "The State's Attorney seems to be the link of community between the Kaiser and the President," he said. "If he is the Kaiser's representative here and his other representative at the press table there is taking down testimony [pointing to Monroe], tell Wilhelm for me that I say 'To hell with the Kaiser and all his cohorts.'"[91]

The Edwardsville attorney embraced a new line of defense that had been used successfully just two months earlier. In one of the Oklahoma shooting deaths of an alleged disloyalist in early 1918, the defense in the case had broached the concept that some laws written in peacetime were not applicable during war. S. L. Miller, an "operative" of the county council of defense in Tulsa, was charged with murder for shooting restaurant waiter Joe Spring. But Miller was found innocent March 26. "It wasn't S. L. Miller that was on trial for murdering Joe Spring yesterday," said a report in the *Tulsa Daily World*. "It was the patriotism of Tulsa and the principle of a new unwritten law that makes it justifiable for a man to slay one who speaks out against the country that shelters and nurtures him."[92]

Williamson would not pass on the opportunity to see if the theory carried weight with the jurors in Madison County too. "The people are the supreme power in America," he stated eloquently. "When the murder law was written we were not at war. America's greatest burden has been that we have been permitted in the past to say what we wanted about the government. There is no room on American soil for any man who is not for the American republic."[93]

The prominent attorney cited another prevailing notion, espoused in the nation's most popular war book, to make his point. James Gerard, the American ambassador to Germany before diplomatic relations were broken off in early 1917, penned *My Four Years in Germany* upon his return to the states.[94] By 1918 it would be the top seller among war books in a nation obsessed with the European conflict, with the story of waning diplomatic relations beating out titles about men in combat and life in the trenches. In the book Gerard tells of a conversation with Arthur Zimmermann, the acting German foreign affairs secretary. The exchange followed the sinking of the *Lusitania*, a period of obvious tension between the two nations.

The diplomats spoke of German submarine warfare and the calls for revenge made by many Americans in 1915. "The United States does not dare do anything against Germany because we have 500,000 German reservists in America who will rise in arms against your government if your government should dare to take any action against Germany," Zimmerman said, repeatedly striking a table with his fist. He was referring to the mandatory military requirement for German men before they were considered reservists who could be recalled for duty, well aware of the great German immigrant population in the states.[95]

Ambassador Gerard was unmoved. "I told him we had 501,000 lamp posts in America, and that is where the German reservists would find themselves if they tried any uprising." After relating the diplomatic conversation to the jurors, Williamson added, "and you can't put a German reservist on a lamp post by due process of law."[96]

Williamson also cited a recent case in Madison County and one federal ruling stating that German aliens had no protection under U.S. laws. He continued his shotgun approach by again hammering the point that the lynching witnesses were as guilty as the defendants; referencing the Germanic names of the judge, the assistant attorney general, and the state's attorney; accusing the state of delaying the trial; complaining that news coverage had been slanted against the defendants; and warning that every pro-German in America would laugh with glee if the men were convicted.[97]

"They will tell you that because of the hanging of Prager, the Kaiser will seek revenge," the fiery Williamson said. "There is nothing in the way of brutality the Kaiser has not done and the Prager case will have no bearing on the Kaiser in his future acts.

If you punish these men for gathering at City Hall, your verdict will stamp you as being opposed to men who are loyal, and in the favor of disloyalty."[98]

"Suppose you were in Collinsville on the night of April 4 and you heard the cry, 'We've caught a German spy?'" Williamson asked while dramatically pointing his finger at the jurors. "Would you have sneered at the idea? Would you have passed it from your memory without a second thought?"[99]

"There isn't a man on trial here who would not shoulder a gun and follow a flag into battle, even to giving up his own life for America," Williamson said. "There are a large number of drafted men leaving Edwardsville tonight for camp to fight the Germans. They are going to halt pro-Germanism. If these men are hanged, think of the contrast."[100]

The attorney asked the eleven defendants to stand at the close of his appeal. "Their lives have been an open book," Williamson told the jurors. "These boys may have made mistakes. But let the men among you who has [*sic*] never made a mistake cast the first ballot to send them to the penitentiary," Williamson said. "Let them return home to supper tonight."[101] When Williamson concluded, the courtroom—the majority of it anyway—burst into applause.

In an era when public speaking was big entertainment and an important part of social discourse, Williamson's words stirred the courtroom. Although both sides made important points, it was Williamson's patriotic oration that would make the strongest impression on those in the courtroom and would be best remembered. A young Collinsville teenager was taken to the trial by his father that day just to hear Williamson's closing words. Sixty years later he wrote that he could still "hear the applause that burst out when the eloquent counsel concluded with a verbal waving of the stars and stripes."[102]

After breaking for lunch, the prosecution had one more opportunity to influence the jurors in the rebuttal made by Illinois assistant attorney general C. W. Middlekauff, who also spoke nearly two hours. He said that he agreed with about three quarters of what Thomas Williamson had said but urged the jury to show its loyalty and patriotism by upholding Illinois law. Middlekauff acknowledged that everyone connected with the case was patriotic—that was not an issue. "If the lynching at Collinsville is permissible, it may occur at any other city. The State is not seeking revenge, but it wishes to prevent like offenses."[103] He touched on the part that conspirators played in the lynching, noting that if Prager had never been taken from his home he would not have been hanged.

"I have no sympathy for Prager, and probably he is in the place where he ought to be," Middlekauff said. "For the sake of argument, let us say that Prager was a German spy, tried and convicted. The question is whether you can afford to set a precedent in Illinois that mobs can go to jails and take out prisoners, try, sentence and execute them in half an hour. If that principle is established, we may as well tear down the courthouse and say to the crowds, 'go to it.'" Middlekauff continued: "I would be glad to see these boys go to their families. But the law and order of the State depends on your conviction of those whom the evidence shows to be guilty."[104]

"There is a big way and a small way to try this case," Middlekauff said. "One way would be to take these men to the city hall at Collinsville, call in their relatives and friends and let them say: 'These are good boys; they may have made a mistake, but we will let them go this time.' Probably half of the residents of Collinsville are in favor of turning them loose. The other way and the right way is to try them before a jury that will enforce the law, and mete out justice to them," Middlekauff said.[105] "The big way is to consider President Wilson's declaration to make the world safe for democracy. Make our laws and enforce them. Before we go to Europe to teach democracy we should maintain it here."[106]

Around 2:30 on Saturday afternoon, the closing arguments concluded, and Judge Bernreuter allowed a ten-minute recess before giving instructions to the jurors. The high temperatures of earlier in the week had abated somewhat, and the eighty-degree weather made the third floor of the courthouse slightly more tolerable.

Besides the hubbub of the trial, it was another patriotic week-end in Edwardsville. After wrapping up the Third War Bond Drive, the town held a send-off on Saturday for forty-one young men leaving for the army. A local manufacturer paid the expenses for twenty-five-member contingent of the Jackie Band, from the Great Lakes Naval Training Center near Chicago, to be in town to help with the festivities. The band traveled throughout the Midwest during the Great War after being formed by John Philip Sousa, who would do his part by enlisting in the navy reserve. Sousa was considered the March King after composing most of the patriotic march songs of the era, not the least of which was "The Stars and Stripes Forever." Though he was now sixty-two years old, there was no better man to organize a marching band.

The Jackie Band came into the courthouse lobby when a brief rain shower passed over, but it had been directed not to play for fear of disturbing the trial. When Judge Bernreuter called the recess, someone took the liberty of informing the band, which again began playing patriotic airs, the first of which was "The Star Spangled Banner."[107] It was almost as if the defense attorneys themselves were scripting the grandiose musical production in the open atrium below.

Joe Riegel, sitting amid the defendants while the trial was in recess, began tearing up as the music ascended into the courtroom from the marching band little more than one hundred feet away. Whether fearing for his own mortality or incarceration, suffering sudden pangs of guilt, experiencing a wave of patriotic emotion—or just for the benefit of the jurors—the rough-and-tumble Riegel had tears streaming down his cheeks for the twelve men to see just before they retired to the jury room.[108]

Bernreuter culled sixteen instructions to the jurors from a laundry list of sixty-six points of information, most submitted by the imaginative defense team. Also provided were definitions from the Illinois statute on murder, manslaughter, and being accessory to a crime. Among the instructions the judge provided were the following:

The jury is free to find some defendants guilty and others innocent, and could choose a different punishment for each defendant, including death, life imprisonment or not less than 14 years prison time on the charge of murder.

The murder had no connection to the war.

Prager was entitled to all protections of Illinois law even though he was an enemy alien.

Those who conspire to commit a crime are as guilty as others charged even though the lynching was not part of their original plan.

Whoever incites a crime is guilty, as an accessory, equally with the principal.

It was not necessary for any defendant to have placed the rope around Prager's neck. Any defendant who aided, assisted, advised or encouraged was equally guilty as an accessory.[109]

It was about 3:15 when the jurors were sent out to make their decision, and it wouldn't take long. The jurors considered the state's case flimsy. For all the testimony that had been provided, most of the suspects had been scarcely connected to the actual lynching. And the jurors were in no frame of mind to convict anyone as an accessory to murder for earlier actions at city hall or elsewhere. Jury foreman Keith Ebey noted that the only man to identify Riegel as having pulled on the rope was Bernhardt Mueller. Yet men who claimed to have left the tree before the lynching, Notley Shoulders and saloon owner William Horstman, would ride the same interurban car back to town as Mueller. It was an apparent contradiction that the state had failed to address in rebuttal, and at this point it was denigrating the most credible witness who had seen Riegel lead the hanging effort. And nothing connected any of the eleven men beyond a reasonable doubt, the jurors said.[110]

Two ballots were taken, the first was 11–1 for acquittal of all eleven defendants. A vote taken minutes later would make it unanimous. In under ten minutes the jury had reached its decision.[111] And in the end, the lack of witnesses to definitively connect the men to the crime would be the undoing of the state's case. What part patriotism or other influences played in the verdicts will never be known.

The defendants had been taken back across North Main Street to the county jail when the jury began its deliberations. No doubt a verdict had been reached before they had an opportunity to settle back into their beds. They were then ordered back to the courtroom. Friends and family members climbed onto benches to get a glimpse of the defendants as they returned to the packed chamber to learn their fate. The jury had been out just forty minutes, the defendants forty-two minutes.

Despite the optimism the attorneys held at the defense table, the atmosphere was tense when foreman Ebey handed the verdict he had written in longhand to Judge Bernreuter.[112] As for his histrionics, Joe Riegel was still crying when he returned to the courtroom. The judge thanked the jurors for their service, particularly for their tolerance in waiting out the tedious jury selection. After the judge silently reviewed the verdict, he passed it to the deputy circuit clerk to be read. The Jackie Band, which had patriotically entertained in the lobby earlier, happened to be leading the parade of new soldiers past the courthouse at the time. And in a surreal moment, the ensemble would be playing "Over There" just as the clerk announced that the men had been found not guilty.[113]

Pandemonium erupted in the courtroom after the verdict was read, with loud cheers and people clapping and stomping their feet. Men threw their hats in the air. The defendants rushed to thank their attorneys before the crowd surged toward the curved wooden railing to embrace them.[114] Virtually the only people not taking part in the wild celebration were the attorneys, the reporters, and the officers of the court. Edwardsville juror John Groshans said, "Well, I guess nobody can say we aren't loyal now," as he waved to the defendants. "We've done justice of the right sort for Madison County."[115] Bernreuter repeatedly rapped his gavel to try to restore order, but the clamor of the raucous crowd drowned out his efforts.[116]

With the help of the attorneys, the crowd finally quieted to grant some level of judicial decorum, allowing Bernreuter to dismiss the jury. The defendants then shook the jurors' hands, thanking them. Within thirty minutes the courtroom was clear. Some of the defendants left arm in arm and joined up, at least briefly, with the patriotic parade that continued to march up and down North Main Street led by the Jackie Band.[117]

None of the court observers was particularly surprised by the verdict.[118] The case was effectively lost in the intimidating undercurrent that washed through Collinsville during April and May 1918, cleansing the grim details from the public consciousness of the one hundred or so witnesses to the lynching. The overblown flag-waving and blind nationalism during the trial probably weren't necessary to win the acquittals, but they were the elements remembered most by those who sat in the courtroom. Forty some years and many criminal trials later, newspaper publisher J. O. Monroe would call the trial simply "a farcical patriotic orgy."[119]

Within minutes of the verdict, word reached Collinsville by phone. A bulletin was placed in front of the *Herald* office on East Main Street, and a five-cent extra edition was on the streets by 6:00 p.m. The defendants rode interurbans or automobiles back to Collinsville with their families and friends. After spending the last month or more in jail, the men "greeted their freedom with unbounded delight."[120]

Hundreds celebrated at Martin Fulton's and other uptown saloons when the acquitted men arrived back in Collinsville. Each of the former defendants had celebrity status now; in some cases they were surrounded by a circle of congratulatory friends as they moved from bar to bar. Drink always flowed freely in the saloons but never so much as on Saturday nights. That the verdict had been rendered late Saturday afternoon seemed nearly divine patriotic intervention. Before the celebration was over, scenes of uproarious drunkenness played out in many of Collinsville's nineteen uptown saloons.[121] But there was reason to celebrate: the miners and their friends had proven that they were above the law—that they were invincible.

And the workingmen of the Collinsville area were celebrating not just the acquittals of the eleven charged men but also the apparent end of official inquiry into the Prager affair. No longer did they have to fear that an unchecked bystander would speak to an investigator or on the witness stand of the scores of others who were intimately involved but not charged—those unnamed men who had taken Prager from his home, beaten him with their fists, goaded the mostly young and drunken crowd into storming city hall, and then prodded the mob to lethal violence as it walked out the St. Louis Road. Those unnamed men and boys who helped raise Robert Prager to his death, they too could breathe a sigh of relief tonight and raise yet another toast to Uncle Sam.

9

It Seems a Nightmare

Those were the sweetless, wheatless, meatless, heatless, and perfectly brainless days when your fathers broke Beethoven's records, boycotted Wagner's music, burned German books, painted German Lutheran churches and Goethe's monument in Chicago the color of Shell filling stations today; strung up a Mennonite preacher in Collinsville, Oklahoma, by his neck until he fainted, repeated the process until he fainted again, and graciously relented; hanged another to the limb of a tree in Collinsville, Illinois, until he was dead.

—Oscar Ameringer, *If You Don't Weaken*

June 3, 1918, was more sobering than most Mondays for the people of Madison County. A one-day strike by the interurban workers didn't help matters. Governor Frank Lowden expressed his disappointment in the Prager trial verdict. "Patriotism was the guise worn by the perpetrators of this crime. The jury seemed to think that it could show its own loyalty by condoning the crime. . . . The result is a lamentable failure of justice," the governor said. "If juries will not convict in cases like this, the local authorities must prevent them from occurring. If in any community they fail in the discharge of this plain duty, nothing remains but to declare martial law in such community."[1] Lowden was concerned enough about the verdict that he asked his assigned Justice Department Bureau of Investigation agent to return immediately to Springfield, in fear that the acquittals would spur other vigilante activity around the state.[2]

State's Attorney Joseph Streuber had decided by Monday morning that he would not prosecute the four policemen. He had seen that county residents were in no mood to convict men in the lynch mob and presumed that the odds of the Collinsville officers being held accountable for their nonfeasance were even worse. He also dropped charges against George Davis, the defendant who had never been located or further implicated.[3]

Streuber would not criticize the jurors' decision, although he felt the evidence showed that four defendants had participated in the lynching and the seven others were implicated. "Neither I nor any other person has the right to say that the jury betrayed their oaths. We may differ as to the conclusions they reached," the state's attorney said. "I have faith in the loyalty and patriotism of the people of Madison County. I have faith in their obedience to, and respect for, the law."[4]

The American criminal justice system still has flaws in the twenty-first century, but it had many more in 1918. Any of a number of courtroom actions in the trial, from the repeated comments in front of the jury questioning Prager's loyalty to the band playing patriotic music outside the trial, could have been grounds for mistrial in today's legal system. And prosecutors and defense attorneys alike probably would have sought separate trials for the defendants, improving the chances of at least a few convictions. But none of that would happen during the Prager trial.

Reaction to the verdict generally brought condemnation of the Madison County legal system, scorn that previously had been reserved for the city of Collinsville and the lynch mob. The *New York Times* said, "The new unwritten law appears to be that any group of men may execute justice, or what they consider justice, in any case growing out of the war."[5]

The *Chicago Daily Tribune* took defense attorneys to task for implying that the legal system had not dealt with a disloyal Prager, so it was appropriate for the mob to act. "The lynching of Prager was reprehensible enough in itself, but the effort to excuse it as an act of 'popular justice' is worse."[6]

"We must save our own soul as a nation," the *St. Louis Star* said. "We cannot let ourselves go in such a way as was done in the

Prager outrage and hold up our heads as civilized people. We are battling for right and humanity and should exhibit those qualities ourselves or be open to the charge of hypocrisy. We cannot successfully battle the Hun if we are to become the Hun ourselves."[7]

The *St. Louis Post-Dispatch* took note of the posttrial finger-pointing: "It does not matter how the blame is distributed for the failure of justice in the Collinsville lynching case. There is enough to go around." It called out one defense ploy in particular. "Everyone who retains a sense of decency deplores the base use which the defendants and their attorneys made of 'patriotism' in the trial of the case. . . . There remains the outstanding shameful fact that a man was murdered in Collinsville, without pretense of concealment, by men who are known, and they have not been punished and there is no prospect that they will be. Law has fallen down in Collinsville."[8]

"Justice has been defeated. Democracy was put on trial in the great State of Illinois and lost its case; democracy has been condemned, convicted and sentenced," said the *St. Louis Labor* newspaper. "Mob rule, lynch law, and defiance of law, order and justice have been sanctioned."[9]

Editors in the smaller communities near Collinsville gave mixed reviews, most attacking the jury decision. "From the verdict of the jury it is evident that Prager committed suicide, as he was found hanging from a tree and no one seems to have had any part therein," said the *Edwardsville Democrat*.[10]

The *Highland Leader* noted the difficulty of obtaining convictions in lynching cases and said, "The prosecutors did their duty and have no occasion to be chagrined at the result. Nor should the learned counsel for the defense get chesty; the eleven lynchers would have been acquitted even if they had relied on the court to appoint their attorney. The lesson the whole thing teaches is that for the time-being, disloyalty classes with such crimes as rape, incest and horse stealing and that a fellow had better let his light so shine that he can't even be suspicioned of any such guilt."[11]

Again the most cutting insights may have been provided by Fred Kern, the feisty editor of the *Belleville News-Democrat*. "The defense consumed its time in condoning the crime, and lifting the lynching aloft into the ethereal realm of the performance of important public duty," Kern said. "The verdict is at variance with the law and the evidence and the instructions of the judge. It is fair warning however, to all people who have a taint of pro-Germanism in their souls, to put the soft pedal on, or to lie low or, better yet, to get right. . . . The lynchers were given a clean bill of health at Edwardsville and may now go out and lynch some more."[12]

A. W. Schimpff, the publisher of the *Advertiser*, called the verdict an "immense relief" in his column and pointed out that the size of the mob made it difficult to single out the actions of any one man. Schimpff called the incident "regrettable" but laid much of the blame on Prager, given his foolish and pro-German views. He also dredged up Prager's prison time and said he was a "white slaver." Schimpff said the lynching had made Americans aware of the dangers of taking the law into their own hands. "Too bad that Collinsville happened to be the place where the crisis should be reached, but it is remarkable that more cases of the kind did not take place in this land."[13]

"His unfortunate fate should be and has been a warning to others who are even more rabid in their disloyalty," Schimpff said. "Previous to the Prager case there were a number of pro-Germans in this City, who on all occasions indicated their hatred for this country and their affection or fear of the Beast of Berlin by open expressions of approval of the most dastardly acts of Prussianism. . . . But there is no more of that in Collinsville, and there is but little of it in surrounding communities. Perhaps after all there are two views of the matter and history will not be so burdened with revenge as to bear too harshly on those who took part."[14]

Schimpff would save his strongest criticism for J. O. Monroe, the young man who had purchased the *Collinsville Herald* less than a year before and greatly improved the newspaper. Monroe took the newsman's role seriously and aggressively covered the Prager affair with extra editions and full-page stories. Schimpff, a former miner, cowered more at pressure from union men and families and gave the trial much less play in his newspaper. Without naming Monroe or the *Herald*, he slammed the competition's prolific coverage of the whole affair, comparing its purveyors to the biblical Pharisees.

> They bawled for revenge and would have continued a condition that would have kept the community in turmoil. The wisest course was to allow the matter to drop into obscurity as soon as possible. Prager was hanged and perhaps met his just desserts. Nothing was to be gained by an effort to railroad another dozen men to the gallows. Nothing was to be gained by raising a hue and cry and by sensational publicity to keep stirring the pot of public feeling.
>
> There has been published in connection with the case column after column of rot that was the veriest bumcombe. Callow youths in the newspaper game have seen a chance for personal gain in the event, and the nimble nickel has been sought with yellow extras. Not to be wondered at when it came from the metropolitan papers, which are absolutely callous of feeling when gain is in sight, but a bird that will befoul its own nest is rather a despicable vulture. . . . They have lost the respect and confidence of the public. They have indulged in a wild orgy of sensationalism and the fiddler must be settled with.[15]

In his column after the trial, Monroe defended the *Herald*'s coverage, saying that most of the defendants were interested in the news and were supplied copies of the *Herald* by friends and relatives. The mother of Charles Cranmer, ill in bed, sent for extra editions of the *Herald* each time they were printed, Monroe said. "Publicity never hurts an honest or innocent man, as is proved by the result of the Prager trial. It is only the guilty who have anything to fear from publicity."[16]

The weekly *Herald* had printed four extras on days when there was testimony and argument in the trial, providing perhaps ten times more coverage than the *Advertiser*. If Monroe was perhaps a little verbose in his reporting, Schimpff and the *Advertiser* underreported and minimized the story of international interest playing out in their own backyard. But at twenty-seven Monroe was already a veteran newsman, having worked at United Press, the forerunner of United Press International, in Springfield and the newspaper in Jacksonville, Illinois. When he had bought the *Herald* from two Collinsville businessmen thirteen months earlier, circulation was just over 400. A year later his weekly circulation was 1,300.[17]

In his column Monroe pointed out weaknesses in the state's case and noted the common feeling in the community that most of the accused were but witnesses to the crime. Having sat on the coroner's jury, Monroe said most of the charges were based on Riegel's confession. He too hammered the point of Prager being immoral and disloyal, as if these alleged defects were both fact more than hopeful imagination.

Collinsville was in a hurry to put the story behind it, to dismiss a wretched night as if it had never happened. And with no relatives or friends walking city streets, Robert Prager had little to prompt any remembrance of him. Monroe related a conversation that was a harbinger of the city's attitude about the lynching for generations to come. After reading a bulletin in front of the *Herald* office that charges had been dismissed against the four police officers, a resident told Monroe: "It's all over now, let's forget it."[18] Then the community did just that.

Many of Collinsville's residents of German lineage were appalled and frightened by what had happened, but they would not publicly speak of it. Nor would the businessmen who depended on the miners and union men as customers. Those who had privately questioned America's need to enter the war, whether they were Socialists or just leery of industrial profiteers, also had no choice but to remain silent and let the matter drop. And it certainly wasn't the proudest moment for the policemen and their families.

Naturally, those with family or friends who had been acquitted also wanted the matter to fade away. As with any other wayward relative or ignominious family event, it would not be discussed, even at the household dinner table.

Those scores of men and boys who had some hand in the affair but were never charged also wanted it forgotten. It was enough just being implicated in the whole mess by whisper and innuendo. That quiet purgatory extended to some young boys, out too late to be up to any good, who tagged along with the mob. They were boys perhaps too young to have a full grasp of what they were doing—yet old enough to grasp the rope and help raise Robert Prager from the ground. The presence of the young boys in the mob had been cited by too many witnesses to ignore. They would live to carry the shame much longer than the old men.

Regret would also burden the men with the mob who knew better, men who could not take their eyes away but failed to utter one word in protest or raise one finger to stop it. Voltaire said, "Every man is guilty of all the good he did not do," and the witnesses too had no desire to dredge up memories of the night when they could have done more.

A U.S. assistant attorney general from the War Emergency Division on April 18 sent Attorney General Thomas Gregory a memo urging the White House make a statement "for the purpose of reassuring the people, quieting their apprehensions, and preventing so far as possible the spread of mob violence, evidence of which is now appearing in all parts of the country."[19] Still Wilson remained quiet on the subject, only saying on April 22 that he was "very deeply concerned" about the treatment of people with different opinions.[20]

Not until July 26, nearly four months after the hanging of Robert Prager, would the president finally speak out about mob action in the United States and subsequent lynchings.[21] Some believed the timing of Wilson's proclamation was driven by Germany's use of the Prager lynching for propaganda purposes in Mexico, South America, and Europe. But the president's timing was probably motivated by a significant increase in the lynching deaths of blacks in southern states; there had been at least thirty just since Prager's lynching. Recent incidents included the late May lynching of eleven blacks in Georgia, allegedly in retaliation for the slaying of a white farmer, and the June lynching of a black woman and her six children in Texas to avenge the reported killing of another white man.[22] In his statement Wilson did not name Collinsville or Prager, or any racial tumult, but spoke solely about the scourge of lynching:

> There have been many lynchings, and every one of them has been a blow at the heart of ordered law and humane justice. No man who loves America . . . can justify mob action while the courts of justice are open and the governments of the States and the Nation are able to do their duty. . . . Germany has outlawed herself among the nations because she has disregarded the sacred obligations of law and made lynchers of her armies. Lynchers emulate her disgraceful example. . . . How shall we commend democracy to the acceptance of other peoples if we disgrace our own by proving that it is, after all, no protection to the weak?[23]

Wilson further urged governors, law enforcement officers, and citizens to end "this disgraceful evil," stating, "It cannot live where the community does not countenance it."[24]

The German press took Wilson to task for what it called his timid—and delayed—reaction to the Prager lynching. "Not a man less will be lynched because Wilson has spoken and, as was the case before, not a lyncher will be sentenced by any court of law. Such a democracy is neither internally sound nor morally strong," said a Cologne newspaper.[25] A Munich newspaper referred to the criminal proceeding as a "mock trial."[26]

The lynching was apparently not reported in German newspapers until May. When it was, one editor attacked the hypocrisy of "the absolutely most free state of the earth." The Hannover newspaper criticized the American government, which allowed the seemingly continual lynchings of blacks, and said, "It is not surprising that a sacrifice has already been made to the rough fury of the illiterate and irritated mob." For all the statements about American refinement and keeping the world safe for democracy, the newspaper said, the United States had failed in both respects. "However difficult it may be for German good nature, we must accustom ourselves to the thought that the Yankee has still an enormous portion of roughness, cruelty and dissoluteness in his blood, which he inherited from the old days, and that a nation which will submit the stain of Collinsville to remain cannot be considered as a nation of culture until the crime has been made good."[27] The Cologne newspaper said that Wilson's comments had been but "crocodile tears" and were driven only by the fear of Germany capitalizing on the lynchings.[28]

It would be mid-June before the German government filed an official complaint about the lynching. Through the Swiss legation, the German government asked for safeguards against similar actions against any German citizens in the States. The Germans contended that the U.S. government was responsible because it "permitted German hatred to be fanned among the American people."[29] It disagreed with the notion that the federal government could not be held accountable for the action, or lack thereof, in state courts.

At no point would President Wilson or his wartime propaganda chief, George Creel of the Committee on Public Information, accept any responsibility for the hysteria they had helped cultivate in 1917 and 1918. They had condemned vigilante action but never seemed to make any connection of it with their federal propaganda programs and the paranoia, persecution, and violence they helped propagate in communities across the nation. Congress, never a fan of Creel's operation, unceremoniously disbanded the CPI on June 30, 1919, without so much as funding the proper closure of the agency.[30]

For all the hysteria foisted on the naive American populace in 1917 and 1918, no bona fide spies or saboteurs would be convicted under the Espionage Act during U.S. involvement in World War I. But the law did prove a valuable weapon for suppressing the opinions of those who *may* have opposed the war for philosophical, political, or religious reasons. By the end of the war, there were about 6,300 warranted arrests, of whom some 2,300 found themselves in jail.[31] They were mostly Socialists and Wobblies, many of whom would have their property permanently taken by the government. The Espionage Act remains federal law, but the Sedition Act amendment, which so severely stifled American civil liberties, was repealed in 1921.

Collinsville's tolerance for dissenting opinion didn't improve after the lynching; perhaps it got worse. Pastor P. G. Spangler, who had seen Prager from the interurban car the night he was lynched, came under fire for initially not allowing Liberty Stamp representatives to speak during his First Baptist Church service. It didn't help that he had objected to military service and offered only to serve in the Salvation Army or the YMCA.[32] He was interviewed by members of the local state council of defense and admitted he may have been "bull-headed," but he continued to hold the belief, like many men of the cloth, that any war was not God's will.[33]

Spangler's troubles weren't nearly as bad as those of John Szillat. He was the city's First Ward alderman and ran a saloon on East Main Street. Szillat was arrested by federal agents and charged with disloyalty in late July after apparently being reported by a neighbor or customer as saying something to the effect of: "This is a rich man's war. If you live in Germany you fight for the Kaiser. If you live in America you have to fight for Wall Street."[34] He also was alleged to have said that America had no business getting into the war, in spite of the *Lusitania* sinking. The U.S. attorney's office in Springfield said that Szillat's saloon was a "clearing house for Socialist propaganda of the lowest type."[35]

Szillat was German by birth, but the fifty-one-year-old had become a naturalized citizen twenty-eight years earlier. When he was arrested, Szillat claimed to be Lithuanian. He was allowed bond and denied the charges, promising to resign as alderman if he was convicted. J. O. Monroe of the *Herald* said that he would not presume Szillat guilty but criticized the continuing unpatriotic talk in the community:

> The surprising thing, it strikes us, is not that there should be here and there a person who cherishes love for German brutality, for some folks are born brutes, but what surprises us is that in this community, where one man was hung on mere suspicion of pro-Germanism, is any man would be lacking in ordinary prudence and common sense as to continue mouthing defense of Germany. It would seem to us that any man with an ounce of sense would

know by this time that not only will the government arrest, convict and punish traitors but that the community itself will not tolerate any propaganda. Any man who continues to prate the arguments, which were permissible two or three years ago, can only be taken for a loose-lipped ignoramus, an ordinary damphool.[36]

The final disposition of the Szillat case is unknown, but most such charges ended up being nolle prosequi, with the defendant unmistakably getting the message that friends and neighbors and the federal government were watching and listening closely.

• • •

Factory whistles blowing in St. Louis just before 3:00 a.m. were the first indication that there was good news, that the armistice had finally been signed on November 11, 1918. As the noise drifted into Collinsville, people knew it was cause for celebration. As residents woke from their sleep, they went outside with every possible noisemaker, from guns to pots and pans.[37] Two men walked about uptown, blasting their coronets as they went. C. H. Dorris made his walk to Webster School to ring the bell. Neither the Chester Knitting Mills nor any of the mines would operate that day, for everyone believed the eleventh-hour agreement worthy of the day off.

It would be difficult to assess how many Americans in 1917 and 1918 truly favored U.S. involvement in the Great War. They undoubtedly supported their soldiers who were being sent abroad. But superpatriotism and vigilante action prevented most people from openly speaking their opinions on overall American involvement—particularly in places like Collinsville, where a mob had murdered a man merely upon rumor and gotten away with it. Open support and public flag-waving didn't necessarily mean that a person genuinely agreed with the nation's involvement. The war's unpopularity was widely believed to be the cause of Republicans winning most elected offices in Madison County and Illinois in the November 1918 elections.[38] At the national level, Woodrow Wilson's Democrats would lose majority control in the Senate and Republicans would increase their advantage in the House.

Wilson's unpopularity and his failure to involve Republicans in peace negotiations ultimately led to U.S. Senate rejection of the Treaty of Versailles. The United States also did not participate in the new League of Nations. Wilson strongly advocated for the league as key to preventing future international conflict, enough so that the president would be awarded the Nobel Peace Prize in 1919, but the United States would not partake. In the end the league proved nearly impotent in preventing the aggression that led to World War II.

Lingering regret over American entanglement in World War I and resentment over the subsequent bank and industrial profits played a large part in the United States' isolationist attitude of the 1930s. Twenty years after the war, in 1937, a Gallup poll showed that 70 percent of Americans thought U.S. intervention in the Great War was, in fact, *a Great Mistake.*[39] That sentiment laid the groundwork for just 7 percent of Americans wanting the nation to get involved militarily in 1940, even after Germany's invasion of France, when Adolph Hitler's intentions were unmistakably clear.[40]

Collinsville's financial support of the Great War improved with the third and fourth Liberty Bond drives. But the intimidating atmosphere in the city no doubt drove up sales to those who feared being called pro-German; such people may have effectively bought the bonds merely as a form of protection. In that respect how much of the community genuinely supported the war effort cannot be determined. After failing to meet its quota for the first two drives, the city more than doubled its expected sales on the third bond drive, which coincidently began the day after the Prager lynching and topped $340,000.[41] It helped too when the miners' unions got more involved after the first two bond drives.

Collinsville ended up 20 percent above quota on the fourth bond sale that closed in October 1918, but when sales stalled the local Liberty Bond Committee briefly considered listing in the newspaper all those who had purchased bonds.[42] A banner ad on the front page of the *Herald* warned, "If you haven't bought or if you bought so little that you'll be ashamed to have the public know about it, you have until Saturday night to redeem yourself."[43] The list would have given a desirable pat on the back to those who had stepped up, but it also could have provided a literal punch list for those in the community bent on harassing suspected pro-Germans or slackers. As it appeared the committee would meet quota late in the drive, it mercifully backed off the idea of publishing any names.

By the time of the 1919 Victory Bond drive to pay off the remaining war debt, Collinsville had once again lost interest, or the suspected pro-Germans no longer felt the need for protection. Faced with a quota of $325,000, individual buyers in the community stepped up for only $100,000 worth of bonds. The city met quota only after the two local banks bought the remaining $225,000 worth.[44]

Hundreds of Collinsville men were drafted into service for the Great War. By August of 1918, the troop trains would also include three of the acquitted defendants, Richard Dukes Jr., Enid Elmore, and Joe Riegel. Madison County would end up registering over 29,000 for the draft, more than 3,700 of whom were inducted and accepted into service.[45] An additional 453 men, and one woman, signed up for the navy, which was all volunteer at the time.[46] Collinsville ended up sending about 700 drafted and enlisted men to fight in World War I.[47] Illinois contributed more than 300,000 of the total 4.7 million enlisted and drafted men who served.[48]

The United States lost over 116,000 men in the Great War, but less than half of those were battle deaths.[49] Still, critics noted the high number of combat losses, although whole American armies were engaged in battle for only six months. Veterans' officials had by 1930 raised the toll to 460,000, citing later disease and injury deaths, including those caused by chemical warfare.[50]

The Collinsville community would not grieve its first battlefield death until Corporal August Karwelat Jr., twenty-four, died July 18, 1918, in the Second Battle of the Marne in France.[51] That battle was one of the final actions in the German spring offensive determined to take advantage before American men and matèriel flooded European battlefields. A few weeks later, the first Collinsville man was wounded in battle in France. He was Cecil Johnson, the son of United Mine Workers board member Mose Johnson.[52]

The Great War claimed the lives of seventeen Collinsville-area men, most dying of pneumonia or influenza.[53] Two of the battle deaths occurred in November, just days before the armistice. Three of the soldiers died of influenza in the training camps during one cruel week in October 1918, when seven people back in Collinsville also succumbed to the virus.[54] In all, forty-four Collinsville-area deaths would be attributed to influenza from approximately one thousand cases reported.[55] The epidemic caused a two-month delay for the grand opening of the magnificent new Miner's Institute and theater building because authorities correctly prohibited large congregating groups in order to stop the spread of disease. The October 1918 outbreak also claimed Madison County's young coroner, Roy Lowe, thirty-three, who was believed to have been infected while handling bodies of the deceased.

In the 1919 city elections, Collinsville's miners tightened their grip on city government by electing James Darmody mayor on the ticket of their newly created Labor Party.[56] The new party name was certainly more palatable than Socialist during the Red Scare era, and its miner candidates would also win two of five aldermanic seats. Mayor John Siegel had run for a third two-year term but was easily defeated by Darmody, who had been an officer in two miners' locals. Also beaten in the election was Alderman Tim Kane, a blacksmith and the only other elected official, besides Siegel, who had stood up and tried desperately to placate the mob one year earlier in front of city hall.

The left-leaning political point of view continued in Collinsville, with Progressive presidential candidate Robert La Follette carrying the township in the 1924 election.[57] He garnered just 17 percent of the vote nationally but 51 percent in Collinsville Township, tallying more votes than Democrats and Republicans combined. Incumbent Republican Calvin Coolidge won that presidential election handily.

The coal miners in Collinsville, however, would go the way of King Coal and gradually fade from power. The year 1918 was the high-water mark for the coal industry in Illinois, which had over ninety thousand miners. Cleaner-burning natural gas slowly grew in popularity and the soft, high-sulfur coal found in the southern Illinois mines became even less desirable. As St. Louis and its industry grew, the city captured the reputation for having the nation's filthiest air, and the readily available southern Illinois coal was largely to blame. After another particularly onerous November day of cut-with-a-knife air pollution in 1939—appropriately dubbed Black Tuesday—St. Louis officials banned the use of Illinois coal.[58]

Even with the wartime coal needs of 1945, Illinois mines produced just sixty-three million tons, about 30 percent less than 1918.[59] And the number of miners statewide dropped to about thirty thousand. Increased mechanization of the mines had further reduced the number of miners to about ten thousand by 1960, when the state was still producing forty-five million tons annually.[60]

The Collinsville mines became more costly to operate after the Great War, as operations extended farther from the main shafts. Just one of the big mines was operating in Collinsville by 1937, employing 378 men.[61] Seven smaller co-op mines operated with 317 men, but the total output was a fraction of what it had been. When Collinsville's last coal mine closed in 1964, it was also the last one operating in Madison County. There are few visible reminders today of Collinsville's coal mining past . . . a barren lot here, a sealed air shaft there, a few vacant grassy areas remediated to stop acid mine drainage. A few areas have been affected by mine subsidence, causing foundation damage to buildings constructed over abandoned coal seams.

But then the mines had always been a blessing, and a curse, for Collinsville. When the shafts were fully operating, primarily in winter, they produced excellent wages. But when the mines were idle, the miners had little money left to spend, and the economic impact rippled throughout the city.[62]

As local coal production faded, so did the repressive grip of the coal miner's unions in the Collinsville area. The United Mine Workers of America solidified its power base nationally after the election of John L. Lewis as president in 1920, and the southern Illinois miners' penchant for administering their own justice would play out to the extreme when twenty strikebreakers and three union men were killed in the Herrin Massacre in 1922. But the UMW fell into disfavor with Illinois miners because of wage concessions, and Collinsville's locals affiliated with the upstart Progressive Miners of America in 1932. Violence continued elsewhere in Illinois while the two rival unions battled for control, but the Collinsville area miners' would be less and less a factor in that struggle.

Blacks were never able to secure the better-paying jobs as coal miners in the Collinsville area, though they continued to constitute a great part of the workforce at the St. Louis Smelting and Refining plant.[63] The Lead Works became less profitable when the lead mines in St. Francis, Missouri, were exhausted and it had to buy ore on the open market. When workers once again tried to organize for higher wages and shorter hours, this time as the Progressive Lead Workers in November 1933, the plant was closed for good.[64] Critical production equipment was shipped off to a facility in South America. The stately manager's homes still remain on what was once Cuba Lane. And some seventy years after the smelter's closing, the EPA ordered the replacement of grass and topsoil in a subdivision that had been built over the site, noting still unacceptably high levels of lead in the ground.

Collinsville was not unlike most towns across the United States during the Great War; all were fed a steady diet of government propaganda and fearmongering. What set it apart was its high percentage of immigrants and the incessant bullying by its coal miners' unions. Fused with patriotic paranoia, they brought out the worst in Collinsville, making it the only American town during World War I where a German immigrant died at the end of a lynching rope. Across the nation other voluntary associations served in authority roles similar to those of the coal miners in Collinsville, but nowhere else were the results so tragic. "The American home front was not a lawless frontier, a police state or a great big meeting of the Elks Club," one Great War historian wrote. "But it looked a little like all of these."[65]

With the perceived need to involve ordinary citizens in keeping the nation secure, perhaps the murder was inevitable. "War always degrades the human mind, especially the mind of the civilian," School Superintendent C. H. Dorris said prophetically, just weeks before the lynching. "The tendency is not so evident with those who do the actual fighting. Soldiers usually speak generously of their foes and quickly forgive those with whom they have measured swords. Not so with those who stay at home. We are apt to be blinded with intolerance and hate."[66]

• • •

Robert Prager was buried in a remote location at St. Matthew Cemetery in St. Louis just after the lynching, but in October 1919 his remains were moved to a better grave site by the same Odd Fellows Lodge that had claimed his body. Harmonie Lodge 353 invited Collinsville Odd Fellows Lodge 43 to attend the service some eighteen months after the lynching. Hundreds gathered as lodge members moved the remains closer to the cemetery entrance, where a fine monument had been erected. "The American flag was insulted and soiled by the men who pretended to be Americans," one speaker said at services that day. "There must have been something wrong with the minds of the people to have allowed such a disgrace."[67]

If no one else cared to remember, the Odd Fellows of St. Louis would not forget Robert Prager. Harmonie Lodge 353 was long gone in 2006, but a member of Lodge 5, also of St. Louis, took note when Prager's old gravestone had become worn and faded after eighty-seven years, and the group replaced it with a new marker. It had the same inscription as the old monument, his fate simply noted as "The Victim of a Mob."[68]

Madison County heard from Prager's father, Karl Heinrich Prager, in a lawsuit filed in 1923 claiming that Robert Prager was his only means of support and asking the county for compensation. The suit was based on a 1918 Illinois Statute that provided for payment of up to $5,000, drawing from the concept of the time that local governments bore some financial responsibility for mob violence. The suit was filed in U.S. District Court in Springfield but dismissed three years later when the St. Louis attorney representing Karl Prager did not appear in court.[69]

The old city hall still stands in Collinsville, but Prager's little shack is long gone, as is the hanging tree, felled in 1962 to clear the way for utility lines. Perhaps appropriately the tree's approximate location is marked by a sign for the expanded St. John Cemetery.

For generations one of the persistent whispers in Collinsville was that a disproportionate number of the men responsible for the Prager lynching had met their fate violently or prematurely, *that they had gotten what was coming to them.* It was civic schadenfreude for a shamed community. But investigation doesn't necessarily bear out the hearsay. Two of the eleven acquitted men died young, but most lived relatively long lives for the era. It could well be that the murmur of the violent, early deaths spoke to the scores of men, and perhaps boys, who had been involved in the lynching affair but were never officially charged or named.

No one knows what drove saloon porter Wesley Beaver, at age twenty-seven, to place a pistol to his right temple and pull the trigger seven months after the trial. He had remained the same happy-go-lucky soul after Prager's murder and never expressed a word of remorse for his involvement in the affair. The morning of January 11, 1919, he told a businessman, "A lot of people think I'm crazy, but I'll have a laugh coming someday."[70] He was discovered that evening in the meeting room above Martin Fulton's Y Saloon with the proprietor's back-bar .38 revolver at his feet. Beaver was involved in one final clamorous procession, his funeral parade to the cemetery led by the Collinsville Concert Band, as he had requested to his many friends.

Enid Elmore, twenty-one years old at the time of the lynching, died of influenza at age twenty-six in Kentucky, where he worked as a butcher.[71] William Brockmeier, forty-one at the time of the lynching, had been an itinerant miner and worked the Collinsville area mines for about two years prior to the lynching. Weeks after the acquittal, he was arrested for failing to pay child support for his family back in Brazil, Indiana, perhaps because he was incarcerated.[72] He had moved on to a mine in Danville, Illinois, some eleven years later when he was killed at the age of fifty-three in a mine ceiling collapse.[73] He was the only charged man known to have died a traumatic death besides Wesley Beaver.

Most of the acquitted men stayed in the Collinsville area, but only one would stay in coal mining, John Hallworth; the others mostly worked out their lives in other blue-collar jobs. Charles Cranmer ended up selling shoes at a department store. Richard Dukes Jr., the biggest and perhaps toughest of the bunch, rarely worked and ended up battling the bottle more than anything else for the rest of his life. He was arrested in 1931 along with the sister of southern Illinois gangsters Bernie and Carl Shelton following a gangland slaying of three men in East St. Louis but was never charged with any crime.[74] For the most part, the men lived quietly, without much talk of the lynching.

The one exception might have been Cecil Larremore, at seventeen years old estranged from his parents and the youngest man charged in the case. He remained very much in the public eye because he and his wife ran a series of restaurants and bars in the uptown area. He was a pleasant and popular man, apparently well liked in the community. Larremore ran for office in a Collinsville Township election once and later worked for the City of Collinsville as parks supervisor. Still, there were those who would not eat in his restaurants because of his involvement in the lynching. Some reported that Larremore was unrepentant about the Prager affair when the matter happened to come up.

A community leader in Collinsville, Bill Jokerst, had adopted the habit in the 1980s of speaking to some Collinsville High School history classes about the Prager lynching.[75] He told the story much as it had been told to him sitting on his father's knee as a young boy. But sharing that particular story didn't sit well with one of Larremore's descendants, who once called and admonished Jokerst for bringing up the topic some seventy years later. *It was something that shouldn't be discussed,* she said. Collinsville High School's American history teachers now lecture on the Prager incident in their classes each year.

The leader of the lynching effort, Joe Riegel, joined the army for two years on July 31, 1918. He was trained, but the armistice would be signed before he could be shipped out, and he was discharged on December 7, 1918. Riegel was still wearing his army uniform December 18 when he appeared before a clerk in Collinsville to get a marriage license with Ruth Kolb of East St. Louis, never mind the fact that he was still married to his first wife, Emma. The next day the eighteen-year-old Kolb returned the license after she learned more of the history of her betrothed, who was ten years her senior. Riegel explained the matter to a newspaper reporter simply as a joke.[76]

Nine months later Riegel signed up for another one-year army stint and ended up extending it another three years when he was assigned to duty in Koblenz, Germany.[77] He was discharged September 1, 1923, at Camp Vail, New Jersey. Despite his total of seven years and four months served in the army, he would never be promoted above the rank of private.

There is no known record that Riegel ever ventured as far west as Collinsville again after his discharge from the army. By 1926 he had apparently settled down and married a woman in Cleveland, Ohio, and helped in raising her three children.[78] He died there in 1947 after working jobs mostly at freight and trucking companies. Riegel was fifty-seven at the time of his death, and after 1918 he apparently had little or no contact with his son, Fred, from the 1915 marriage in Illinois.[79] The child was raised by Riegel's parents in their Collinsville home.

J. O. Monroe went on to build the *Collinsville Herald* into a fine family-owned community newspaper. He also served many years as an Illinois state senator. Five years after the lynching, he once again got a chance to stand up to mob action and intimidation after a large Ku Klux Klan rally near Monk's Mound in May 1923, and this time there was no hesitation on his part.[80] Awakened by the blaring horns of a midnight Klan parade around Main and Clay Streets, Monroe wrote down the license numbers of all the cars he could see and outed those in the procession in the next edition of his newspaper. He did not recoil from heavy criticism for identifying the members of the clandestine group. "Presumably the Klan is something to be spoken of in a whisper and not out loud," he said in his column.[81] And after a lifetime of publishing and Democratic politics, Monroe's views on the Prager affair changed completely.

One week after the men were acquitted in 1918, Monroe wrote his column under the heading "The Whole City Is Glad." He went on to relate the opinion that many in the city held at the time.

> Outside a few persons who may still harbor Germanic inclinations, the whole City is glad that the 11 men indicted for the hanging of Robert P. Prager were acquitted. . . . The community is well-convinced that he was disloyal. The City does not miss him. The lesson of his death has had a wholesome effect on the Germanists of Collinsville and the rest of the nation. In this day and time when human life is being sacrificed by the thousands for principle, Prager's death may be regarded as a cheap price to pay for the silencing of Germanic tongues.[82]

After raising five children and retiring from politics and publishing, Monroe in 1962 wrote the memoirs of his long career and reflected on the Prager affair. Forty-four years later, with the mature clarity only given an old man, he revisited the biggest story he had ever covered:

> Looking back on the whole horrible thing, it seems a nightmare. It began with gossip, fear and hate for the alien. It grew with idleness, rabble-rousing talk and excessive misguided patriotism, and

the temper of drunkenness. It was made possible by the surprise and carelessness of the police, and unfortunate miss-guesses on what to do with the man.

When the crowd first got to the victim, no one really thought of hanging. Tar and feathers were intended. The tar was not found. A rope was. By now there were over 200 yelling men, flushed with beer, hot from marching over a mile, confused, and muddled with mob psychology.[83] Nowhere appeared a sober, clear-headed man to say "no," and make it stick. And so came violence, death, tragedy and shame.[84]

Appendix

Collinsville, Ill., 4-4-18
Proclamation to the Members of Local Union 1802, Maryville, Ill.

Dear Brothers:

In regards to affairs of last night, I am compelled to make this statement in public to you. My name is Robert P. Prager of 208 1/2 Vandalia Street, Collinsville, Ill. The statements uttered by your president of your Local No. 1802, Mr. J. Fornero; and also the action taken by him to take away my daily bread in such a manner as herein stated, is not the action or will of your people as a workingman's union. I have respect for your officials if on legal duty and will obey their commands to the letter. I have been a union man at all times and never once a scab in all my life, and for this reason I appeal to you. An honest working man as myself is entitled to a fair hearing of your committee. I ask you in the name of humanity to examine me to find out what is the reason I am kept out of work. I have kept the union informed from the very beginning of my employment at the Maryville mine. I have put in and signed up two applications, the first with Mr. Wilhelm and the second with Mr. Ben Kettle. I have also had my application signed by three of your good standing members who have worked with me at various mines. I do not claim to be a practical miner, but do claim to have worked over four years in the mines as a laborer, most of this time as a timberman. In regard to my loyalty, I will state that I am heart and soul for the good old U.S.A. I am of German birth, which accident I cannot help, and also have declared my intention of U.S. citizenship. My second papers are due to be issued very soon if I am granted same. Please give this appeal due consideration and allow me to return to work.

Yours in respect,
Robt. P. Prager

I further wish to state that I was branded as a liar in public by your president, Jim Fornero. By him I was branded a German Spy, which he cannot prove. Also this gentleman tried to have me arrested at Edwardsville, Maryville and Collinsville, Ill., and did not succeed in any of these places. Mr. Fornero tried to have an angry mob deal with me. I also was informed by him to leave my home at once and never again come to Maryville if I knew what was good for my health. Also please state to your union for what reason you have kept a brother working man that is honest, law-abiding and loyal and take his bread away.

Collinsville Advertiser, April 6, 1918
St. Louis Post-Dispatch, April 5, 1918

Notes

This account of the Collinsville community in 1917 and 1918, the lynching itself, and the trial was primarily derived by synthesizing information gathered from more than fifteen newspapers that had reporters in the area prior to, during, or after the incident, or at the trial in Edwardsville. Only by compiling the accounts of these newspapers can we clearly understand the psyche of the community during that era.

As is still the case today, initial reporting was naturally more prone to error, given the rush to get the story out. Many facts were not publicly revealed until the trial. Other information would scarcely warrant an initial mention yet shed critical light on the incident when examined in context with other events. Newspaper reporters of the era often did not precisely quote a speaker, instead settling for an approximation of what was said. When newspapers had differing versions of quotations from the same speaker, the author utilized that which was most plausible given the oratorical or conversational style of a century ago.

1. It's Plain Murder

1. *Collinsville Herald*, April 28, 1918.
2. *St. Louis Globe-Democrat*, May 30, 1918.
3. *Collinsville Advertiser*, May 18, 1918.
4. *Edwardsville Intelligencer*, April 24, 1918.
5. *Collinsville Herald*, April 26, 1918.
6. *Collinsville Advertiser*, April 6, 1918.
7. *Collinsville Herald*, April 12, 1918.
8. *Collinsville Advertiser*, April 6, 1918.
9. *Collinsville Herald*, April 12, 1918; *Edwardsville Intelligencer*, April 8, 1918.

10. *Belleville News-Democrat*, April 12, 1918.

11. *St. Louis Post-Dispatch*, June 2, 1918.

12. *St. Louis Republic*, May 30, 1918.

13. *Collinsville Herald*, May 29, 1918.

14. *Belleville News-Democrat*, April 12, 1918.

15. *St. Louis Star*, April 11, 1918.

16. *Collinsville Advertiser*, April 6, 1918.

17. *St. Louis Star*, April 11, 1918.

18. Editorial, *Collinsville Advertiser*, April 13, 1918.

19. *Collinsville Advertiser*, April 6, 1918.

20. *Collinsville Advertiser*, April 6, 1918.

21. *St. Louis Post-Dispatch*, April 9, 1918.

22. *Collinsville Advertiser*, April 6, 1918.

23. *Collinsville Herald*, April 5, 1918.

24. *Collinsville Advertiser*, April 6, 1918.

25. *St. Louis Post-Dispatch*, April 12, 1918.

26. *Collinsville Herald*, May 28, 1918.

27. *Collinsville Herald*, April 12, 1918.

28. *Collinsville Herald*, April 12, 1918.

29. *St. Louis Post-Dispatch*, April 11, 1918.

30. *St. Louis Globe-Democrat*, May 29, 1918.

31. *Belleville News-Democrat*, April 12, 1918.

32. *St. Louis Globe-Democrat*, May 29, 1918.

33. *St. Louis Star*, April 5, 1918.

34. *St. Louis Post-Dispatch*, May 29, 1918.

35. *Collinsville Advertiser*, April 6, 1918.

36. *Collinsville Advertiser*, April 6, 1918.

37. *St. Louis Star*, April 10, 1918.

38. *St. Louis Post-Dispatch*, May 29, 1918.

39. *Collinsville Advertiser*, April 6, 1918.

40. *St. Louis Globe-Democrat*, April 5, 1918.

41. *Collinsville Herald*, April 12, 1918.

42. *St. Louis Post-Dispatch*, April 11, 1918.

43. *St. Louis Republic*, May 30, 1918.

44. *Collinsville Advertiser*, April 6, 1918.

45. *St. Louis Post-Dispatch*, May 29, 1918.

46. *St. Louis Star*, April 5, 1918.

47. *St. Louis Star*, April 5, 1918.

48. *St. Louis Post-Dispatch*, May 29, 1918.

49. *St. Louis Star*, May 29, 1918.

50. *St. Louis Post-Dispatch*, May 29, 1918.

51. Robert Prager, final note, Collinsville Historical Museum. Translated by Carmen Freeman.

52. Cranmer wrote "Tresten, Germany" on the note, his erroneous understanding of "Dresden, Germany."

53. *St. Louis Star*, April 11, 1918.

54. *St. Louis Post-Dispatch*, April 11, 1918.

55. *St. Louis Star*, April 11, 1918.

56. *St. Louis Star*, April 11, 1918.

57. *Collinsville Advertiser*, April 6, 1918.

58. *St. Louis Star*, April 11, 1918.

59. *St. Louis Star*, April 5, 1918.

60. *Collinsville Advertiser*, April 6, 1918.

61. *Collinsville Advertiser*, April 6, 1918.

2. A Small Town, a Great War

1. Chenoweth, Elrick, and Barrett, *Directory of Coal Mines*, 32. Local historians cite the first Collinsville mine as being sunk in 1857 or 1859, but these dates could not be confirmed.

2. Killinger, "Collinsville Our Heritage," 9, Collinsville Memorial Public Library.

3. Gill, "Historical Survey," 59, Collinsville Memorial Public Library.

4. Illinois Department of Mines and Minerals, *36th Annual Coal Report*; Illinois Department of Mines and Minerals, *37th Annual Coal Report*.

5. U.S. Bureau of the Census, *14th Census*, 261–65.

6. *Collinsville Herald*, March 30, 1917.

7. J. O. Monroe, "So Far, So Good: 50 Years of Memoirs of Printing, Publishing, Politics and People," *Collinsville Herald*, August 2, 1962.

8. *Collinsville Advertiser*, April 7, 1917.

9. Monroe, "So Far, So Good," *Collinsville Herald*, August 2, 1962.

10. *Collinsville Herald*, June 22, 1917.

11. Monroe, "So Far, So Good," *Collinsville Herald*, August 2, 1962.

12. Axelrod, *Selling the Great War*, 44.

13. Axelrod, *Selling the Great War*, 57.

14. Axelrod, *Selling the Great War*, 57, 43.

15. Kennedy, *Over Here*, 11–12.

16. Monroe, "So Far, So Good," *Collinsville Herald*, August 2, 1962.

17. Emerson, *Blue Book*, 578.

18. Feldman, *Manufacturing Hysteria*, 11–12.

19. Feldman, *Manufacturing Hysteria*, 14.

20. Kennedy, *Over Here*, 14.

21. Peterson and Fite, *Opponents of War*, 22, 43.

22. Kennedy, *Over Here*, 144.

23. Kennedy, *Over Here*, 147.

24. U.S. Bureau of the Census, *14th Census*, 4.

25. Axelrod, *Selling the Great War*, 184.

26. Kennedy, *Over Here*, 41.

27. Fleming, *Illusion of Victory*, 94.

28. Axelrod, *Selling the Great War*, 63.

29. Axelrod, *Selling the Great War*, 104.

30. Axelrod, *Selling the Great War*, 108.

31. Fleming, *Illusion of Victory*, 120.

32. Axelrod, *Selling the Great War*, 142.

33. Axelrod, *Selling the Great War*, 146–47.

34. Axelrod, *Selling the Great War*, 157.

35. Axelrod, *Selling the Great War*, 160–68.

36. Axelrod, *Selling the Great War*, 169.

37. Kennedy, *Over Here*, 55.

38. Feldman, *Manufacturing Hysteria*, 35.

39. Feldman, *Manufacturing Hysteria*, 35.

40. Lohrmann, "Experiences in the Parsonages," Concordia Historical Institute.

41. *Collinsville Advertiser*, May 26, 1917.

42. *Collinsville Advertiser*, May 26, 1917.

43. *Collinsville Herald*, June 8, 1917.

44. *Collinsville Advertiser*, June 9, 1917.

45. *Collinsville Herald*, June 8, 1917.

46. *Collinsville Herald*, June 8, 1917.

47. *Collinsville Advertiser*, June 9, 1917.

48. Mead, *Doughboys*, 71.

49. Jenison, *War-Time Organization of Illinois*, 5–6.

50. Mead, *Doughboys*, 71.

51. *Collinsville Herald*, June 8, 1918.

52. *Collinsville Herald*, May 12, 1917.

53. *Collinsville Herald*, July 13, 1917.

54. *Collinsville Herald*, May 12, 1917.

55. Mead, *Doughboys*, 71.

56. *Collinsville Herald*, July 17, 1917.

57. J. O. Monroe, "So Far, So Good: 50 Years of Memoirs of Printing, Publishing, Politics and People," *Collinsville Herald*, July 30, 1962.

58. *Collinsville Herald*, July 27, 1917.

59. *Collinsville Herald*, August 3, 1917.

60. *Collinsville Herald*, July 27, 1917.

61. *Collinsville Herald*, August 17, 1917.

62. Charles Maurer letter, Illinois State Historical Library.

63. *Collinsville Herald*, August 31, 1917

64. *Collinsville Herald*, June 2, 1917.

65. *Collinsville Herald*, September 7, 1917.

66. Robert Johann, interview with author, July 7, 2014.

67. *Collinsville Herald*, May 4, 1917.

68. *Collinsville Herald*, June 2, 1917.

69. *Collinsville Herald*, October 12, 1917.

70. *Collinsville Herald*, September 7, 1917.

71. *Collinsville Herald*, July 20, 1917.

72. *Collinsville Advertiser*, September 22, 1917.

73. *Collinsville Herald*, September 21, 1917.

74. Editorial, *Collinsville Herald*, September 28, 1917.

75. *Collinsville Herald*, October 5, 1917.

76. *Collinsville Herald*, October 5, 1917.

77. *Collinsville Herald*, November 16, 1917.

78. Charles Maurer letter.

79. *Collinsville Herald*, December 21, 1917.

80. Kennedy, *Over Here*, 157.

81. Editorial, *Collinsville Advertiser*, September 1, 1917.

82. Charles Maurer letter.

83. *Collinsville Herald*, March 1, 1918.

84. Mead, *Doughboys*, 148.

85. *Collinsville Herald*, March 22, 1918; Mead, *Doughboys*, 71.

86. *Collinsville Herald*, May 19, 1917.

87. Mead, *Doughboys*, 173.

88. "Income Tax," *United Mine Workers Journal*, January 10, 1918, 16.

89. Axelrod, *Selling the Great War*, 149.

90. *Collinsville Herald*, July 6, 1917.

91. Editorial, *Collinsville Herald*, June 15, 1917.

92. Liberty Loan Organization, *Subscriptions*.

93. *Collinsville Herald*, October 19, 1917.

94. *Collinsville Herald*, October 19, 1917.

95. Kennedy, *Over Here*, 106.

96. *Collinsville Herald*, April 27, 1917.

97. *Collinsville Herald*, May 4, 1917.

98. St. Louis Smelting and Refining Collection, Collinsville Historical Museum.

99. *East St. Louis Daily Journal*, August 12, 1917.

100. *Collinsville Herald*, August 17, 1917.

101. *Collinsville Herald*, July 6, 1917.

102. *Collinsville Herald*, December 7, 1917.

103. *Collinsville Herald*, June 29, 1917.

104. *Collinsville Herald*, March 1, 1918.

105. Monroe, "So Far, So Good," *Collinsville Herald*, August 2, 1962.

106. *Collinsville Herald*, June 2, 1917.

107. Baseball Almanac, "1917 World Series."

108. Mead, *Doughboys*, 91.

109. Kennedy, *Over Here*, 175–76.

110. Mead, *Doughboys*, 103.

111. Mead, *Doughboys*, 127.

112. Mead, *Doughboys*, 128.

113. Kennedy, *Over Here*, 169.

114. Mead, *Doughboys*, 105.

115. Mead, *Doughboys*, 163.

116. *Washington Post*, November 27, 1917.

117. Farwell, *Over There*, 108.

118. Farwell, *Over There*, 108.

119. Beals, "Collinsville World War I Casualties," Collinsville Memorial Public Library.

120. Dorris, "Schoolmaster and the War," Mary Sue Schusky collection.

121. *Collinsville Advertiser*, December 29, 1917.

122. *Collinsville Herald*, January 4, 1918.

123. *Collinsville Advertiser*, January 26, 1918.

124. *Collinsville Herald*, February 15, 1918.

125. Feldman, *Manufacturing Hysteria*, 64.

126. *Collinsville Herald*, January 4, 1918.

127. *Collinsville Herald*, March 1, 1918.

128. Mead, *Doughboys*, 11.

129. *St. Louis Times*, May 24, 1918.

130. Dorris, "Schoolmaster and the War."

131. Dorris, "Schoolmaster and the War."

132. *Collinsville Herald*, September 7, 1917.

133. *Collinsville Advertiser*, November 24, 1917.

134. *Collinsville Advertiser*, November 24, 1917.

135. *Collinsville Advertiser*, December 1, 1917.

136. *Collinsville*, Ill. *City Directory 1916*.

137. *Collinsville Herald*, December 7, 1917.

138. *Collinsville Herald*, December 7, 1917.

139. Dorothy (Dorris) Dilliard memoirs, 6–7, Mary Sue Schusky collection.

140. Capozolla, *Uncle Sam Wants You*, 84.

141. Coit, "History of Collinsville, Illinois Chapter," Collinsville Historical Museum.

142. Jenison, *War-Time Organization of Illinois*, 5–419.

143. C. H. Dorris Collection, Collinsville Historical Museum.

144. Kennedy, *Over Here*, 123.

145. Kennedy, *Over Here*, 124.

146. *Collinsville Herald*, January 18, 1918.

147. *Collinsville Advertiser*, January 19, 1918.

148. Kennedy, *Over Here*, 124.

149. *Collinsville Advertiser*, January 26, 1918.

150. Fleming, *Illusion of Victory*, 173.

151. Fleming, *Illusion of Victory*, 234–35.

152. Fleming, *Illusion of Victory*, 151.

153. Kennedy, *Over Here*, 117

154. Okrent, *Last Call*, 99.

155. Kennedy, *Over Here*, 117.

156. *Collinsville Advertiser*, February 9, 1918.

157. *Collinsville Herald*, January 4, 1918.

158. Editorial, *Collinsville Herald*, February 15, 1918.

159. *Collinsville Advertiser*, February 16, 1918.

160. Editorial, *Collinsville Herald*, February 15, 1918.

161. Axelrod, *Selling the Great War*, 120.

162. *Collinsville Advertiser*, February 9, 1918.

163. Axelrod, *Selling the Great War*, 124.

164. Peterson and Fite, *Opponents of War*, 93.

165. C. H. Dorris Collection.

166. Dorothy (Dorris) Dilliard memoirs, 6.

167. Dorris, "Schoolmaster and the War."

168. *Collinsville Herald*, July 13, 1917.

169. *Collinsville Herald*, December 7, 1917.

170. *Collinsville Herald*, February 22, 1918.

171. *Collinsville Advertiser*, April 13, 1918.

172. *Collinsville Herald*, March 8, 1918.

3. United We Stand

1. Chenoweth, Elrick, and Barrett, *Directory of Coal Mines*.

2. Maryville Centennial Committee, *Maryville, Illinois*, 13–15, Collinsville Memorial Public Library.

3. Vernetti, *Old King Coal*, 49.

4. *Collinsville Coal Mines*, Collinsville Historical Museum.

5. *Collinsville Coal Mines*.

6. Killinger, "Collinsville Our Heritage," 10.

7. "Vivid Memory," Irving Dilliard Collection, Collinsville Historical Museum.

8. Morton, "Day in the Mine," 16.

9. Chenoweth, Elrick, and Barrett, *Directory of Coal Mines*.

10. Chenoweth, Elrick, and Barrett, *Directory of Coal Mines*.

11. Morton, "Day in the Mine," 17.

12. Morton, "Day in the Mine," 17.

13. Morton, "Day in the Mine," 16.

14. Abbott, *Immigrant and Coal Mining Communities*, 42.

15. Vernetti, *Old King Coal*, 49.

16. Illinois Department of Mines and Minerals, *36th Annual Coal Report of Illinois*, 50.

17. Emerson, *Blue Book*, 375.

18. Illinois Department of Mines and Minerals, *37th Annual Coal Report*, 2.

19. Illinois Department of Mines and Minerals, *37th Annual Coal Report*, 206.

20. Illinois Department of Mines and Minerals, *37th Annual Coal Report*, 206.

21. *United Mine Workers Journal*, January 10, 1918, 8. Mindful of its high immigrant membership, the weekly UMW *Journal* in 1918 had sections with critical news items also printed in Italian and Slovak.

22. *United Mine Workers Journal*, February 21, 1918, 11.

23. *Collinsville Herald*, November 16, 1918.

24. *Collinsville Herald*, March 1, 1918.

25. Scott Richardson, "100 Years Later, Tragedy of Cherry Mine Disaster Still Hits Home," *Bloomington (IL) Pantagraph*, April 11, 2009.

26. Illinois Department of Mines and Minerals, *36th Annual Coal Report*; Illinois Department of Mines and Minerals, *37th Annual Coal Report*.

27. Illinois Department of Mines and Minerals, *37th Annual Coal Report*, 199.

28. Abbott, *Immigrant and Coal Mining Communities*, 33.

29. Illinois Department of Mines and Minerals, *37th Annual Coal Report*, 2.

30. Illinois Department of Mines and Minerals, *37th Annual Coal Report*, 1.

31. Illinois Department of Mines and Minerals, *36th Annual Coal Report*; Illinois Department of Mines and Minerals, *37th Annual Coal Report*.

32. Illinois Department of Mines and Minerals, *37th Annual Coal Report*, 1.

33. Illinois Department of Mines and Minerals, *37th Annual Coal Report*, 110.

34. Abbott, *Immigrant and Coal Mining Communities*, 42.

35. Abbott, *Immigrant and Coal Mining Communities*, 33.

36. U.S. Bureau of the Census, *14th Census*, Illinois Abstract, 42.

37. Gib Killinger Collection, Collinsville Historical Museum.

38. U.S. Bureau of the Census, *14th Census*, Illinois Abstract, 33.

39. Gill, "Historical Survey," 111.

40. London, *John Barleycorn*, 35.

41. *Collinsville, Ill. City Directory 1916*; *Collinsville Herald, 1919 City Directory*.

42. *Collinsville Advertiser*, May 4, 1918.

43. *Collinsville Herald*, February 22, 1918.

44. Powers, *Faces along the Bar*, 67.

45. Powers, *Faces along the Bar*, 45.

46. Powers, *Faces along the Bar*, 13.

47. Powers, *Faces along the Bar*, 210.

48. Powers, *Faces along the Bar*, 17.

49. Powers, *Faces along the Bar*, 30.

50. Powers, *Faces along the Bar*, 44.

51. Powers, *Faces along the Bar*, 83.

52. Powers, *Faces along the Bar*, 83.

53. Powers, *Faces along the Bar*, 53.

54. *East St. Louis Daily Journal*, April 18, 1917.
55. Okrent, *Last Call*, 94.
56. Okrent, *Last Call*, 104.
57. Okrent, *Last Call*, 106.
58. Okrent, *Last Call*, 83.
59. Illinois Department of Mines and Minerals, *37th Annual Coal Report*, 206.
60. Dow, "Miner's Institute Building."
61. Miner's Institute Nomination, Collinsville Historical Museum.
62. *Collinsville Herald*, April 20, 1917.
63. Jenison, *War-Time Organization of Illinois*, 5–256.
64. *Collinsville Herald*, August 3, 1917.
65. *Collinsville Herald*, August 3, 1917.
66. *Collinsville Herald*, August 3, 1917.
67. *Collinsville Herald*, August 3, 1917.
68. *Collinsville Herald*, August 3, 1917.
69. *Collinsville Herald*, August 10, 1917.
70. *Collinsville Advertiser*, August 11, 1917.
71. *Collinsville Herald*, August 10, 1917.
72. *Edwardsville Intelligencer*, August 3, 1919.
73. Editorial, *Collinsville Herald*, August 10, 1917.
74. Editorial, *Collinsville Advertiser*, August 11, 1917.
75. *East St. Louis Daily Journal*, August 14, 1917.
76. *Collinsville Herald*, August 17, 1917.
77. *Collinsville Herald*, August 17, 1917.
78. *Collinsville Herald*, August 17, 1917.
79. *Collinsville Herald*, August 24, 1917.
80. *Collinsville Herald*, August 24, 1917.
81. *Collinsville Herald*, September 7, 1917.
82. *Collinsville Herald*, September 7, 1917.
83. *Collinsville Herald*, September 14, 1917.
84. *United Mine Workers Journal*, October 11, 1917, 6.
85. *United Mine Workers Journal*, October 18, 1917, 4.
86. *United Mine Workers Journal*, October 25, 1917, 4.
87. *St. Louis Post-Dispatch*, October 19, 1917.
88. *St. Louis Post-Dispatch*, October 19, 1917.
89. Jenison, *War Documents and Addresses*, 6–195.
90. *Collinsville Herald*, October 19, 1917.
91. *Collinsville Herald*, October 19, 1917.
92. *Collinsville Herald*, October 19, 1917.
93. *Collinsville Herald*, October 19, 1917.
94. *Collinsville Herald*, November 2, 1917.
95. Jenison, *War Documents and Addresses*, 6–195.

96. Editorial, *Collinsville Herald*, November 2, 1917.

97. Illinois Department of Mines and Minerals, *36th Annual Coal Report*, 32; Illinois Department of Mines and Minerals, *37th Annual Coal Report*, 26.

98. *United Mine Workers Journal*, January 10, 1918, 11.

99. United Mine Workers Local 264, election results and documents, Southern Illinois University–Edwardsville Lovejoy Library.

100. *Collinsville Advertiser*, January 5, 1918.

101. Abbott, *Immigrant and Coal Mining Communities*, 42.

102. *Collinsville Herald*, December 21, 1917.

103. *Collinsville Herald*, February 22, 1918.

104. *Collinsville Herald*, February 8, 1918.

105. *Collinsville Herald*, January 11, 1918.

106. *United Mine Workers Journal*, January 17, 1918, 3.

107. *Collinsville Herald*, January 11, 1918.

4. You Are Either for Us or against Us

1. McCartin, *Labor's Great War*, 39.

2. National Industrial Conference Board, *Strikes in American Industry*, 3.

3. St. Louis Smelting and Refining Collection.

4. U.S. Bureau of the Census, *14th Census*, field collection forms.

5. *Collinsville Herald*, April 6, 1917.

6. St. Louis Smelting and Refining Collection.

7. *Collinsville Herald*, June 2, 1917.

8. *Collinsville Herald*, August 3, 1917.

9. *Collinsville Herald*, August 3, 1917.

10. *Collinsville Advertiser*, August 4, 1917.

11. *Collinsville Herald*, August 3, 1917.

12. *Collinsville Herald*, August 3, 1917.

13. *Collinsville Herald*, August 10, 1917.

14. *Collinsville Herald*, August 10, 1917.

15. *Collinsville Herald*, August 17, 1917.

16. *Collinsville Herald*, August 17, 1917.

17. *Collinsville Herald*, August 24, 1917.

18. *Collinsville Advertiser*, August 25, 1917.

19. *Collinsville Advertiser*, September 1, 1917.

20. U.S. Bureau of the Census, *14th Census*, field collection forms.

21. *Collinsville Advertiser*, April 7, 1917.

22. *Collinsville Herald*, August 31, 1917.

23. *Collinsville Herald*, September 7, 1917.

24. *Collinsville Herald*, September 14, 1917.

25. *Collinsville, Ill. City Directory 1916*; *Collinsville Herald*, *1919 City Directory*.

26. *Collinsville Herald*, September 28, 1917.

27. *Collinsville Herald*, September 28, 1917.

28. *Collinsville Herald*, September 28, 1917.
29. *East St. Louis Daily Journal*, September 28, 1917.
30. *Collinsville Herald*, September 28, 1917.
31. *Collinsville Herald*, September 28, 1917.
32. *Collinsville Herald*, September 28, 1917.
33. Barnes, *Never Been a Time*, 210.
34. Barnes, *Never Been a Time*, 210.
35. Editorial, *Collinsville Advertiser*, July 7, 1917.
36. Editorial, *Collinsville Herald*, July 6, 1917.
37. *Collinsville Herald*, October 5, 1917.
38. *Collinsville Herald*, October 5, 1917.
39. Editorial, *Collinsville Herald*, October 5, 1917.
40. *Collinsville Herald*, October 5, 1917.
41. *Collinsville Herald*, October 5, 1917.
42. *Collinsville Herald*, October 12, 1917.
43. *Collinsville Herald*, October 12, 1917.
44. *Collinsville Herald*, October 12, 1917.
45. *Collinsville Herald*, October 12, 1917.
46. *Edwardsville Intelligencer*, August 31, 1912.
47. *Edwardsville Intelligencer*, March 30, 1918.
48. *Edwardsville Intelligencer*, April 30, 1918.
49. Dechenne, "Labor and Immigration," 101.
50. *East St. Louis Daily Journal*, October 16, 1917.
51. *East St. Louis Daily Journal*, October 17, 1917.
52. *Collinsville Advertiser*, October 20, 1917.
53. *East St. Louis Daily Journal*, October 18, 1917.
54. *Collinsville Herald*, October 19, 1917.
55. *Collinsville Herald*, October 26, 1917.
56. *Collinsville Advertiser*, October 20, 1917.
57. *Collinsville Herald*, October 19, 1917.
58. *Collinsville Advertiser*, October 13, 1917.
59. Illinois Department of Mines and Minerals, *42nd Annual Coal Report*, 214.
60. *Collinsville Herald*, October 26, 1917.
61. *Collinsville Herald*, November 2, 1917.
62. *Collinsville Herald*, November 2, 1918.
63. *Collinsville Advertiser*, November 3, 1917.
64. *Collinsville Herald*, November 2, 1917.
65. *Collinsville Herald*, November 2, 1917.
66. *Collinsville Herald*, November 2, 1917.
67. Editorial, *Collinsville Herald*, November 9, 1917.
68. *Collinsville Herald*, October 26, 1917.
69. Editorial, *Collinsville Herald*, November 16, 1917.
70. *Collinsville Herald*, November 30, 1917.

71. *Collinsville Herald*, November 23, 1917.

72. *Collinsville Herald*, November 30, 1918.

73. *Collinsville Herald*, November 30, 1917.

74. "Minutes of October 15, 1917 Meeting," United Mine Workers Local 685 Collection, Collinsville Historical Museum.

75. *Collinsville Herald*, November 23, 1917.

76. *Collinsville Herald*, November 30, 1917.

77. *Collinsville Herald*, November 30, 1917.

78. *Collinsville Herald*, November 23, 1917.

79. *St. Louis Post-Dispatch*, December 24, 1917.

80. *Collinsville Herald*, November 16, 1917.

81. *Collinsville Herald*, January 11, 1918.

82. *Collinsville Herald*, October 26, 1917.

83. *Collinsville Herald*, November 16, 1917.

84. *Collinsville Advertiser*, December 15, 1917.

85. *Collinsville Advertiser*, January 19, 1918.

86. *Collinsville Herald*, December 28, 1917.

87. *Collinsville Herald*, November 30, 1917.

88. *Collinsville Herald*, December 14, 1917.

89. *Illinois State Register*, December 15, 1917.

90. United Mine Workers Local 826, records, 1918, Southern Illinois University–Edwardsville Lovejoy Library.

91. *Collinsville Advertiser*, November 17, 1917.

92. *Collinsville Herald*, November 23, 1917.

93. *Collinsville Herald*, December 28, 1917.

94. *Collinsville Herald*, February 1, 1918.

95. *Collinsville Herald*, February 15, 1918.

96. *Collinsville Herald*, March 15, 1918.

97. *Collinsville Advertiser*, September 8, 1917; *Collinsville Herald*, February 8, 1918.

98. Editorial, *Collinsville Herald*, February 1, 1918.

99. Jenison, *War-Time Organization of Illinois*, 5–6.

100. *St. Louis Post-Dispatch*, March 2, 1918.

101. *St. Louis Post-Dispatch*, March 2, 1918.

5. A Little Tar Might Help

1. U.S. Department of Homeland Security, *Yearbook of Immigration Statistics*, 6.

2. U.S. Bureau of the Census, *14th Census*, "Population by Country of Birth," 63.

3. U.S. Bureau of Census, *14th Census*, "Population by Country of Origin," 65.

4. Kennedy, *Over Here*, 68.

5. U.S. Bureau of Census, *14th Census*, "Population of Principal Cities," 56.

6. Howard, *Illinois*, 438.

7. Detjen, *Germans in Missouri*, 15.

8. Detjen, *Germans in Missouri*, 23.

9. Detjen, *Germans in Missouri*, 31.

10. Detjen, *Germans in Missouri*, 27.

11. Detjen, *Germans in Missouri*, 158.

12. *Collinsville Herald*, March 8, 1918.

13. Lohrmann, "Experiences in the Parsonages," 3.

14. *Collinsville Herald*, March 12, 1918.

15. *Collinsville Herald*, March 19, 1918.

16. Kennedy, *Over Here*, 24.

17. Wilson, "Third Annual Message."

18. Peterson and Fite, *Opponents of War*, 81.

19. Kennedy, *Over Here*, 67.

20. Kennedy, *Freedom from Fear*, 14.

21. Abbott, *Immigrant and Coal Mining Communities*, 6.

22. *St. Louis Post-Dispatch*, September 28, 2014.

23. Peterson and Fite, *Opponents of War*, 196.

24. Lloyd, "Liberty Philosophy," 499.

25. Peterson and Fite, *Opponents of War*, 81.

26. Kennedy, *Over Here*, 14.

27. *Collinsville Advertiser*, December 29, 1917.

28. Feldman, *Manufacturing Hysteria*, 23.

29. Kennedy, *Over Here*, 25.

30. Feldman, *Manufacturing Hysteria*, 32.

31. Peterson and Fite, *Opponents of War*, 19.

32. Feldman, *Manufacturing Hysteria*, 24.

33. Feldman, *Manufacturing Hysteria*, 23.

34. Peterson and Fite, *Opponents of War*, 151.

35. Capozolla, "Only Badge Needed," 1360.

36. Feldman, *Manufacturing Hysteria*, 23.

37. Peterson and Fite, *Opponents of War*, 182.

38. Peterson and Fite, *Opponents of War*, 215.

39. Feldman, *Manufacturing Hysteria*, 59.

40. Peterson and Fite, *Opponents of War*, 148.

41. Adams, "Anti-German Sentiment," 14.

42. Adams, "Anti-German Sentiment," 14.

43. Adams, "Anti-German Sentiment," 16.

44. *East St. Louis Daily Journal*, March 29, 1918.

45. Adams, "Anti-German Sentiment," 35.

46. *East St. Louis Daily Journal*, March 30, 1918.

47. Feldman, *Manufacturing Hysteria*, 20.

48. Peterson and Fite, *Opponents of War*, 249.

49. Kennedy, *Over Here*, 83.

50. Burton, "Espionage and Sedition Acts," 49.

51. Peterson and Fite, *Opponents of War*, 183.

52. Detjen, *Germans in Missouri*, 164.

53. Burton, "Espionage and Sedition Acts," 47–48.

54. Burton, "Espionage and Sedition Acts," 43.

55. Peterson and Fite, *Opponents of War*, 182.

56. Peterson and Fite, *Opponents of War*, 182.

57. *Edwardsville Intelligencer*, March 9, 1918.

58. *East St. Louis Daily Journal*, March 31, 1918.

59. National Civil Liberties Bureau, *War-Time Prosecutions and Mob Violence*.

60. National Civil Liberties Bureau, *War-Time Prosecutions and Mob Violence*.

61. Lohrmann, "Experiences in the Parsonages," 2.

62. National Civil Liberties Bureau, *War-Time Prosecutions and Mob Violence*, 9.

63. National Civil Liberties Bureau, *War-Time Prosecutions and Mob Violence*, 8.

64. National Civil Liberties Bureau, *War-Time Prosecutions and Mob Violence*, 7.

65. National Civil Liberties Bureau, *War-Time Prosecutions and Mob Violence*, 8.

66. National Civil Liberties Bureau, *War-Time Prosecutions and Mob Violence*, 7.

67. National Civil Liberties Bureau, *War-Time Prosecutions and Mob Violence*, 6.

68. National Civil Liberties Bureau, *War-Time Prosecutions and Mob Violence*, 9.

69. National Civil Liberties Bureau, *War-Time Prosecutions and Mob Violence*, 5.

70. Peterson and Fite, *Opponents of War*, 194.

71. National Civil Liberties Bureau, *War-Time Prosecutions and Mob Violence*.

72. "Lynching and Mob Murders, 1917," *Crisis: A Record of the Darker Races*, February 1918; "Lynching Records for the Year 1918," *Crisis: A Record of the Darker Races*, February 1919. *The Crisis* is the official magazine of the NAACP.

73. "The Burning at Dyersburg" (an NAACP investigation), *Crisis: A Record of the Darker Races*, February 1918. Some research and literature refer to Lation Scott as Ligon Scott.

74. *Collinsville Herald*, April 13, 1917.

75. *East St. Louis Daily Journal*, April 18, 1917.

76. *Collinsville Herald*, January 25, 1918.

77. Dechenne, "Recipe for Violence," 229–30.

78. *Edwardsville Intelligencer*, February 18, 1918.

79. Dechenne, "Recipe for Violence," 233.

80. Peterson and Fite, *Opponents of War*, 201, italics added.

81. *Collinsville Herald*, March 1, 1918.

82. *Collinsville Advertiser*, March 2, 1918.

83. *Collinsville Herald*, March 1, 1918.

84. *Edwardsville Intelligencer*, February 27, 1918.

85. Editorial, *Collinsville Herald*, March 1, 1918.

86. Editorial, *Collinsville Herald*, March 1, 1918.

87. Chicago Civil Liberties Committee, *Pursuit of Freedom*, 112.

88. Gov. Frank Lowden telegram to U.S. Attorney General Thomas Gregory, Illinois State Archives.

89. Lowden telegram to Gregory.

90. Hutchinson, *Lowden of Illinois*, 1–375.

91. *St. Louis Post-Dispatch*, April 26, 1918.

92. *Edwardsville Intelligencer*, March 2, 1918.

93. *Edwardsville Intelligencer*, March 4, 1918.

94. *Edwardsville Intelligencer*, March 4, 1918.

95. *St. Louis Globe-Democrat*, May 9, 1918.

96. Editorial, *Collinsville Herald*, March 8, 1918.

97. *Edwardsville Intelligencer*, March 21, 1918.

98. Peterson and Fite, *Opponents of War*, 201.

99. *Belleville News-Democrat*, March 26, 1918.

100. *St. Louis Post-Dispatch*, March 25, 1918.

101. *Belleville News-Democrat*, March 29, 1918.

102. *Belleville News-Democrat*, March 26, 1918.

103. *Belleville News-Democrat*, March 26, 1918.

104. *Belleville News-Democrat*, April 9, 1918.

105. *Belleville News-Democrat*, March 29, 1918.

106. *East St. Louis Daily Journal*, April 2, 1918.

107. Dechenne, "Recipe for Violence," 233.

108. *East St. Louis Daily Journal*, August 16, 1917.

109. Peterson and Fite, *Opponents of War*, 199.

110. Peterson and Fite, *Opponents of War*, 200.

111. National Civil Liberties Bureau, *War-Time Prosecutions and Mob Violence*, 7.

112. Peterson and Fite, *Opponents of War*, 197.

113. National Civil Liberties Bureau, *War-Time Prosecutions and Mob Violence*, 7.

114. *St. Louis Globe-Democrat*, March 4, 1918.

6. I Am for the Good Old USA

1. *Collinsville Advertiser*, March 30, 1918.

2. Editorial, *Collinsville Herald*, March 29, 1918.

3. *Collinsville Herald*, April 5, 1918.

4. *Collinsville Herald*, April 5, 1918.

5. *Edwardsville Intelligencer*, March 22, 1918.

6. *Montgomery News*, March 22, 1918.

7. *Greenville Advocate*, April 1, 1918.

8. *East St. Louis Daily Journal*, March 24, 1918.

9. *East St. Louis Daily Journal*, March 29, 1918.

10. *East St. Louis Daily Journal*, April 7, 1918.

11. *Collinsville Herald*, March 29, 1918.

12. *Belleville News-Democrat*, March 30, 1918.

13. *Belleville News-Democrat*, March 25, 1918.

14. *Belleville Daily Advocate*, April 13, 1918.

15. Birth certificate of Robert Paul Prager, Saxony State Archives. Translation by Carmen Freeman.

16. Records of U.S. Customs Service for ss *Breslau*, National Archives.

17. *St. Louis Post-Dispatch*, April 19, 1918.

18. Robert Prager record collection from Indiana Reformatory, Indiana Commission on Public Records.

19. *St. Louis Post-Dispatch*, April 19, 1918.

20. *St. Louis Globe-Democrat*, June 1, 1918.

21. *Collinsville Advertiser*, May 18, 1918.

22. Omaha Directory Co., *City Directory*.

23. *St. Louis Star*, April 6, 1918.

24. *St. Louis Post-Dispatch*, January 31, 1917.

25. *St. Louis Post-Dispatch*, April 5, 1918.

26. U.S. Department of Labor Naturalization Service, "Declaration of Intention to Become U.S. Citizen."

27. *St. Louis Star*, April 6, 1918.

28. *St. Louis Star*, April 9, 1918.

29. *St. Louis Post-Dispatch*, April 5, 1918.

30. *Edwardsville Intelligencer*, May 24, 1918.

31. *Edwardsville Intelligencer*, April 6, 1918.

32. *St. Louis Republic*, April 6, 1918.

33. *Edwardsville Intelligencer*, April 6, 1918.

34. *St. Louis Times*, April 6, 1918.

35. *St. Louis Post-Dispatch*, April 7, 1918.

36. *St. Louis Globe-Democrat*, April 6, 1918.

37. *Collinsville Herald*, April 5, 1918.

38. Abbott, *Immigrant and Coal Mining Communities*, 20.

39. *St. Louis Post-Dispatch*, April 12, 1918.

40. *St. Louis Times*, April 11, 1918.

41. *St. Louis Star*, April 5, 1918.

42. *St. Louis Star*, April 11, 1918.

43. *Collinsville Herald*, December 21, 1917.

44. *Collinsville Advertiser*, February 2, 1918.

45. *Edwardsville Intelligencer*, April 5, 1918.

46. *East St. Louis Daily Journal*, April 5, 1918.

47. *St. Louis Star*, April 5, 1918.

48. *Collinsville Herald*, April 5, 1918.

49. *St. Louis Post-Dispatch*, April 5, 1918.

50. *St. Louis Post-Dispatch*, April 7, 1918.

51. *St. Louis Post-Dispatch*, April 7, 1918.

52. *Collinsville Herald*, April 12, 1918.

53. *St. Louis Post-Dispatch*, April 6, 1918. The Prager statement was reprinted in numerous publications.

54. *Edwardsville Intelligencer*, April 5, 1918.

55. *St. Louis Post-Dispatch*, April 5, 1918.

56. *St. Louis Post-Dispatch*, April 5, 1918.

57. *St. Louis Post Dispatch*, May 31, 1918.

58. *St. Louis Times*, May 31, 1918.

59. Chicago Civil Liberties Committee, *Pursuit of Freedom*, 112.

60. *St. Louis Post-Dispatch*, April 7, 1918.

61. Chicago Civil Liberties Committee, *Pursuit of Freedom*, 112.

62. Louis Jackstadt, interview with author, June 13, 2014.

63. *Collinsville Herald*, April 5, 1918.

64. *Collinsville Herald*, April 12, 1918.

65. *St. Louis Post-Dispatch*, May 31, 1918.

66. *Collinsville Herald*, May 31, 1918.

67. *St. Louis Post-Dispatch*, May 31, 1918.

68. *Collinsville Herald*, May 29, 1918.

69. *Collinsville Herald*, April 12, 1918.

70. *Collinsville Herald*, May 28, 1918.

71. *Edwardsville Intelligencer*, April 5, 1918.

72. *Edwardsville Intelligencer*, April 5, 1918.

73. *Collinsville Herald*, April 6, 1918.

74. *Collinsville Herald*, April 5, 1918.

75. *St. Louis Post-Dispatch*, April 11, 1918.

76. "Minutes of October 1, 1917 Meeting," United Mine Workers Local 685 Collection, Collinsville Historical Museum.

77. *St. Louis Star*, April 11, 1918.

78. *Belleville News-Democrat*, April 12, 1918.

79. *Collinsville Herald*, April 12, 1918.

80. *Collinsville Herald*, May 31, 1918.

81. *Collinsville Advertiser*, April 13, 1918.

82. *St. Louis Star*, April 5, 1918.

83. *Collinsville Herald*, April 5, 1918.

84. *Collinsville Herald*, April 5, 1918.

85. *Collinsville Herald*, April 5, 1918.

86. *St. Louis Times*, May 28, 1918.

87. *Collinsville Herald*, May 29, 1918.

88. Editorial, *Collinsville Advertiser*, April 13, 1918.

89. *Collinsville Herald*, April 12, 1918.

90. *St. Louis Post-Dispatch*, April 7, 1918.

91. *St. Louis Post-Dispatch*, April 11, 1918.

92. *St. Louis Post-Dispatch*, April 28, 1918.

93. *St. Louis Post-Dispatch*, April 6, 1918.

94. *St. Louis Star*, April 11, 1918.

95. *Belleville News-Democrat*, April 11, 1918.

96. *St. Louis Star*, April 11, 1918.

97. Wesley Beaver draft registration card, World War I Selective Service System draft registration cards, National Archives.

98. *St. Louis Star*, April 11, 1918.

99. *Collinsville Herald*, April 12, 1918.

100. *Collinsville Advertiser*, April 6, 1918.

101. *St. Louis Post-Dispatch*, April 7, 1918.

102. *St. Louis Post-Dispatch*, April 9, 1918.

103. *St. Louis Post-Dispatch*, April 7, 1918.

104. *Collinsville Herald*, April 12, 1918.

105. *St. Louis Post-Dispatch*, April 9, 1918.

106. *Collinsville Herald*, May 29, 1918.

107. *Collinsville Herald*, May 29, 1918.

108. Robert Johann, interview with author, July 7, 2014.

109. *St. Louis Post-Dispatch*, April 7, 1918.

110. *St. Louis Star*, April 5, 1918.

111. *St. Louis Star*, April 11, 1918.

112. *St. Louis Post-Dispatch*, May 28, 1918.

113. *Collinsville Herald*, April 12, 1918

114. Phillip Herr, interview with author, October 20, 2014.

7. I Want to Tell

1. *Edwardsville Intelligencer*, April 5, 1918.

2. *St. Louis Post-Dispatch*, October 5, 1919.

3. J. O. Monroe, "So Far, So Good: 50 Years of Memoirs of Printing, Publishing, Politics and People," *Collinsville Herald*, August 13, 1962.

4. *Collinsville Herald*, April 5, 1918.

5. *St. Louis Star*, April 6, 1918.

6. *St. Louis Post-Dispatch*, October 5, 1919.

7. *Collinsville Herald*, April 12, 1918.

8. *Collinsville Herald*, April 12, 1918.

9. *Collinsville Advertiser*, May 18, 1918.

10. *St. Louis Star*, April 6, 1918.

11. *St. Louis Globe-Democrat*, April 6, 1918.

12. *Collinsville Herald*, April 12, 1918.

13. Frank Lowden address at Liberty Bond Rally, Illinois State Archives.

14. *St. Louis Star*, April 5, 1918.

15. *East St. Louis Daily Journal*, April 5, 1918.

16. *St. Louis Times*, April 8, 1918.

17. *St. Louis Times*, April 8, 1918.

18. Monroe, "So Far, So Good," *Collinsville Herald*, August 13, 1962.

19. *St. Louis Post-Dispatch*, April 12, 1918.

20. *St. Louis Star*, April 6, 1918.

21. *Collinsville Herald*, April 6, 1918.

22. *St. Louis Star*, April 6, 1918.

23. *St. Louis Times*, April 6, 1918.

24. *St. Louis Star*, April 6, 1918.

25. *St. Louis Times*, April 8, 1918.

26. *Collinsville Herald*, April 6, 1918.

27. *Collinsville Herald*, April 6, 1918.

28. *Collinsville Herald*, April 6, 1918.

29. *St. Louis Post-Dispatch*, April 7, 1918.

30. *Collinsville Herald*, April 12, 1918.

31. *St. Louis Post-Dispatch*, April 7, 1918.

32. Editorial, *Belleville News-Democrat*, April 8, 1918.

33. *St. Louis Star*, April 10, 1918.

34. *St. Louis Post-Dispatch*, April 7, 1918.

35. *St. Louis Post-Dispatch*, April 6, 1918.

36. *St. Louis Post-Dispatch*, April 9, 1918.

37. *Chicago Daily Tribune*, April 9, 1918.

38. *St. Louis Post-Dispatch*, April 6, 1918.

39. *St. Louis Star*, April 11, 1918.

40. Quotations from newspapers taken from "The First War Lynching," *Literary Digest*, April 20, 1918.

41. Editorial, *Washington Post*, April 12, 1918.

42. Editorial, *Washington Post*, April 11, 1918.

43. "Lynching: An American Kultur?," *New Republic*, April 13, 1918.

44. Editorial, *St. Louis Argus*, April 19, 1918.

45. Editorial, *Westliche Post*, April 6, 1918.

46. Editorial, *Belleville News-Democrat*, April 5, 1918.

47. Kroeker, "In Death," 82–83.

48. *Edwardsville Intelligencer*, April 8, 1918.

49. *Edwardsville Intelligencer*, April 8, 1918.

50. "Lynching of Robert Paul Prager," Irving Dilliard Collection, Collinsville Historical Museum.

51. *Collinsville Herald*, April 12, 1918.

52. Meier, *125 Years of Service*, 19, Collinsville Memorial Public Library.

53. *Collinsville Herald*, April 6, 1918.

54. *St. Louis Post-Dispatch*, April 8, 1918.

55. *St. Louis Times*, April 9, 1918.

56. *St. Louis Post-Dispatch*, April 8, 1918.

57. *Collinsville Herald*, April 12, 1918.

58. *St. Louis Post-Dispatch*, April 9, 1918.

59. *Collinsville Herald*, April 12, 1918.

60. *Collinsville Herald*, April 12, 1918.

61. *Collinsville Herald*, April 12, 1918.

62. *St. Louis Post-Dispatch*, April 11, 1918.

63. *Collinsville Advertiser*, April 14, 1918.

64. *St. Louis Star*, April 11, 1918; *Collinsville Herald*, April 12, 1918.

65. *St. Louis Post-Dispatch*, April 11, 1918.

66. *Belleville News-Democrat*, April 12, 1918.

67. *Collinsville Herald*, April 12, 1918.

68. *Collinsville Herald*, April 12, 1918.

69. *Collinsville Herald*, April 12, 1918.

70. *Collinsville Herald*, April 12, 1918.

71. *St. Louis Star*, April 12, 1918.

72. *St. Louis Republic*, April 9, 1918.

73. *St. Louis Republic*, April 11, 1918.

74. *St. Louis Republic*, April 11, 1918.

75. *Edwardsville Intelligencer*, May 3, 1918.

76. *Edwardsville Intelligencer*, April 14, 1918.

77. *Collinsville Herald*, April 19, 1918.

78. *Edwardsville Intelligencer*, April 18, 1918.

79. *St. Louis Star*, April 27, 1918.

80. *Collinsville Herald*, May 3, 1918.

81. *Collinsville Herald*, May 3, 1918.

82. *St. Louis Star*, April 27, 1918.

83. *Edwardsville Intelligencer*, April 28, 1918.

84. *Illinois Complied Statutes*, chapter 38, Criminal Code, §255 and §256u. 1917.

85. *Edwardsville Intelligencer*, April 26, 1918.

86. *Collinsville Herald*, April 26, 1918.

87. *Collinsville Herald*, May 3, 1918.

88. *Edwardsville Intelligencer*, May 2, 1918.

89. Hutchinson, *Lowden of Illinois*, 1–375.

8. A Farcical Patriotic Orgy

1. Bernreuter, *Jacob Bernreuter Family in America*, 96–97.

2. *St. Louis Post-Dispatch*, May 13, 1918.

3. *Collinsville Herald*, May 17, 1918.

4. *St. Louis Post-Dispatch*, May 13, 1918.

5. *St. Louis Post-Dispatch*, May 13, 1918.

6. *St. Louis Post-Dispatch*, May 13, 1918.

7. *St. Louis Post-Dispatch*, May 14, 1918.

8. *Edwardsville Intelligencer*, May 13, 1918.

9. *Edwardsville Intelligencer*, May 13, 1918.

10. *Collinsville Herald*, May 24, 1918.

11. *St. Louis Post-Dispatch*, May 14, 1918.

12. *St. Louis Times*, May 15, 1918.

13. *East St. Louis Daily Journal*, May 15, 1918.

14. *St. Louis Post-Dispatch*, May 15, 1918.

15. *Edwardsville Intelligencer*, Madison County Centennial edition, August 31, 1912.

16. Third Judicial Circuit Court document collection from Robert Prager murder trial, Madison County Historical Museum and Archival Library.

17. *Edwardsville Intelligencer*, May 15, 1918.

18. *Edwardsville Intelligencer*, May 15, 1918.

19. *St. Louis Times*, May 17, 1918.

20. *Edwardsville Intelligencer*, May 15, 1918.

21. *Collinsville Herald*, May 17, 1918.

22. Norton, *History of Madison County*, 2:718–19.

23. *St. Louis Post-Dispatch*, May 16, 1918.

24. Jenison, *Illinois in the World War*, 5–7.

25. *Edwardsville Intelligencer*, May 16, 1918.

26. *Edwardsville Intelligencer*, May 17, 1918.

27. *Edwardsville Intelligencer*, May 18, 1918.

28. *Edwardsville Intelligencer*, May 20, 1918.

29. *St. Louis Times*, May 21, 1918.

30. *St. Louis Times*, May 15, 1918.

31. *St. Louis Post-Dispatch*, April 16, 1918.

32. *Edwardsville Intelligencer*, May 20, 1918.

33. *Belleville News-Democrat*, April 6, 1918.

34. *Edwardsville Intelligencer*, May 23, 1918.

35. *St. Louis Times*, May 23, 1918.

36. *St. Louis Post-Dispatch*, May 23, 1918.

37. *Edwardsville Intelligencer*, May 25, 1918.

38. *St. Louis Times*, May 25, 1918.

39. *Edwardsville Intelligencer*, May 25, 1918.

40. *St. Louis Times*, May 16, 1918.

41. *St. Louis Times*, May 22, 1918.

42. *St. Louis Times*, May 24, 1918.

43. *Edwardsville Intelligencer*, May 28, 1918.

44. *St. Louis Times*, May 28, 1918.

45. *St. Louis Times*, May 28, 1918.

46. *Edwardsville Intelligencer*, May 28, 1918.

47. *St. Louis Times*, May 28, 1918.

48. *Edwardsville Intelligencer*, May 28, 1918.

49. *Edwardsville Intelligencer*, May 28, 1918.

50. *Edwardsville Intelligencer*, May 28, 1918.

51. *St. Louis Post-Dispatch*, May 29, 1918.

52. *St. Louis Star*, May 28, 1918.

53. *St. Louis Star*, May 28, 1918.

54. *Edwardsville Intelligencer*, May 29, 1918.

55. *Collinsville Herald*, May 28, 1918.

56. *Collinsville Herald*, May 28, 1918.

57. *Edwardsville Intelligencer*, May 29, 1918.

58. *Collinsville Herald*, May 29, 1918.

59. *Collinsville Herald*, May 29, 1918.

60. *Collinsville Herald*, May 29, 1918.

61. *Collinsville Herald*, May 29, 1918.

62. *St. Louis Times*, May 30, 1918.

63. *St. Louis Republic*, May 30, 1918.

64. *Collinsville Herald*, May 29, 1918.

65. *Collinsville Herald*, May 29, 1918.

66. *St. Louis Times*, May 31, 1918.

67. *Edwardsville Intelligencer*, May 29, 1918.

68. *Collinsville Herald*, May 31, 1918.

69. *St. Louis Post-Dispatch*, May 31, 1918.

70. *Collinsville Herald*, May 31, 1918.

71. *Collinsville Herald*, May 31, 1918.

72. *Collinsville Herald*, May 31, 1918.

73. *Collinsville Herald*, May 31, 1918; *St. Louis Post-Dispatch*, May 31, 1918.

74. *Collinsville Herald*, May 31, 1918.

75. *Collinsville Herald*, May 31, 1918.

76. *Edwardsville Intelligencer*, June 1, 1918.

77. *Collinsville Herald*, May 31, 1918.

78. *St. Louis Post-Dispatch*, June 2, 1918.

79. *Edwardsville Intelligencer*, June, 3, 1918.

80. *St. Louis Post-Dispatch*, June 1, 1918.

81. *Collinsville Herald*, June 1, 1918.

82. *Edwardsville Intelligencer*, June 3, 1918.

83. *Edwardsville Intelligencer*, June 3, 1918.

84. *Collinsville Herald*, June 1, 1918.

85. *St. Louis Star*, June 1, 1918.

86. *Collinsville Herald*, June 1, 1918.

87. *Collinsville Herald*, June 1, 1918.

88. *Collinsville Herald*, June 1, 1918.

89. *Belleville News-Democrat*, June 3, 1918.

90. *Collinsville Herald*, June 1, 1918.

91. *Collinsville Herald*, June 1, 1918.

92. Peterson and Fite, *Opponents of War*, 200.

93. *Collinsville Herald*, June 1, 1918.

94. Gerard, *My Four Years in Germany*, 173–74.

95. Gerard, *My Four Years in Germany*, 173.

96. *Collinsville Herald*, June 1, 1918.

97. *Collinsville Herald*, June 1, 1918.

98. *St. Louis Star*, June 1, 1918.

99. *St. Louis Star*, June 1, 1918.

100. *Belleville News-Democrat*, June 3, 1918.

101. *Collinsville Herald*, June 1, 1918.

102. "Lynching of Robert Paul Prager."

103. *Edwardsville Intelligencer*, June 3, 1918.

104. *Collinsville Herald*, June 1, 1918.

105. *St. Louis Post-Dispatch*, June 2, 1918.

106. *Edwardsville Intelligencer*, June 3, 1918.

107. *St. Louis Post-Dispatch*, June 2, 1918.

108. *Edwardsville Intelligencer*, June 3, 1918.

109. *St. Louis Post-Dispatch*, June 2, 1918.

110. *St. Louis Post-Dispatch*, June 2, 1918.

111. *St. Louis Globe-Democrat*, June 2, 1918.

112. *Belleville News-Democrat*, June 3, 1918.

113. *Edwardsville Intelligencer*, June 3, 1918.

114. *Edwardsville Intelligencer*, June 3, 1918.

115. Chicago Civil Liberties Committee, *Pursuit of Freedom*, 113.

116. *St. Louis Globe-Democrat*, June 2, 1918.

117. *East St. Louis Daily Journal*, June 1, 1918.

118. *Edwardsville Intelligencer*, June 3, 1918.

119. J. O. Monroe, "So Far, So Good: 50 Years of Memoirs of Printing, Publishing, Politics and People," *Collinsville Herald*, August 16, 1962.

120. *Collinsville Herald*, June 1, 1918.

121. *St. Louis Post-Dispatch*, June 3, 1918.

9. It Seems a Nightmare

1. *Edwardsville Intelligencer*, June 4, 1918

2. Adjutant General Frank Dickson telegram to J. Herbert Cole, National Archives.

3. *St. Louis Post-Dispatch*, June 3, 1918.

4. *Edwardsville Intelligencer*, June 3, 1918.

5. Editorial, *New York Times*, June 3, 1918.

6. Editorial, *Chicago Daily Tribune*, June 5, 1918.

7. Editorial, *St. Louis Star*, June 3, 1918.

8. *St. Louis Post-Dispatch*, June 3, 1918.

9. *St. Louis Labor*, June 8, 1918. *St. Louis Labor* was the Socialist Party newspaper.

10. Editorial, *Edwardsville Democrat*, June 6, 1918.

11. Editorial, *Highland Leader*, June 4, 1918.

12. Editorial, *Belleville News-Democrat*, June 3, 1918.

13. Editorial, *Collinsville Advertiser*, June 8, 1918.

14. Editorial, *Collinsville Advertiser*, June 8, 1918.

15. Editorial, *Collinsville Advertiser*, June 8, 1918.

16. Editorial, *Collinsville Herald*, June 7, 1918.

17. *Collinsville Herald*, June 7, 1918.

18. Editorial, *Collinsville Herald*, June 7, 1918.

19. John Lord O'Brian memo to Attorney General Thomas Gregory, University of Buffalo Archives.

20. Peterson and Fite, *Opponents of War*, 206.

21. Woodrow Wilson proclamation of July 26, 1918, Library of Congress.

22. "Lynching Records for the Year 1918," *Crisis: A Record of the Darker Races*, February 1919.

23. Woodrow Wilson proclamation.

24. Woodrow Wilson proclamation.

25. *Kölnische Volkszeitung*, September 6, 1918, U.S. Department of State.

26. *Münchner Neueste Nachrichten*, U.S. Department of State.

27. *Hannoverscher Kurier*, U.S. Department of State.

28. *Kölnische Volkszeitung*, August 22, 1918, U.S. Department of State.

29. *St. Louis Post-Dispatch*, June 12, 1918.

30. Axelrod, *Selling the Great War*, 216.

31. Feldman, *Manufacturing Hysteria*, 31, 55.

32. *Collinsville Herald*, January 18, 1918.

33. *Collinsville Herald*, July 19, 1918.

34. *Collinsville Herald*, July 26, 1918.

35. *Collinsville Herald*, July 26, 1918.

36. Editorial, *Collinsville Herald*, July 26, 1918.

37. *Collinsville Herald*, November 15, 1918.

38. J. O. Monroe, "So Far, So Good: 50 Years of Memoirs of Printing, Publishing, Politics and People," *Collinsville Herald*, August 6, 1962.

39. Boyer et al., *Enduring Vision*, 767.

40. Johnstone, *Against Immediate Evil*, 75.

41. *Collinsville Herald*, May 10, 1918.

42. *Collinsville Herald*, October 25, 1918.

43. *Collinsville Herald*, October 18, 1918.

44. *Collinsville Herald*, May 16, 1919.

45. Jenison, *War-Time Organization of Illinois*, 5–372.

46. Jenison, *War-Time Organization of Illinois*, 5–376.

47. J. O. Monroe, "So Far, So Good: 50 Years of Memoirs of Printing, Publishing, Politics and People," *Collinsville Herald*, August 20, 1962.

48. Howard, *Illinois*, 440; DeBruyne and Leland, "American War," 2.

49. DeBruyne and Leland, "American War," 2.

50. Fleming, *Illusion of Victory*, 307.

51. Beals, "Collinsville World War I Casualties."

52. *Collinsville Herald*, August 16, 1918.

53. Coit, "History of Collinsville, Illinois Chapter."

54. *Collinsville Herald*, December 6, 1918.

55. Coit, "History of Collinsville, Illinois Chapter."

56. *Collinsville Herald*, April 15, 1919.

57. *Collinsville Herald*, November 7, 1924

58. Tim O'Neil, "1929 'Black Tuesday' Spurred Crackdown on Coal Pollution," *St. Louis Post-Dispatch*, November 29, 2009.

59. Illinois Department of Mines and Minerals, *64th Annual Coal Report*.

60. Illinois Department of Mines and Minerals, *79th Annual Coal Report*.

61. Illinois Department of Mines and Minerals, *56th Annual Coal Report*.

62. Gill, "Historical Survey."

63. David Hoskin, interview with author, February 9, 2017.

64. St. Louis Smelting and Refining Collection.

65. Capozolla, *Uncle Sam Wants You*, 7, 12.

66. Dorris, "Schoolmaster and the War."

67. *St. Louis Post-Dispatch*, October 5, 1919.

68. Merkel, *Suburban Journals*.

69. *Illinois State Journal*, June 15, 1926.

70. *Collinsville Herald*, January 17, 1919.

71. Enid Elmore certificate of death, Kentucky Department for Libraries and Archives.

72. *Edwardsville Intelligencer*, June 18, 1918.

73. Illinois Department of Mines and Minerals, *48th Annual Coal Report*, 80.

74. *Belleville Daily News-Democrat*, February 3, 1931.

75. William Jokerst, interview with author, May 27, 2014.

76. *St. Louis Post-Dispatch*, December 22, 1918.

77. Military personnel records of Joseph Riegel, National Archives, National Personnel Records Center.

78. Marriage license for Joseph Riegel and Anna Cannon, Cuyahoga County Archive.

79. Phyllis Kesler, interview with author, April 15, 2016.

80. *Collinsville Herald*, June 1, 1923.

81. Editorial, *Collinsville Herald*, June 8, 1923.

82. *Collinsville Herald*, June 7, 1918.

83. The size of the mob at the time of the lynching was approximately one hundred participants and bystanders.

84. Monroe, "So Far, So Good," *Collinsville Herald*, August 16, 1962.

Bibliography

Archival Sources

Collinsville Historical Museum, Collinsville IL.

C. H. Dorris Collection. Documents, ephemera, and photographs.

Coit, Carolyn Dudley. "History of Collinsville, Illinois Chapter of the American Red Cross."

Collinsville Coal Mines. Map and legend.

Gib Killinger Collection. Ephemera and photographs.

Irving Dilliard Collection.

"The Lynching of Robert Paul Prager in World War I: An Instance of Anti-German Hysteria." Address to Southwestern Illinois Conference on Local and Community History at Southern Illinois University–Edwardsville, March 26, 1980.

"Vivid Memory: Long Procession of Miners' Lamps." *Collinsville Herald*, n.d.

Miner's Institute Nomination for National Park Service National Register of Historic Places.

Prager, Robert. Final note to Karl Prager (copy), April 5, 1918.

St. Louis Smelting and Refining Collection. Collinsville IL, 1904–33. Documents and photographs.

United Mine Workers Local 685 Collection. Minutes, documents, and other records.

Collinsville Memorial Public Library, Collinsville IL.

Beals, Eugene. "Collinsville World War I Casualties."

Gill, James. "A Historical Survey of the City of Collinsville."

Killinger, Gib. "Collinsville Our Heritage: History of Collinsville."

Maryville Centennial Committee. *Maryville, Illinois 1902–2002*.

Meier, Louise. *125 Years of Service 1848–1973*. (History of Holy Cross Lutheran Church, Collinsville, Illinois.)

Concordia Historical Institute, Department of Archives of the Lutheran Church–Missouri Synod, St. Louis.

Lohrmann, Rev. Dr. Martin, trans. "Experiences in the Parsonages of the Lutheran Church in Southern Illinois during the War Years of 1917–1918. Described by an eye and ear witness at the request of the officers of the historical society." (Original document by Rev. Justus Lohrmann.)

Cuyahoga County Archive, Cleveland OH.

Marriage license for Joseph Riegel and Anna Cannon, March 11, 1926.

Illinois State Archives, Springfield.

Governor Frank Lowden Collection.

Lowden, Frank. Address at Liberty Bond Rally, Rock Island IL, April 6, 1918.

Lowden, Frank. Telegram to U.S. Attorney General Thomas Gregory, February 28, 1918.

Illinois State Historical Library, Springfield.

Maurer, Charles. Letter to Dr. Wayne Stevens, January 24, 1921. War Records Section, box 19, folder: Local Board–Madison County.

Indiana Commission on Public Records, Indianapolis.

Prager, Robert. Record collection from Indiana Reformatory at Jeffersonville.

Kentucky Department for Libraries and Archives, Frankfort.

Elmore, Enid. Certificate of death, September 19, 1922.

Library of Congress, Rare Books and Special Collections Division, Washington DC.

Wilson, Woodrow. Proclamation of July 26, 1918.

Madison County Historical Museum and Archival Library, Edwardsville IL.

Third Judicial Circuit Court document collection from Robert Prager murder trial (copy).

Mary Sue Schusky private collection, Collinsville IL.

Dilliard, Dorothy (Dorris). Memoirs.

Dorris, C. H. "The Schoolmaster and the War." Address to Madison County Teacher's Association at Edwardsville IL, February 2, 1918.

National Archives, National Personnel Records Center, St. Louis.

Riegel, Joseph. Military personnel records.

National Archives, Washington DC.

Dickson, Adjutant General Frank. Telegram to J. Herbert Cole, U.S. Treasury Department Bureau of Investigation, June 4, 1918. General Investigative Records of the Bureau of Investigation, 1908–22.

Records of U.S. Customs Service for ss *Breslau*. Manifest of Alien Passengers for the U.S. Immigration Officer at Port of Arrival from Bremen, Germany, in Baltimore MD, April 3, 1905. (Prager is incorrectly listed as Robert Trager.)

World War I Selective Service System draft registration cards, Madison County IL.

Saxony State Archives, Dresden, Germany.

Prager, Robert Paul. Birth certificate issued March 3, 1888, with February 28, 1888, date of birth.

Southern Illinois University–Edwardsville Lovejoy Library. Louisa Bowen Archives and Special Collections.

United Mine Workers Local 264, election results and documents. Records of Progressive Mine Workers of America Local Union 3, box 1, folder 5.

United Mine Workers Local 826, records, 1918. Records of Progressive Mine Workers of America Local Union 3, box 1, folder 25.

University of Buffalo Archives, Charles B. Sears Law Library, Buffalo NY.

O'Brian Collection.

O'Brian, John Lord. Memorandum to U.S. Attorney General Thomas Gregory, April 18, 1918.

U.S. Department of State, Washington DC.

Hannoverscher Kurier (Hannover), July 9, 1918, translated. Records of the Department of State relating to World War I and Its Termination, 1914–29. https://www.fold3.com.

Kölnische Volkszeitung (Cologne), August 22, 1918, and September 6, 1918. Records of the Department of State relating to World War I and Its Termination, 1914–29. https://www.fold3.com.

Münchner Neueste Nachrichten (Munich), June 18, 1918, translated. Records of the Department of State relating to World War I and Its Termination, 1914–29. https://www.fold3.com.

Published Sources

Abbott, Grace. *The Immigrant and Coal Mining Communities of Illinois.* Springfield: Illinois Department of Registration and Education, 1920.

Adams, Frank. "Anti-German Sentiment in Madison and St. Clair Counties: 1916–1918." MA thesis, Eastern Illinois University, 1966.

Ameringer, Oscar. *If You Don't Weaken.* New York: Henry Holt, 1940.

Axelrod, Alan. *Selling the Great War: The Making of American Propaganda.* New York: Palgrave MacMillan, 2009.

Barnes, Harper. *Never Been a Time: The 1917 Race Riot That Sparked the Civil Rights Movement.* New York: Walker Books, 2008.

Baseball Almanac. "1917 World Series." http://www.baseball-almanac.com/ws/yr1917ws.shtml.

Bernreuter, Robert. *The Jacob Bernreuter Family in America*. State College PA: Self-published, 1987.

Boyer, Paul, Clifford Clark, Karen Halttunen, Joseph Kett, Neal Salisbury, Harvard Sitkoff, and Nancy Woloch. *The Enduring Vision: A History of the American People*. Vol. 2, *Since 1865*. 7th ed. Boston: Wadsworth, Cengage Learning, 2011.

Burton, Shirley. "The Espionage and Sedition Acts of 1917 and 1918: Sectional Interpretations in the United States District Courts of Illinois." *Illinois Historical Journal* 87, no. 1 (Spring 1994): 41–50.

Capozolla, Christopher. "The Only Badge Needed Is Your Patriotic Fervor: Vigilance, Coercion, and the Law in World War I America." *Journal of American History* 88, no. 4 (March 2002): 1354–82.

———. *Uncle Sam Wants You: World War I and the Making of the Modern American Citizen*. New York: Oxford University Press, 2008.

Chenoweth, Cheri, Scott Elrick, and Melony Barrett. *Directory of Coal Mines in Illinois: 7.5 Minute Quadrangle Series: Collinsville Quadrangle Madison and St. Clair Counties*. Champaign: Illinois State Geological Survey, 2005.

Chicago Civil Liberties Committee. *Pursuit of Freedom: A History of Civil Liberty in Illinois 1787–1942*. Chicago: Chicago Civil Liberties Committee, Illinois Civil Liberties Committee, 1942.

Collinsville, Ill. City Directory 1916. Collinsville IL: Welch & Davis, 1916.

Collinsville Herald. 1919 City Directory: Collinsville, Illinois. Collinsville IL, 1919.

DeBruyne, Nese, and Anne Leland. "American War and Military Operations Casualties: Lists and Statistics." U.S. Congressional Research Service. January 2, 2015.

Dechenne, David. "Labor and Immigration in a Southern Illinois Mill Town, 1890–1937." PhD diss., Illinois State University, 1989.

———. "Recipe for Violence: War Attitudes, the Black Hundred Riot, and Superpatriotism in an Illinois Coalfield, 1917–1918." *Illinois Historical Journal* 85, no. 4 (Winter 1992): 221–38.

Detjen, David. *The Germans in Missouri, 1900–1918: Prohibition, Neutrality and Assimilation*. Columbia: University of Missouri Press, 1985.

Dow, Charles. "Miner's Institute Building to Celebrate 75th Anniversary." In *Concerning Coal: An Anthology*, edited by Magdalen Mayer, Mara Lou Hawse, and Paula J. Maloney, 36–37. Carbondale: Coal Research Center, Southern Illinois University at Carbondale, 1997.

Emerson, Louis, ed. *Blue Book of the State of Illinois, 1917–1918*. Springfield: State of Illinois.

Farwell, Byron. *Over There: The United States in the Great War, 1917–1918*. New York: Norton, 1999.

Feldman, Jay. *Manufacturing Hysteria: A History of Scapegoating, Surveillance, and Secrecy in Modern America*. New York: Pantheon Books, 2011.

Fleming, Thomas. *The Illusion of Victory: America in World War I*. New York: Basic Books, 2003.

Gerard, James. *My Four Years in Germany*. New York: Grosset & Dunlap, 1917.

Howard, Robert. *Illinois: A History of the Prairie State*. Grand Rapids MI: William B. Eerdmans, 1972.

Hutchinson, William. *Lowden of Illinois: The Life of Frank O. Lowden*. Chicago: University of Chicago Press, 1957.

Illinois Department of Mines and Minerals. *36th Annual Coal Report of Illinois: 1917*. Springfield, 1917.

———. *37th Annual Coal Report of Illinois: 1918*. Springfield, 1918.

———. *42nd Annual Coal Report of Illinois: 1923*. Springfield, 1923.

———. *48th Annual Coal Report of Illinois: 1929*. Springfield, 1929.

———. *56th Annual Coal Report of Illinois: 1937*. Springfield, 1937.

———. *64th Annual Coal Report of Illinois: 1945*. Springfield, 1945.

———. *79th Annual Coal Report of Illinois: 1960*. Springfield, 1960.

Jenison, Marguerite Edith. *War Documents and Addresses*. Illinois in the World War 6. Springfield: Illinois State Historical Society, 1923.

———. *The War-Time Organization of Illinois*. Illinois in the World War 5. Springfield: Illinois State Historical Society, 1923.

Johnstone, Andrew. *Against Immediate Evil: American Internationalists and the Four Freedoms on the Eve of World War II*. Ithaca NY: Cornell University Press, 2014.

Kennedy, David. *Freedom from Fear: The American People in Depression and War, 1929–1945*. New York: Oxford University Press, 1999.

———. *Over Here: The First World War and American Society*. 25th Anniversary ed. New York: Oxford University Press, 2004.

Kroeker, Marvin. "In Death You Shall Not Wear It Either." In *An Oklahoma I Had Never Seen Before: Alternative Views of Oklahoma History*, edited by Davis Joyce, 82–83. Norman: University of Oklahoma Press, 1998.

Liberty Loan Organization. *Subscriptions to the Second Liberty Loan in That Part of the State of Illinois Located in the Eighth Federal Reserve District*. St. Louis, n.d.

Lloyd, Brian. "Liberty Philosophy: Nationalism and the Making of American Pragmatism." *Science and Society* 73, no. 4 (October 2009): 498–531.

London, Jack. *John Barleycorn, or, Alcoholic Memoirs*. London: Mills & Boon, 1914.

McCartin, Joseph. *Labor's Great War: The Struggle for Industrial Democracy and the Origins of Modern American Labor Relations, 1912–1921*. Chapel Hill: University of North Carolina Press, 1997.

Merkel, Jim. *Suburban Journals of Greater St. Louis*. December 12, 2008. http://www.stltoday.com/suburban-journals/world-fellows-restore-gravestone-of-german-american-member-lynched-by/article_c0a2f04-e5d4-59c2-9c93-dd8b4ff4ea6e.html.

Mead, Gary. *The Doughboys: America and the First World War*. New York: Overlook Press, 2000.

Morton, Chester. "A Day in the Mine with My Father, Thomas Morton, in the Years 1900 to 1929." In *Tell Me a Story: Life around the Coal Fields of Illinois*, 16–18. Carbondale: Coal Research Center, Southern Illinois University at Carbondale, 1992.

National Civil Liberties Bureau. *War-Time Prosecutions and Mob Violence involving the Rights of Free Speech, Free Press and Peaceful Assemblage from April 1, 1917 to March 1, 1919*. New York: National Civil Liberties Bureau, 1919.

National Industrial Conference Board. *Strikes in American Industry in Wartime: April 6 to October 6, 1917*. Research Report 3, March 1918.

Norton, W. T., ed. *History of Madison County and Its People*. Vol. 2. Chicago: Lewis, 1912.

Okrent, Daniel. *Last Call: The Rise and Fall of Prohibition*. New York: Scribner, 2010.

Omaha Directory Co. *City Directory of Omaha and South Omaha 1915*. Omaha NE, 1915.

Peterson, H. C., and Gilbert Fite. *Opponents of War 1917–1918*. Seattle: University of Washington Press, 1971.

Powers, Madelon. *Faces along the Bar: Lore and Order in the Workingman's Saloon, 1870–1920*. Chicago: University of Chicago Press, 1998.

U.S. Bureau of the Census. *14th Census of the United States, 1920*.

———. *14th Census of the United States, 1920*. Collinsville Township census field data collection forms.

U.S. Department of Homeland Security. *Yearbook of Immigration Statistics: 2015*. Washington DC: Office of Immigration Statistics, 2016.

U.S. Department of Labor Naturalization Service. "Declaration of Intention to Become U.S. Citizen Number 15982," filed in St. Louis, April 3, 1917.

Vernetti, Mary. "Old King Coal." In *Tell Me a Story: Life around the Coal Fields of Illinois*, 49–50. Carbondale: Coal Research Center, Southern Illinois University at Carbondale, 1992.

Wilson, Woodrow. "Third Annual Message." December 7, 1915. The American Presidency Project. http://www.presidency.ucsb.edu/ws/index.php?pid=29556.

Index